Contents

Introduction

This book is written for students of management and marketing, managers at all levels in small or large firms and trainers in management or business studies. For students with a particular interest in marketing the topics cover those basic subjects that make up the main framework of marketing and are embraced by most syllabi for professional examinations. For industrial managers, not necessarily involved in the marketing function, these basics deal with the modern concept of marketing, through market segmentation, pricing, product modification, deletion and addition of new offerings. Reference material is given which deals with particular topics in more detail. The book offers information on International Marketing as well as the enormous amount of help currently available to firms intent on extending their products/services to the Single European Market. One objective of this book was to provide a training aid, not only for students but for all managers in any type or size of organisation. In order to facilitate training, questions are added after each chapter to reinforce the readers' understanding of the particular topic using the self-assessment method.

The author, who is a management consultant and lecturer in marketing, has found that the subject of marketing is ill-understood by students and client companies. It is sometimes assumed that marketing is simply equated with selling and distribution and is a 'hotch-potch' of subjects not easily related. A further objective is to show that subjects under the umbrella of marketing are clearly related and form a sensible framework starting with an understanding in, and the evolution of, the consumer orientation to marketing as distinct from the production or sales orientations.

The book concludes by suggesting further readings on various marketing topics and defines some useful marketing terms to aid students and aspiring marketers in industry.
In conclusion the author thanks Mrs Ciceley Johnson for her effort in typing and carrying out some investigations and Dr D W Brough for his help and encouragement.

D H Booth 1990

INTRODUCTION TO THE MARKETING CONCEPT

British Industry is taking steps to improve its international competitiveness and in many areas such as quality and design, is making significant progress. In terms of marketing however, our performance is often way behind that of our major competitors despite an increasing volume of literature and advice on the subject. Until many more firms become market orientated in the widest sense, national economic recovery will be slow.

There is much information and help available and the recent Support for Marketing Initiative by the D.T.I., aimed at helping the smaller firm by providing subsidised external advice, is enjoying a good response (1).

DEFINITIONS OF MARKETING

A lack of understanding of marketing on the part of new and existing firms retards their progress. Failure to properly research market needs and study those segments most likely to NEED and buy their products are key initial elements for any enterprise. Many case studies in the literature on marketing draw attention to the failure of companies who have given insufficient attention to these fundamentals. Many firms do not know how to present their product and get it in front of the right buyer at the right time and skills in communicating with the prospect are often of a low order. Marketing has received many definitions, but can simply be stated as:

- A total business philosophy aimed at improving profit performance by identifying customer/client needs

and - Designing the correct service/product to satisfy these needs, delivering it on time and providing a sound after-sales service.

For brevity the word customer will include client and product will include service where applicable.

Marketing has been defined as the management process responsible for anticipating and satisfying client/customer needs – at a profit. A delightfully simple description of marketing is that "it is a way of making it easier for customers to do business with you!"

Before stressing the central position of the customer in marketing and dealing with those factors that establish a market orientation, it is worthwhile considering how the marketing concept evolved and clarifying the difference between marketing and selling.

EVOLUTION OF THE MARKETING CONCEPT

Some time ago marketing was equated with distribution and the central problem was considered to be that of ensuring that the factory output was available in widely dispersed markets. Business was considered to be about producing things and it was assumed that insatiable demand would provide ready markets. After the last war, demand was often greater than product availability and selling many goods was a relatively easy task. It was considered at this time that business success would flow from efficient production and therefore LOW COST products. This theme of the job of marketing can be called a 'production orientation' with an essentially passive marketing contribution. Decisions about the product, price and distribution were shaped mainly by production considerations and decisions about promotion, if any, were added later.

Some firms went to market with inappropriate products or services being based on what they could produce well and not necessarily what the customer actually wanted or needed. Many sad examples of this era are available to illustrate this point and it is difficult nowadays to see how such firms could be so myopic. At that time, industry became increasingly separated from consumers. It was no longer possible for manufacturers to be in close contact with customers and so markets were assumed to exist. Even today, some firms operate on this basis paying little attention to customer needs and detailed requirements.

Technological progress and mass production gave yet another view of the role of marketing. It was recognised that business could not carry on by endlessly producing and a new credo of sales orientation emerged. Output had to be sold and if there was insufficient demand it had to be created by hard selling. More intensive competition was offset by developing the role of Sales Manager with a field sales force. Production considerations still dominated decisions on the product range but it was apparent that products did not easily sell themselves.

Advertising, sales promotions and branding increased and product differentiation became significant as a means of distinguishing products from those of competitors. In some industries great attention was given to special product features as a major competitive device; these were formulated as 'unique selling propositions.' All this occurred without proper market research and the seller's perception still pervaded.

These facts relate to an era long ago but still remain the guiding ethos for many firms, i.e. the product or sales orientation. It is evident in many firms that marketing is still equated with selling and their organisation structures reveal this. A variation of this attitude is the firm with a strong selling function and a marketing department which is subservient and carrying out ill-defined functions. Insurance companies provide examples of those who accented hard selling but many are now remedying this approach through properly researching market segments to find real needs and introducing specific products to satisfy them.

The modern marketing concept probably emerged in the 1950's and has a CONSUMER ORIENTATION since it was directed at the fundamental importance of the consumer. This concept suggests that the best way to make a profit and stay in business in the long term is to initially define what the customer/client NEEDS in detail – and then design the product(s)/service(s) to satisfy this need. Consumer satisfaction is thus the means to corporate ends of profit, expansion and survival. The real marketing approach advocates that firms should produce what the customer needs and wants rather than attempt to persuade the customer to buy what they produce. An essential requirement is therefore to define customer/client requirements through market research and then to aim the firm's offerings at specific sections of the total market with a 'marketing mix' (product, price, promotion and distribution method) designed for that segment. The acceptance of this concept has been paralleled by an enormous growth and sophistication in market research.

Marketing can no longer be considered to be an appendage but something that reaches the heart of the business. There are those who suggest that "marketing is the proper business of business." Firms cannot survive without customers and the marketer needs to have special access to customer aspirations and needs. Proper research gives a direct channel to these aspirations and needs. Many firms dominated by the marketing concept take the view that delivery of customer/client satisfaction is the sole preserve of the marketing function. In fact, all members of the firm should be involved in marketing the product/service. The extreme marketing enthusiast regards the business almost as an appendage to marketing!

The well known writer on marketing, Levitt (2) comments that "marketing must undoubtedly have a say, but to suggest that simply because it knows the market, it should have the **most** say about the firm's reactions to the market – this is to go too far."

COMPONENTS OF MARKETING

Marketing is thus about:
- Recognising demand   – Satisfying demand
- Planning to meet demand   – Stimulating demand

The ambitious firm needs to become market orientated or 'customer driven' rather than product or sales orientated. In the simple diagram below the customer is placed CENTRAL and directed at this centre are those broad areas that this book deals with.

Recognising Demand   Planning to meet Demand

THE CUSTOMER

Stimulating Demand   Satisfying Demand

Recognising demand requires the firm to carry out market research, make some forecasts based on current sales statistics and listen to customer's detailed requirements. Research may be a relatively simple process or can be carried out by those agencies with special skills/experience in this field. References will be made to outside agencies in Chapter 3 which deals with research.

Planning to meet demand follows from market research and will involve:
- modifying, possibly deleting some existing products/services and developing new offerings based on research and customer intelligence.
- segmenting the total market by taking a 'bits' approach to define precisely which section(s) of the market the product(s) will be directed at.

This is the subject of Chapter 2.

Stimulating demand requires an understanding of methods of communicating with the prospect. Communication is a fundamental matter in any business. Poor communication or its breakdown is the cause of war, strikes, divorce and other unpleasant happenings. To develop, sustain and grow a profitable business requires special understanding and skills in communication. This important topic which embraces publicity, advertising, P.R., personal selling and the many ways of communicating with potential customers is dealt with in Chapter 4.

Satisfying demand requires a number of obvious basic matters such as responding with speed to the customer's enquiry, delivering his requirements on time and providing a quality of after sales service that distinguishes it from competing firms. Product/service pricing is one of the major components of the 'marketing mix' and frequently not given the attention and study it deserves is dealt with under this heading. See chapter 2. In continuing to satisfy customer demand the firm ambitious to grow and increase profitability will constantly monitor its range of products/services to maintain a balance based on client needs.

Reasons for the increasing importance of marketing are, briefly:
- The increasing affluence of customers and the rise in discretionary incomes.
- Greater competition.
- Increased emphasis on intangible aspects of products/services.

The development of new offerings incurs substantial costs, a matter dealt with in the chapter on new product development. The ordinary man in the street has more money to spend on 'non-essentials' i.e. his discretionary income has increased, and firms increasingly strive to capture a greater share of consumer's discretionary income. Because the demand for 'basic goods' in many areas has reached near saturation, efforts often need to be directed at the replacement market, e.g. Central Heating in the home is now common with more than 60% of houses enjoying this 'luxury'.

Manufacturers are now devoting efforts to producing systems that reduce energy costs as well as the replacement market. Buying behaviour is often affected by the wants of individuals and influenced by their need to accent status and individuality. Many writers stress that once basic physiological needs have been satisfied, consumers desire esteem, status and 'self actualization.' These matters are much in the mind of firms when designing and promoting offerings such as cars, cosmetics, clothing, foods and cigarettes etc.

THE NEED TO RESPOND SPEEDILY TO CHANGES

Firms are under continued threat from technological innovations. The environment within which firms operate is constantly changing and there is always the possibility of new competition, changes in the Law and the availability of particular skills and/or raw materials. Such matters require the firm to have an eye open for changes outside which may present problems in the future – or conversely present opportunities if acted on with speed and imagination. The escalating cost of energy in recent years has forced many companies to reappraise their energy needs and learn more about energy management to minimise costs. Those firms who have responded to these needs, and particularly those who produce energy saving products/ services, have better prospered. Many firms need to look outside at the changing world and ask themselves "Precisely what business are we in?" "What products/services should we now be developing for the future to sustain our growth and profitability?"

The Product Life Cycle concept, discussed in Chapter 7, deals with the stages of the development of a new product, its growth, maturity and decline. This cycle applies also to a firm as a whole. Where is your firm in this cycle? All enterprises need to develop new products/services and rejuvenate offerings to replace those existing and which are entering the decline phase. This subject is dealt with in Chapters 6, 7 and 9.

The need for companies to be adaptive to changes in the environment has been emphasised by Levitt (2) and others who argue that many companies tend to focus on products rather than needs. A good deal has been written by Kotler (3) et al on the marketing environment, a subject inadequately considered by many firms who may fail to see opportunities even if, at first sight, they come disguised as problems. The marketing environment is the sum of all those factors and institutions which are external but potentially relevant to the firm.

There are several parts of the environment for consideration:

The TASK environment consists of those organisations that assist the firm to carry out its task – suppliers, distributors, buyers. The COMPETITIVE environment consists of organisations that compete for customers and resources (labour, materials and expertise especially if they are in short supply). The PUBLIC environment and those institutions, that watch and regulate the firm's activities. The **MACRO** environment concerns those trends that can affect marketing activities and embrace:

- demography
- economics
- natural resources
- technology
- legislation
- social factors/customs

The macro environment has been changing rapidly and produces problems associated with inflation, shortages, the escalating cost of energy and high unemployment. Consumer, environmental and womens' liberation movements also need to be reckoned with. Some companies have needed to modify their product(s) and methods of marketing and selling to take account of one or more of these factors above. The components of the environment change or alter at different rates and products and methods that were sound in a successful period in the organisation's history have had to be modified or discarded at a later stage to take account of changing needs, social factors or legislation in a particular country.

Firms need to accept that sometimes the environment is turbulent and not stable and evolving at modest pace. As a consequence the time span between the introduction of new appliances and peak production is reducing. The art of forecasting requires firms to more frequently revise forecasts. Political and cultural development are particularly difficult to forecast.

In terms of the demographic environment, facts of particular importance such as population changes and the size and location of individuals present problems which require organisations to reappraise their methods of distribution. The world's population in many areas is showing explosive growth, in others a decline. When populations change so do needs; however those countries with a high population growth can least afford to satisfy these needs. Products in this case may need to be designed to use cheaper raw materials or a substitute offered. In parts of the world such as in the UK there is an increasing elderly population, a fact of great importance to suppliers of goods, services and appropriate accommodation for the old. In some areas of the world, the aspirations and needs of customers are changing. This arises through improving education, better methods of communications with the world at large, and changing needs and wants here make further demands on the firm's marketing function. In terms of the economic environment marketers need to better understand purchasing powers in the population; income difference as well as income trends are important. Per capita income is not the best measure of purchasing power which is a function of current income, prices, savings and the availability of credit.

Whilst the technological environment spawns new and major industries it destroys others and affects consumers through the concern about the irreparable damage caused by industrial activity and the depletion of many natural resources such as minerals, wood, oil and coal. Increasing pollution and increasing energy costs are matters for concern and means of reducing them present opportunities for the many organisations that use energy and produce energy saving products and/or systems.

Marketing in these changing times must concern itself with longer term possibilities and be involved in converting potential threats into opportunities whilst carrying out its task of gathering market data, developing and commercialising new products as well as dealing with the pricing, advertising, promoting, distributing and branding of both new and existing products.

Marketing does not apply only to commercial operations; it can be applied to non-profit organisations (4) such as charities, libraries and even political parties!

MARKETING VERSUS SELLING

This introductory section concludes by spelling out the difference between marketing and selling. Selling focuses on the needs of the seller, marketing on the needs of the buyer. Selling is preoccupied with the seller's need to convert his product to cash, marketing with the idea of satisfying the needs of the customers by means of the product(s) and the whole cluster of things associated with creating, delivering and finally consuming it. If the firm's customers grow so will its suppliers. High expenditure on selling or sales promotion can be successful in persuading people to try the product – but maybe only once. Unless the product satisfies fully the needs of the consumer he will not repeat his purchase – and may actively communicate adverse comments to other potential purchasers. Marketing is seizing a wider role in business and there are increasing signs that firms in the U.K. are receiving this message (5).

REFERENCES

1. "Support for Marketing," initiative introduced by the Department of Trade and Industry for small/medium companies. Detail from the D.T.I. or Institute of Marketing, Moor Hall, Cookham, Maidenhead, Berks.
2. Levitt T. Marketing Myopia, Harvard Business Review, July/August 1960.
3. Kotler P. Marketing Management Analysis, Planning and Control, 2nd Edition, Prentice/Hall International Editions.
4. Kotler P. Strategies for Introducing Marketing into Non-Profit Organisations, J. Marketing, January 1979.
5. McBurnie T. Marketing Seizes a Wider Role, Sunday Times, 26th July 1987.

QUESTIONS

1. List the main reasons why more firms need to develop their understanding of the marketing concept. What kinds of organisations

particularly need to become more market orientated and what organisations do not need this orientation?

2. What kind of help is available currently from government sources to assist a firm's marketing effectiveness? What other sources of low cost help are available to assist the small firm?

3. What is meant by the marketing environment and what is its importance to the marketing function of a firm? Give some examples.

4. What is the difference between marketing and selling?

5. List some major threats and opportunities facing the:
   a) Railway passenger market.
   b) The Hotel Industry.
   c) The Car Industry.
   d) Suppliers of training services.

MARKET SEGMENTATION: TARGET MARKETING

Market segmentation is an important and increasingly used technique to assist in target marketing. It is NOT concerned with distinguishing product possibilities but with distinguishing relevant customer groups and their needs and interests. Segmentation is about sub-dividing the total market into 'bits' or sub-sets of potential buyers and selecting these sub-sets as target markets. The firm's products can then be offered to those segments with a distinct 'marketing mix' appropriate to that segment.

MARKETING MIX

The term marketing mix refers to the main variables available to the selling company to match the benefits sought by buyers. The marketing mix is often referred to as the "Four-P's" and made up of:

    Product (or service)
    Price
    Promotion
    Place (distribution)

Each major variable for all the firm's offerings requires careful research and study before short and long term marketing plans can be evaluated. The emphasis to be placed on each 'P' will vary according to the size and nature of the business.

The marketing mix should not be confused with 'product mix' – the range of products that may be marketed by a given firm, for example a range of paints and wallpapers. The most appropriate marketing mix for a given product is selected from a large number of variables; some cannot be altered in the short term but others can. Each enterprise needs to tailor the easily adjusted variables in the short term with longer term plans, e.g. on product deletion, modifications, addition, demand and competition. Decisions on pricing, promotion, communication and distribution are included in the marketing mix as indicated in Fig.1 overleaf where reference to appropriate chapters dealing in detail with them are included.

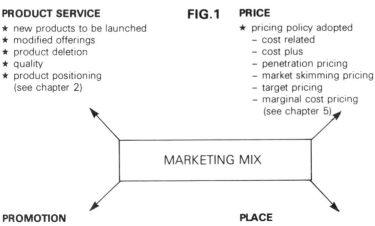

PRODUCT SERVICE
* ★ new products to be launched
* ★ modified offerings
* ★ product deletion
* ★ quality
* ★ product positioning
  (see chapter 2)

FIG.1

PRICE
* ★ pricing policy adopted
  - cost related
  - cost plus
  - penetration pricing
  - market skimming pricing
  - target pricing
  - marginal cost pricing
    (see chapter 5)

MARKETING MIX

PROMOTION
* ★ role/size of personal selling staff
* ★ advertising/promotion programmes
* ★ methods of integration methods of communication/budgets
* ★ use of exhibitions/frequency
* ★ PR programme/use of agencies
  (see chapter 4)

PLACE
* ★ changes in methods of distribution
* ★ expansion/modification/deletion of intermediaries
* ★ reappraisal of service levels and costs
  (see chapter 9)

The 'Four P's' illustrated in Figure 1 that constituted the marketing mix may be considered to be an oversimplification. Jefkins in his book, **Modern Marketing** (12) lists and discusses a "twenty-element mix" which includes:

> The product life cycle
> Marketing research
> Product image
> Packaging
> Distribution
> Sales force
> Market education
> Corporate and financial PR
> Test marketing
> Advertising etc.

These topics are discussed in this text.

Segmentation requires the marketer to understand and use the many bases available for segmenting the total market, the three major strategies that can be adopted and the ways in which the attractiveness of different segments can be evaluated.

The creative use of this simple but powerful technique allows the marketer to develop an offer for specific market segments whose needs are not satisfied by the mass market. A disciplined approach to the subject will discover the heterogeneity of the total market – and thus the opportunities for the firm through sensible targeting.

Some of the reasons for adopting a strategy of segmentation or target marketing are basic commonsense. The firm needs to commit its resources efficiently i.e. maximise its income for a given outlay. The writer is a middle-aged male not much interested in baby foods – why then direct the baby food manufacturer's efforts at me? Why waste his money communicating with a disinterested party?

AIMS OF SEGMENTATION

Careful segmentation helps the firm to spot opportunities in the market place and be able to capitalize on them speedily. The whole character of the firm will become outward looking, attempting to achieve its own objectives by giving specific chosen customer groups satisfaction and developing customer loyalty.

Again the customer is central to the adoption of a strategy based on market segmentation. Too many firms remain inward-looking, having a selling orientation and basing their approach on a definition of product(s) rather than on the needs of the chosen market segments.

An often quoted example is that of a manufacturer of slide rules who should have identified himself more favourably with market needs and spotted opportunities by defining himself as being in the 'problem solving' business rather than in the slide rule market. The market need is to solve problems; a slide rule is only one of the many pieces of apparatus available to aid in doing this. The firm could have extended its product range by marketing products such as a calculator or an abacus having identified itself as being in the problem solving business, thus identifying itself better and permitting the enterprise to extend its product range now and in the future.

VARIABLES USED AS THE BASIS FOR SEGMENTATION

Many variables are used as a basis for dividing the total market into segments. Geographic and other variables include:

- Density (urban, rural, suburban)
- Climate
- Age, Sex
- Family size
- Income
- Occupation
- Educational level
- Social class
- Ethnic group

Psychographic and behaviouristic variables would include:

- Life style, personality
- Benefits sought
- User status
- Usage rate
- Loyalty status

The marketer may aim at the largest part of the total market with a MARKETING MIX designed to attract as many prospects as possible; this is called UNDIFFERENTIATION marketing.

Attacking a limited number of segments only is another strategy i.e. one of DIFFERENTIATED marketing. Another approach would be to target on one narrow segment, developing an ideal offer and marketing mix for CONCENTRATED marketing.

When a firm's resources are limited, it may be considered appropriate to aim for concentrated marketing. When a firm's competitors are using undifferentiated marketing, it could be appropriate to concentrate on differentiated marketing.

THREE IMPORTANT BASICS FOR PRACTICAL SEGMENTATION

Before dealing with some examples of segmentation it is necessary to stress the three important criteria that need to be satisfied if a market segmentation exercise is to yield maximum benefit.

According to Kotler (1) the first requirement is that the segment(s) should be MEASURABLE. Market segments based on geographic, demographic or socio-economic variables are relatively cheap and easy to measure from published data sources. Segments based on personality or user behaviour variables are less easy to quantify and relatively expensive to carry out by field surveys. The segment(s) must be ACCESSIBLE and this implies cost effectiveness. Mass media advertising may reach the target audience – but at a high cost. The target market must be communicated with at the lowest possible cost e.g. through the use of journals or specialist magazines bought by the target group(s). It can be very costly to promote certain goods and services on T.V. to attract a specific group; better to supply literature and samples to places where potential buyers meet to discuss their hobby, sport or interest.

Lastly the chosen segment(s) must be SUBSTANTIAL or viable i.e. large enough to be able to support significant sales.

Some segments such as students may only be viable and substantial at a later date. Expenditure by banks to attract potential supporters would be regarded as a sound investment.

AN EXAMPLE

Examples of segmenting the market are provided by the banks who wish to aim services tailored for personal clients and corporate markets. (2)

In targeting on the corporate market, variables used in isolating prospects may include:

- Type of enterprise (industrial, commercial, charitable)
- Size (measured by Number of employees, Balance sheet value, Turnover, or Profitability)
- Geographic location

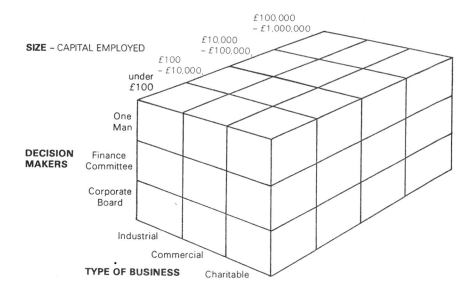

- Turnover or Profitability
- Management structure (type of decision making unit)

These variables or bases are hypothetical but nevertheless provide a starting point to illustrate how the market can be broken down. A starting point is the construction of a 3-dimensional model as shown.

This simple grid identifies 4 × 3 × 3 = 36 segments. In practical terms some segments do not (or rarely) exist and the number of segments is correspondingly reduced. It may be practical to combine two or more segments making the final total more meaningful and actionable. In the above example two segments would be discarded, e.g.

- An industrial establishment with a capital employed of less than £100 whose decisions are made by a corporate board.
- An enterprise with a capital of greater than £1m where decision making is the responsibility of one man.

Other segments however will remain for selection on the basis of the criteria discussed i.e. measurability, accessibility, if they are substantial.

PERSONAL CLIENTS

Aiming services at personal bank clients will require the construction of grids using such variables as AGE, SEX, MARRIED, UNMARRIED, FAMILIES WITH/WITHOUT CHILDREN, DIVORCED INDIVIDUALS, WIDOWS, RETIRED COUPLES.

A package which deals specifically with the researched needs of the chosen segments can then be set down and directed at the appropriate segment.

Banks and other organisations that approach the total market in this way demonstrate their understanding of the marketing concept by studying NEEDS and designing an offering to meet these needs. They also communicate with their customers in the most cost effective way.

The approach of insurance/financial services providers often follows a similar approach. Local authorities can benefit from a disciplined approach to segmenting the market for their services. A useful article by D.A. Yorke (3) which deals with the marketing of leisure services by local authorities details a useful approach based on the above principles.

METHODS FOR CLASSIFICATION

Classifying people by social class provides a set of variables which will be referred to in the chapter dealing with research. In recent years, alternative methods of consumer targeting have been widely publicised and used. C.A.C.I. Market Analysis Division (4) launched ACORN (A Classification Of Residential Neighbourhoods) which provides a significant advance in market segmentation.

ACORN classifies every address in Great Britain into one of 38 types according to the demographics of its immediate neighbourhood. This provides customer lists and survey databases to identify the types of neighbourhood with the heaviest usage of any media, product or service. Having established target types ACORN uses computer systems to give the town, and small areas within them, that provide best prospects for any product. According to C.A.C.I. literature this organisation has developed with media owners, services that maximise return on advertising and sales promotion budgets by targeting selectively on a geographic basis.

The Royal Mail provides further valuable information under its publication on The Consumer Location System C.L.S. (5). "C.L.S. is a computerised system for analysing people's purchasing, reading and viewing habits, and relates these to the neighbourhoods in which they live. It provides a consumer profile related to propensity to consume and also produces media performance evaluations related to cost effective research of the specific target audience." (C.L.S. literature)

C.L.S. uses the ACORN classification system and comments and provides useful information on sources of contact with:
- A.G.B. Home Audit Database
- The super profile area classification system
- The Pin profile classification system

Whether a firm supplies a service, one or more products, related or unrelated, the technique of segmenting the total market using appropriate variables and then deciding a market strategy (concentrated, differentiated, or undifferentiated marketing) will be invaluable in propagating and expanding the business profitably.

PRODUCT POSITIONING

Product (Brand) positioning (or re-positioning) provides another ___ __ __ ....ᵤ in fixing on the target market(s) and differentiating its product/service. Using the 'positioning' concept the marketing function focuses the attention of potential buyers in the chosen segment(s) on the fact that their product/brand is designed to meet a clear and specific purpose. The Marketing Manager will need to carefully, and in detail, set down his approval since it has to be communicated precisely to all professionals associated with communicating with all potential customers. Prior to this it will be important to carefully research the customer's perceptions and attributes of the offering which is intended to best match customer needs in detail.

Product (Brand) positioning refers to the place a product occupies in a given market and is related to the work of economists on market structure, competitive position of the firm and the concepts of competition and substitution among products. Whilst marketing is concerned with product differentiation and market position analysis more recently attention has been given to the firm and its product image. Thus a new perspective on positioning that concentrates on potential buyers' perceptions concerning the place a product occupies in a given market. Positioning implies:
- The place the offering occupies in its market.
- How the offering ranks against its competitors in various dimensions that can be quantified.

and
- The attitude of the end users (cognitive, affective and action tendencies) towards the product.

Positioning therefore requires an assessment of the potential buyers' perceptions and preferences for the product or brand in relation to its competitors.

PROFILE CHARTS

The traditional approach to the direct measurement of the perceived positioning of a firm's products and services has been a profile chart of brands by attributes and an example is given in Fig.3. This simple method provides a profile of the strengths and weaknesses of the firm's product and one (or more) of its competitors. The difficulty with this method is that it is only able to show a few products and no information is provided on the relationship amongst the attributes – although these can be overcome by factor-analysing them to produce a series of charts for the company against each of its competitors (or group of competitors). A more informative approach is to use multi-dimensional techniques. For details of these and other approaches to product positioning strategies the reader is referred to texts that detail the alternative approaches to the measurement of product positioning (6) (7) (8).

AN EXAMPLE

An example of segmentation, product positioning and the use of a profile chart can be illustrated by reference to a specialised vehicle marketed by a small firm with limited financial resources (9). This vehicle was designed to provide an 'economical, durable and practical work-horse' and benefits claimed by the manufacturer were:

- Low fuel consumption.
- Simple maintenance
- Capital saving through a unique body replacement scheme.
- A payload of 6cwt in a large area over the drive wheels.
- Fold-flat tailgate for easy loading.
- Low insurance grouping.
- Twelve months warranty on parts and labour.
- The engine supplied by a well-known manufacturer who could supply spares nationwide through 200 major dealers.

The vehicle offered different adjustable seat options with a very comfortable driving position. The vehicle had good acceleration, cornered firmly and was agile and manouverable for both country and town driving. Competing vehicles were more costly to purchase and maintain and fuel consumption was higher.

Because the firm had limited resources and a homogeneous sole product, undifferentiated marketing could not be considered and the approach had to be via –

- concentrated marketing on a narrow segment.

or   • differentiated marketing to several segments with an attractive offer and marketing mix for each.

Because the vehicle was at the beginning of its life cycle the firm's approach was one of developing primary demand initially (concentrated marketing) with differential marketing in its second phase.

Of the segmentation variables available the marketing function gave consideration to:

1. Geographic variables. The vehicle would operate equally well in town or country but could not be recommended for long distance work. The export market possibilities could only be considered when the firm had greater resources.
2. Demographic variables. The target age group was not considered too relevant if the vehicle was to be aimed initially at the user type. Since the vehicle seats only two its use as a family car would be small although there remained a possible market amongst the 'country-set' who currently had one or more other vehicles.
3. The social class variable would be relevant in indicating at least one segment.

and   4. The life style variable in conjunction with one or more other factors could indicate another segment.

Because the firm and its product were new, customer loyalty to competitors' products required special consideration. The vehicle (and its competitors') are purchased only on special occasions and purchasers would mainly be first-time buyers, another factor in segmenting. The first view of segmentation possibilities considered:

a) User type
b) Geographic location
c) Number of 'establishments'

Factor (c) was considered to be more relevant than a consideration of potential sales since it could be more readily measured. Under (a) the private user would be included although it would be more difficult to quantify.

Rather than explore a 3-dimensional framework, factors (a) and (b) only provided the information on target markets and National (10) and local directories were employed to provide data on numbers of potential users in each category and their location. The final selection of segments was determined by obtaining:

- The most appropriate size of target geographic areas bearing in mind the current level of production.
- An estimate of the response rate and conversion to sales through direct mailing.
- The resources available for personal selling.
- Costs associated with appointing specialised distributors.

TARGET MARKETS, SELLING/PROMOTION

It was decided that house builders and similar firms would not provide target segments since they normally carry loads in excess of the vehicle on offer. From such considerations the most likely segments were isolated. From the 'Mark 1' prospection plan frequent review and monitoring was adopted, adding or deleting segments as experience and sales accumulated. Promotion and selling was initially through –

- Direct mail
- Personal selling
- Advertising in specific trade and other journals
- Trade exhibitions, agricultural and other shows.

Having selected target groups a 'statement of intent' was produced which set down those decisions whose object was to cause the potential purchasers to recognise that the product was designed to meet his specific needs. These decisions had to be wholly consistent with each other for the external and internal agencies who provided support to achieve these objectives.

The format for the product embraced:

- The derivation of a product name and logo.
- A description of the main attributes of the vehicle and how it differed from competitors.
- A list of competitive vehicles to help identify the source of sales.
- Details about the main target groups.

- A description of the functional benefits offered compared with competitors and in accordance with user needs.
- The physical characteristics compared with competitive products.
- The emotional (intangible) benefits offered to satisfy status, confidence in the reliability of the offer, reassurance etc.
- Pricing policy compared with competitors.
- The options including paint work types offered.
- Promotional, advertising and selling methods.

This kind of discipline forced the marketing function to take a view of customer perceptions and pose the fundamental question, "Is our offer something really needed by the chosen segments?"

POSITIONING

A 'positioning statement' for the vehicle was prepared after giving the vehicle a name, a distinctive logo and showing it widely in attractive colours being driven by a well-known rally driver. The statement listed the main characteristics:

- Low purchase price
- Reliability – traditionally engineered with a well-proven engine.
- Low running costs.
- Versatility.
- Agility – fun to drive.
- Cheap and easy to maintain.

There was no direct competitor in the price range but its close competitors were listed. Selected target groups were:

End User	Geographic Area
Small farmers	The North West up to Carlisle to Stoke in the South
Small holdings	Staffordshire/Cheshire
Market gardeners	Staffordshire/Cheshire
Grocery wholesalers/retailers	Cheshire
Large transport firms for the economic delivery of small loads	Staffs., Cheshire, North West
'Young' country-set private users	The North West
Etc.	Etc.

'Head-on' advertising comparing competitive products was adopted as well as a campaign directed at the private sector to those 'young' men and women, irrespective of age, who liked a 'fun-vehicle' with appropriate 'extras' and special paintwork.

The product positioning profile chart was designed with the aid of a Mintel car report which listed owner's views about his car's advantages. At this time there was a particular interest in economy and reliability.

Owner's view of his car's advantages
Mintel 1974/78 (11)

	Nov '74	**Jan '78**
Economy	1	2
Reliability	2	1
Comfort	3	3
Space	4	4
Handling/road holding	5	5
Smartness/style	6	6
Accessories	7	7
Safety	9	9

Comparing the attributes of the vehicle on offer with competitors was assisted by the preparation of the above chart which permitted a semi-quantative comparison of perceived attributes. In the example shown only one competing vehicle is included for simplicity.

FIG. 3

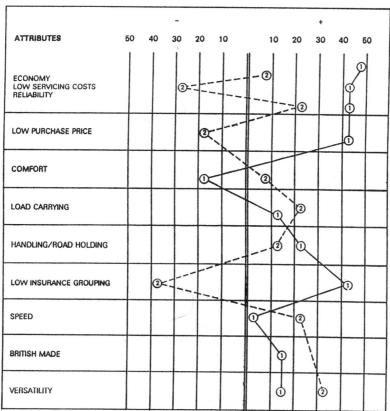

The Marketing Manager intent on ensuring that his product is successful in achieving planned market share and profit objectives will use the discipline of market segmentation to enable him to centre activity on the most lucrative targets. In differentiating the product and aiming it with maximum accuracy a close study of competitor's offering is required. In drawing up a positioning statement it will be important to ensure that decisions are wholly consistent and provide sufficient clear information so that his associates and top management can play the most appropriate part in ensuring that the product achieves success and reinforces the company's corporate objectives.

REFERENCES

1. Kotler, P., Marketing Management Analysis, Planning and Control, 2nd Edition, Prentice/Hall International Editions.
2. Yorke, D.A., The definition of Market Segments for Banking Services. European Journal of Marketing, Vol. 16 No. 3. 1982.
3. Yorke, D.A., Local Authorities and the Marketing of Leisure Services, The Service Industries Journal, Vol. 4, November 1984, No., 3.
4. Consumer Targeting from C.A.C.I. Market Analysis Division, 59/62 High Holborn, London. WC1V 6DX.
5. The Consumer Location System, The Post Office Headquarters, 33 Grosvenor Place, London. SW1X 1PX.
6. Wind Yoram, Product policy, concepts, methods and strategy. Addison and Westley 1982.
7. Kotler, P., Chapter 12. Marketing Analysis, Planning and Control. 2nd Edition. Prentice/Hall.
8. Johnson, R.M., Market Segmentation: A Strategic Management Tool, Journal of Marketing Research, February 1971.
9. Booth, D.H., Unpublished research project.
10. Kompass. Yellow Pages.
11. Mintel. Owner's View of His Car's Advantages, 1974/78.
12. Jefkins, F., Modern Marketing, M. and E. Handbooks (Macdonald and Evans), 1983.

QUESTIONS

1. In terms of your firm's offerings, list relevant segmentation variables and construct a 3-dimensional grid. Isolate the segments most suitable and in line with criteria that they should be measurable, accessible and substantial. Repeat the exercise using different sets of variables.
2. What important criteria need to be adhered to in effectively segmenting the market(s) for a given product? Give an example relating to one of your own products.
3. How would you segment the market for:
   a) Washing powders
   b) Tea
   c) Animal feeds
   d) Bicycles
   e) Fertilisers

4. List the methods for segmenting industrial markets.
5. What is product/service positioning and what is its relevance for target marketing?

MARKET RESEARCH

With the increasing acceptance of the marketing concept which places client/customer NEEDS as central to the task of marketing, research to determine these needs in detail has expanded enormously over recent years. The number of companies having their own market research department varies by industry, such departments being most common in consumer companies. Information published in the early 1970's for the U.S.A. gave the percentage of companies having their own research department as:

Consumer companies	64%
Publishers/Broadcasters	60%
Industrial companies	58%
Advertising agencies	46%
Retailers/Wholesalers	40%

For those firms without research expertise there are available many specialist consulting firms which fall into several categories:

1. Full-time market research firms whose clients are too small to have their own research department.
2. Specialist firms concentrating in particular areas such as –
   - Market analysis/forecasting
   - Survey research work
   - Packaging research
   - Brand name testing

   and who specialise in either consumer or industrial goods.
3. Information selling firms who gather continuous trade or consumer data to sell to client companies on a fee-subscription basis. Many firms sell customer lists and these will be referred to in Chapter 4.

DEFINITION

Market research can be defined as, The process of systematic investigation into markets to:

a) Establish present and potential demand for consumer and industrial products

and

b) Provide a basis for management decisions.

Information from research reduces the element of uncertainty and thus sets limits on the decisions which have to be made.

Research undertaken needs to be sound and scientific i.e. logical in method and OBJECTIVE in outlook; it must be careful not to give a false sense of security. Judgement still has to be exercised – JUDGEMENT and NOT GUESSWORK. Many small companies have attempted superficial research and used some optimistic 'guesswork' – with fatal results. Some firms have employed researchers and are reluctant to believe the results since they do not 'fit in' with their ideas. This may be because the client company does not know its market although it is possible that incorrect bases have been employed in the survey.

SOURCES

Sources of information can include the firms own sales statistics, information published by competitors and Trade Associations. Government statistics can provide useful sources of information although some care is necessary in using this source in terms of the need to check definitions carefully. Many general publications such as newspapers, The Economist and trade journals provide further sources.

Interviews of many types provide detailed information on needs, preferences and perceptions which may take the form of:
● Personal interviews carried out by independent consultants or interviewers from a specialist agency.
● Group interviews and discussion which can be very useful in ascertaining attitudes.
● Consumer panels. Members of such panels need to be changed frequently for a number of obvious reasons.
● Telephone surveys are popular, particularly in the U.S.A. for consumer surveys. Often a telephone call may be used to discover if a visit would be worthwhile.

Surveys by post can be unsuccessful since they may be dealt with by someone of little importance and without suitable detailed knowledge. Many questionnaires are thrown in the waste paper basket, whilst others get an irrelevant replay.

It is worthwhile at this point distinguishing briefly, industrial from consumer market research.

Consumer research is used in the highly competitive consumer market for foodstuffs, soap powders, cosmetics, toothpastes etc. Only a small sample of consumers can be questioned and the sample must therefore be statistically representative. Questions asked are normally predetermined and fixed for the survey. Attitudes may be tested as well as buying characteristics.

Industrial research. The number of businesses in an industry are relatively limited, and purchasers of equipment and materials are generally experienced and knowledgeable in the trade. These circumstances call for quite a different approach to that followed for consumer research. Information is obtained by personal interview and the interviewer must be experienced and able to ask relevant questions and note pertinent data which may be revealed in the course of the meeting. Much relevant information can be obtained from other sources, but care must be exercised to keep within the terms of reference. Such terms must be clear and specify whether, for instance, all products of a class are to be examined or only one; one market or all markets.

MARKETING RESEARCH METHODOLOGY

This can be summarised by considering the stages in the research process.

1. **Problem definition** is a preliminary statement of the research objectives which are normally to provide information: INFORMATION NEEDS are here identified.
   The information is to be found from:
   a) Secondary data sources from outside the firm and from within.
   b) Primary data sources from 'fieldwork'.
   What information is needed? This may be about products, brands, companies, retail stores, service and charitable organisations as well as about individuals. Information needed may relate to:

   * Opinions
   * Value
   * Beliefs
   * Motivations
   * Attitudes
   * Intentions
   * Knowledge
   * Behaviour
   * Lifestyle
   * Social grades
   * Minority groups

2. **Secondary Source Data** is available from:
   * Company records and previous research findings
   * Research organisations and government departments, trade and professional organisations
   * Market research agencies
   * Trade/professional conferences, seminars
   * Technical literature, periodicals, government statistics, newspapers

3. **New or primary information** will be obtained through:
   * Surveys by personal interview, telephone or post
   * Observation and experimentation
   * Motivational research methods from in-depth interviewing and group discussion/interviewing.

Other stages in the process will:

4. Define the research method, location(s), and size/type of sample.

5. Collect the data.

6. Analyse the data.

7. Evaluate the results and set down recommendations for action.

FIELD RESEARCH

Field and laboratory experiments are used to evaluate the affect of changes in the product/service, its price, type of packaging, outlet or method of advertising and promotion. Controlled field experiments relate the change in resulting sales arising from changes in these variables. Laboratory experiments provide a controlled method of determining the effect of price, packaging and other stimuli on individual consumers or groups/panels. Whilst laboratory tests are somewhat artificial, valuable information can be made available to suppliers of goods in terms of measured attitudes to the product, price, packaging, advertising and promotion compared with competing products. Such tests provide an indication of customer reaction/behaviour in the market place.

Selective observations of people sometimes using mechanical devices can provide valuable insight to behaviour although not to motivations. Observations in shops, children's reactions to toys or clothes provides information on attitudes, preferences and intentions. Interviews are not conducted and there are obvious problems associated with the interpretation of observations. Mechanical devices such as eye cameras, which measure changes in pupil size, can measure interest and reactions to adverts. A tachistoscope, a projection device to present visual stimuli for a brief period, can be used to measure brand-name awareness. The use of tape recordings of discussions between sales staff and customers, the use of movie cameras and video tapes can all provide valuable research data. The use of traffic counters and television and radio audimeters are other examples of physical phenomena observed by mechanical devices.

Physical phenomena observed by people include the use of store/retail audits, 'pantry' audits, information on brand/stock levels. Products and brands on hand provide basic information for the supplier company.

SURVEY WORK-METHODS

Surveys using questionnaires are widely used – and often abused. Surveys may be carried out by mail, telephone or personal interview and the method used will be dependent on type of information sought, amount of information needed, cost, accuracy required and the ease of questioning. The decision will require determining sample size and the method of analysing results.

In surveys by mail, matters to be considered require answers to the questions:
● Who is the respondent? Industrial buyer, consumer, professional adviser?
● Will motivation to respond be high?
● What will be the length of the questionnaire and will it be simple to complete?
● What sample size is required?
● If a rented or purchased list is used, how up to date and accurate is it?
● Will a reply device be enclosed?
● What will be the response rate?

The covering letter will be important and ask for co-operation and possibly give instruction and guidance.

A good response provides a relatively low cost method but the speed of response may be slow; reminders may be necessary to speed up and increase response.

For telephone surveys similar considerations will apply and this topic is further discussed in Chapter 4. The telephone is increasingly used as a relatively quick and cheap method of communicating with the prospect but suffers from the disadvantage of being impersonal and usually only permits speaking to one person when the respondent cannot consult other people, company records etc. Personal interviews are usually associated with high cost and discussed more fully in Chapter 4.

The respondent may be interviewed in the home, office, in the street or in a theatre queue and the factors affecting motivation to participate in an interview are numerous and will include:

- Pressure of competing activities, embarrassment or ignorance, consequences, invasion of privacy.
- Liking for interviewer, interest in content, loneliness, prestige of research agency.

QUESTIONNAIRES

The preparation of a questionnaire requires considerable skill and in industrial selling often a good deal of technical knowledge. Too many open-ended questions will invite many responses and make analysis difficult. Questions may be structured – Yes/No, multiple choice, rankings or paired comparisons. In wording questions it is important to avoid ambiguity so that the question means exactly the same to all respondents. The respondent's ability to answer depends on his education and language and he may exhibit an unwillingness to answer blunt questions on personal matters.

In posing questions it is necessary to use language that does not influence the answer. In sequencing questions the initial questions need to be designed to provide motivation and encourage co-operation. There is a need for a logical order, from general to specific and the rotation of questions and sub-questions will eliminate bias. Personal questions may be left to the end or inserted in the middle when appropriate.

MOTIVATED RESEARCH TECHNIQUES

Motivated research techniques try to find the underlying motives, desires and emotions of consumers that relate to their behaviour. The techniques penetrate below the level of the conscious mind and uncover motives which consumers are not aware of or tend to hide. Two approaches to motivated research are:

a) The psychoanalytical approach. This technique relies on what is drawn from individuals in depth interviews and projective tests.

b) The psychosociological approach relies on group behaviour of consumers and the impact of culture and environment on their opinions and reactions.

The techniques used are:

Depth interviewing which uses interviewing and observational methods. The interviewer chooses topics for discussion and through non-structured indirect questions, leads the respondent to free expression of .motives, attitudes, opinions, experience and habits in relation to adverts, products, brands, services etc.

Group interviewing where the interviewer stimulates and moderates group discussion to encourage freedom of expression and interaction between individuals.

Projective techniques. Here the respondent sometimes reveals what he may cover up in direct questioning. Verbal projectives may seek answers to questions such as "What do you think people do in a situation . . . . ?" When a person is asked about someone else, their answer may reveal their own view. Other methods use word association tests, response to pictures, and sentence completion of the type "people buy on credit when . . . . "

NEED TO BE THOROUGH AND UNBIASED, USE OF OUTSIDERS

Marketing texts and most sources of advice on the subject stress the importance of thoroughly researching the market for the firm's products/services before their launch. Market research is a scientific business which can be carried out most effectively by skilled and experienced professionals. This help can be expensive for the smaller firm. A prestigious research company (1) gives some examples of the type of work undertaken with an indication of cost (1985 values). Three examples given by the firm are summarised below:

1. How do I define and forecast my markets, improve marketing strategy? Executive interviews with competitors and end-users was undertaken. The report showed present and projected market size and segments, company and product image versus competition, competitor policies and future product/service developments. The report set out realistic targets, and the sales and product development strategy (or acquisition strategy) with priorities for action. £12 – 18,000.

2. How do I find and develop new markets quickly from an open brief? The research company worked successfully with the client to generate a list of new product ideas, surveyed them by desk research and telephone enquiries, then carried out interviews at a high level amongst companies operating in the promising markets. The report concentrated on product design and marketing methods for the best products. £12 – 16,000.

3. Is my product/service right for the market? Through group discussions, telephone and individual interviews, the research company found out how the product/service was chosen,

what features appealed and how it should be designed and presented. A detailed product/service brief was prepared. £10 – 15,000. The many services covered by the research company fell in the fee range £10 – 17,000.

For a small firm with limited financial resources, there are lower cost methods and for those firms with ambitions to export a considerable amount of help available through government agencies at low or nil cost.

OTHER SURVEY METHODS, COSTS

Omnibus surveys ask questions on behalf of many different client companies and thus cut costs since the individual client pays only for his particular questions. Several research firms conduct surveys on a regular basis and client companies list their questions and receive the answers usually in the form of a computer print-out. The surveys are carried out by personal interview or telephone. General omnibus surveys and specialist surveys are available; the former interview is a representative sample of 1000–2000 people on a regular weekly or monthly basis. Because some clients may require less than the whole sample, or require a sample composed of females only (such as housewives) this can be made available at a lower cost.

Specialist surveys are sold to companies who are interested in a specific market sector; farmers, motorists etc. Omnibus surveys allow a firm to test the reaction to a modified product or a new method of packaging. The use of a regular omnibus survey will allow a firm to gauge if it is gaining market share and who from or who else is reducing its market share.

Most omnibus survey providers charge an initial entry fee followed by a charge per question asked. Help is offered by the survey firms in designing the form of question. The initial fee is payable usually on a once-only basis. For general omnibus surveys using personal interviews the entry fee is of the order of £100. Telephone surveys as well as some specialist surveys do not charge an entry fee.

Question charges are priced depending on:
- The size of sample required
- The number of questions to be asked
- The number of people answering

and
- The type of question to be asked

General omnibus surveys charge £150 – 250 per question for 'pre-coded' questions and for specialist surveys £90 – 350. A list of some of the firms who carry out general omnibus surveys, is given below:

Survey	Firm	Frequency	Entry Fee Aug. 1986	Cost/precoded question (sample of 1000)
Access	British Market Research Bureau	Weekly	£100	£165
Gallup omnibus	Social Surveys	Weekly	£195	£170
GB omnibus	Market & Opinion Research	Fortnightly	£140	£190
Household survey	Survey Force	Monthly	sometimes	£140
Random omnibus	NOP Market Research	Weekly	£130	£230
Telephone omnibus (Telephone survey)	NOP Market Research	Weekly	None	£225

Specialist surveys carried out less frequently than general surveys are offered by firms such as Martin-Hamblin Research's Mediline for medical and pharmaceutical matters, samples GP's. The same firm's Telepharm uses a telephone panel of 250 retail pharmacists; prices are £90 to question 200 GP's plus £450 entry fee. Taylor Nelson's Pharmacy Pointer charges £200 per question and a £200 entry fee. Travel and Tourism Research offer a Travel Agent's Omnibus Survey: 200 agents and minimum fee £500. Produce Studies Omnifarm is a panel of 1000 farmers, minimum fee £500. Research Surveys of Great Britain offers a Motoring Omnibus; 1000 motorists, entry fee £150 and £250 per question. Many survey providers exist and a list of addresses is given in the reference section.

OTHER SOURCES

Firms seeking the answers to questions addressed to other business can use:
(i)   Key Directors Omnibus from Audience Selection, a quarterly survey of 600 decision-makers from the top British businesses.
(ii) Telebus from Market Research Enterprises (a quarterly telephone survey of 1200 business people).
(iii) Business Line from Business Decisions who question 2000 small businesses.

Omnibus surveys are less costly than commissioning a market research firm with a specific brief. If the firm requires answers to a large number of questions however, an omnibus survey can be costly. Respondents to a specially commissioned questionnaire are in fact concentrating solely on the questions specifically required by the firm and in this sense can be more effective. The omnibus survey providers will not give the degree of assistance normally offered by a firm commissioned specially in the sense of helping with the basics of formulating the (buying firms) correct questions and discussing in detail the implications of the findings.

Omnibus surveys are of no value in extracting information from certain very specialised groups where no such survey exists but for a relatively low cost (under £1000) an omnibus survey will obtain answers to a limited number of questions asked by professional market research practitioners.

ASSISTANCE WITH EXPORTING see also chapter 11

As an introduction to exporting, the Small Firm's Service offer a free and very useful booklet 'How to start Exporting' which can be obtained free by telephoning Freefone 2444. A good deal of literature is also available from the main High Street Banks, which deal with export finance, foreign exchange, letters of credit and associated topics. Local export clubs can also provide valuable information and practical help.

The British Overseas Trade Board (BOTB) is a good source of information and provides free booklets on many overseas markets giving detailed information which is regularly updated. There is currently available, free of charge, from the BOTB a new edition of its Export Wall Map which shows all British diplomatic posts offering commercial services. This useful map can be obtained from the nearest BOTB regional office.

Foreign Embassies and Consulates are another useful source of market information and can, if properly asked, save a firm's time and money in researching the market abroad for its products/services.

The Statistics and Market Intelligence Library at the Department of Trade and Industry is a source of information about the needs of countries overseas and their development plans, and this can be invaluable to the exporter. Also at this London based library, is the BOTB's Product Data Store which provides data on very many products around the world. The data is stored under 3000 different product headings according to the Standard Industrial Classification.

The BOTB can very much reduce the effort on the part of the firm's ambitions to export and who wish to find the potential for their product in specific countries. The Market Prospects Service and Export Representative Service have been profitably used by firms starting to export and needing information on the prospects for their product/service, competing products, identifying potential customers as well as advice on price, quality and distribution methods. The reports cost less than £200 and if the firm is encouraged to visit the country this fee is refunded as a contribution to travel costs. Full details of this service can be obtained from the nearest BOTB office.

The Export Representative Service will give assistance in selecting agents and distributors in a particular country. This service is very cheap and again the fee is refunded should the firm visit the country to visit the recommended agent(s).

Market Research at low cost is available through the BOTB's Export Marketing Research Scheme. The scheme contributes to the cost of market research commissioned from consultants, and a contribution to travel costs for employees of the firm carrying out research outside the EEC as well as substantial financial help towards research commissioned by trade associations. Details of help available and impartial advice on researching overseas markets can be obtained from the Export Marketing Research Section at 1 Victoria Street, London SW1H 0ET.

Having chosen a potential overseas representative to handle the firm's product or service, the BOTB can supply at very low cost, an assessment of the agent or distributor through its Overseas Status Report Service. This report, obtainable from the local BOTB office, gives detail of the interests and capabilities of the overseas company, its commercial standing, territorial coverage and facilities.

OTHER SOURCES

Further help is available from The British Standards Institution from its department which supplies Help to Exporters, giving information on foreign standards and requirements; a translation service is also available. Some help is given free of charge but the BSI will charge for detailed research. Information and help from this service can be obtained from BSI, Longford Wood, Milton Keynes MK14 6LE.

A useful article by Professor T. Faulkner titled 'Researching Your Market on a Small Budget' is included in The National Westminster Bank's Small Business Digest, issue No. 26, July 1987. This short paper draws attention to the two kinds of research, Desk Research and Field Research and lists sources of information already in existence for the smaller business through:

- Libraries
- Trade Associations, Chamber of Commerce
- CBI Industrial Training Boards etc.
- Central Government Departments
- Local Government Departments
- Banks
- Special agencies which exist to help small firms
- Newspapers such as The Financial Times
- Specialist trade and other magazines
- Suppliers/Customers

This list whilst not exhaustive does offer an indication of the wide range of free or low cost sources of available information. Brief but pertinent comments on Field Research are also included in this article which concludes with the statement that, "Marketing Research takes time, even money, but so does the failure which can result from poorly informed marketing decisions!"

A list of sources of further sources of information and useful addresses is given below.

REFERENCES AND FURTHER READING

1. Research Associates, Stone, Staffordshire.
2. The Industrial Market Research Society, Bird Street, Lichfield, Staffs.
3. Tupper & Mills 1975. Sources of UK Marketing Information, Ernest Benn.
4. Government Statistics. A Brief Guide to Sources. HMSO.
5. The Economist Intelligence Unit, 27 St. James Place, London SW1.
6. Mintel Publications, 20 Buckingham Street, London WC2N 6BR.
7. The IPC Consumer & Industrial Marketing Manual. IPC Publications. The Market Research Society, 37 Hertford Street, London.
8. Statistics & Marketing Intelligence Library, 50 Ludgate Hill, London EC8 7HU.
9. Trade & Industry (Weekly) HMSO London.

ADDRESSES

Audience Selection, 10-14 Macklin Street, London WC2B 5NF.

British Market Research Bureau Ltd., 53 The Mall, Ealing, London W5 3TE.

Business Decisions, 25 Wellington Street, London WC2E 7DW.

Carrick James Market Research, 11 Great Marlborough Street, London W1.

Harris Research Centre, Holbrooke House, Holbrooke Place, 34-38 Hill Rise, Richmond, Surrey TW10 6UA.

Market & Opinion Research International, 32 Old Queen Street, London SW1H 9HP.

Marplan Ltd., Bridgewater House, 5-13 Great Suffolk Street, London SE1 0NS.

Martin-Hamblin Research, Mulberry House, 36 Smith Square, London SW1P 3HL.

NOP Market Research Ltd., Tower House, Southampton Street, London WC2E.

Research Surveys of Great Britain Ltd. Research Centre, West Gate, London W5 IEL.

Sample Surveys Ltd., 82 Bishops Bridge Road, London W2 6BB.

Social Surveys (Gallup Poll) Ltd., 202 Finchley Road, London NW3.

Taylor Nelson Medical, 44-46 Upper High Street, Epsom, Surrey KT17 4QS.

Travel & Tourism Research, Lector Court, 151-153 Farringdon Road, London EC1R 3AD.

QUESTIONS

1. Comment on the main differences between Consumer Markets and Industrial Markets from the point of view of obtaining market information.

2. List the main sources of information for carrying out Desk Research.
3. What are the main methods available for Field Research?
4. What are the main sources of information and help available to firms ambitious to export their products?
5. Summarise the main steps in any market research assignment.
6. Comment on the problems involved in preparing a sensible and practical research questionnaire.

COMMUNICATING WITH THE CUSTOMER – PRINCIPLES

GENERAL

Success in business is dependent on having not only a good product/service, a determination to succeed, some money (and sometimes a bit of good luck) but on certain fundamental skills. Heading the list of necessary skills is the ability to COMMUNICATE. For a firm to succeed it needs to learn the types of communication best suited to its needs and how to INTEGRATE these methods in the most cost effective way to get its image and product/service details in front of those firms or individuals most likely to buy.

Previous chapters have dealt with methods of targeting on the most likely groups of buyers and methods for researching needs; this chapter deals firstly with some fundamental considerations in communicating with methods available and concludes by summarising an INTEGRATED approach to communicating in chapter 6.

INFORMATION NEEDS

The amount of information generated by business and directed at people and business is vast and growing, being swollen by information from and demands for information from government agencies, regulations and statutes, consumer movements, banks and competitors. In this scene the company must get its message across despite the 'noise' in the surrounding atmosphere.

For simplicity, communicating can be divided in the main areas of:–

INFORMING — Obtaining, selecting and interpreting information, exchanging information and selecting and using appropriate forms of transfer of information to other people.

PERSUADING — The preparation of rational arguments, identifying false arguments, responding flexibly to personal factors which enter into communications and engaging in constructive discussion.

OPERATING — Understanding the communication systems of organisations, selecting and using appropriate media and adapting messages to the needs and capacities of the various recipients in the buying organisation.

CO-OPERATING — Understanding the constraints and opportunities of working with the potential customer and responding constructively to the contributions of other people/agencies who may assist a firm's marketing efforts.

MARKETING IS ABOUT COMMUNICATION

Marketing is about communication and described by one writer (1) as a twofold process involving technical and social factors. Marketing aims at changing purchase behaviour, but before this is achieved the potential purchaser is considered to pass through a series of stages before deciding to purchase. It is critical that the marketer understands the "buyer – readiness" stages and situation pertaining to the audience at a particular time.

MODELS

The marketing task may be to seek a COGNITIVE, AFFECTIVE or CONATIVE (behavioural) response, the purpose of which may be to:-
- inject something in the potential purchaser's mind
- change an attitude

or
- induce the potential purchaser to undertake a specific action such as trial and evaluation of the firm's product.

Several communication 'models' are discussed at length in the literature on marketing and these are summarised here. It is also necessary to understand the complex area of industrial **buyer behaviour,** a subject of extreme importance to those engaged in industrial marketing, and draw attention to the interactive approach to marketing in this situation.

THE COMMUNICATION PROCESS

The communication process aims to deal with the basic questions: WHO is to say WHAT . . . . . . in WHICH communication CHANNEL . . . . . . to WHOM and with WHAT EFFECT? (2).

These fundamental questions first posed by Lasswell may be re-phrased by describing communications as consisting of a SENDER transmitting a MESSAGE through MEDIA to a RECEIVER who RESPONDS.

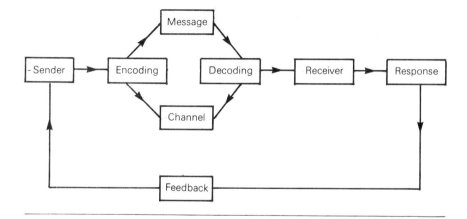

The communicator's role will be to analyse the source (himself), the message, media, audience and response for a particular situation. A communication model offered by Kotler embraces this idea:

The elements in the process may be briefly defined as:

SENDER	The party sending the message (also called source or communicator).
ENCODING	The process of putting thought in suitable (symbolic) form.
MESSAGE	The set of symbols that the sender transmits.
MEDIA	The paths through which the message moves from sender to receiver.
DECODING	The process by which the receiver assigns meaning to the symbols transmitted.
RECEIVER	The party receiving the message sent by another party (also called audience or destination).
RESPONSE	The reactions of the receiver after having been exposed to the message.
and FEEDBACK	That part of the receiver's response which is communicated back to the sender.

Such a model indicates the factors in effective communication. Senders must know what audiences they want to reach and what responses they want. They must be skilful in encoding messages that take account of how the target audience tends to decode messages. They must transmit the message over cost-effective media that reach the target audience – and they must develop feedback channels so that they can monitor whether the audience received the intended message.

AUDIENCE RESPONSE

This model is not meant to convey the idea of a passive audience. Because of the decoding process the audience does not necessarily receive all the message or receive it in the intended way. The audience can show a wide variety of responses after interpreting the message. Most importantly the audience may initiate or control the feedback to the sender, thus playing the role of a communicator. The audience then plays an active part in the dialogue with the marketer.

The above model provides a good framework for the marketing communicator in his planning and focusing attention on the elements which require decision, i.e.

● who is the target audience?
● what response is sought?
● what message is to be developed?
● what source attributes should accompany the message?
● what feedback should be collected?

Before making a buying decision the purchaser needs, in the most general sense, three types of information. Firstly, the potential purchaser must be AWARE of the product and thus needs information about its existence and availability. Secondly, information which gives a reason for becoming interested is required and thirdly, information which assists in evaluating the product in terms of satisfying the needs of the potential purchaser. Three types of information source are available to satisfy information needs.

Marketer dominated channels of communication are those means of communicating which are under the direct control of the marketer: the product itself, advertising, promotion, distribution channels, personal selling etc. **Consumer dominated** channels are all interpersonal sources of information which are not under the direct control of the marketer. Thirdly, there are **neutral sources** not directly influenced by either the marketer or the consumer, such as consumer reports, magazine and newspaper articles about products, government agencies e.g. The Energy Efficiency Offices.

OPINION LEADERS

A good deal of research and literature deals with the concept of the two-step flow of information (sometimes called multi-step flow) which provides the classical model of the link between mass media and interpersonal communication. This concept which has been modified and elaborated over the past 20 years postulates that influences and ideas, "flow from (mass media) to **opinion leaders** and from them to the less active sections of the population." The two-step flow concept thus adds an intermediary or relay point – the opinion leader – to the communications process, i.e. the model suggests that information is fed by change agents to opinion leaders within the community who in turn influence the more passive audience segment thus:

This simple two-step flow suggests that people receive information from interpersonal sources, instead of, or in addition to, mass media sources; the initiative in the transmission of information being assumed to lie with the communicator. If it is assumed that the audience is passive, which source – formal or interpersonal – has the most influence on buyer behaviour? The two types of information channels are often competitive rather than complementary.

Several studies in consumer behaviour lead the researchers to suggest that personal influence is the more powerful force in convincing consumers to buy new products, or switch brands.

FORMAL/INFORMAL CHANNELS

If formal and informal channels are competitive and the latter are the more effective of the two, the marketer will need to consider the problem of stimulating opinion leaders. They could be prestigious firms or individuals.

The two-step concept presents only a partial picture of the way in which the audience obtains information as has been indicated. Friends and interpersonal sources are generally deemed to be more trustworthy – even if not particularly knowledgeable. Neutral sources may be deemed to be more trustworthy and knowledgeable.

It may be concluded therefore that for providing information to create awareness and knowledge the interpersonal (marketer dominated) channels must play a major role. Audiences however are often seekers of information especially where:

- the product investment is high;
- perceived risk is high;
- the product has significant social and symbolic value.

An example of intense information seeking might be typified by the farmer considering the purchase of innovative and expensive machinery. A potential heat pump purchaser would likewise seek information from interpersonal and neutral sources to provide the basis for trial and adoption.

INFORMATION FLOW

The simple two-step model may be redrawn thus:

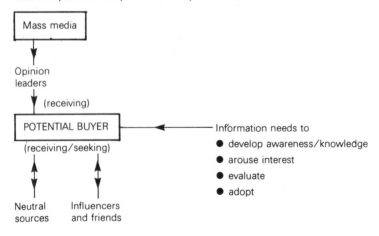

THE RESPONSE

Receivers of information differ in their cognitive complexity depending on their basic intelligence, experience and education. An educated audience will be able to handle more complex information than will a group with a poor educational background and the communicator will need to know the tendencies of the target audience toward selective perception, distortion and recall since this will determine the effectiveness of the message. The communicator will be particularly interested in the degree to which various groups are persuasible. Intelligence is widely considered to be negatively correlated with persuasibility, but the evidence is inconclusive. Women have been found to be more persuasible than men, but men who feel socially inadequate show this trait. Persons who are low in self-confidence are thought to be more persuasible but research has shown a curvilinear relationship between self-confidence and persuasibility, with those moderate in self-confidence being most persuasible.

The vital task for the communicator however is to define the response sought. As already stated, the marketer may be seeking a cognitive, affective or conative response and several models are available in the literature to underline this point. Four models are reproduced below.

RESPONSE HIERARCHY MODELS

STAGES	AIDA (3) model	Hierarchy – (4) of – effects model	Innovation – Adoption model	Communications model
COGNITIVE	Attention ↓	Awareness ↓ Knowledge	Awareness ↓	Exposure ↓ Reception ↓ Cognitive– response ↓
AFFECTIVE	Interest ↓ Desire	Liking ↓ Preference ↓ Conviction	Interest ↓ Evaluation	Attitude ↓ Intention ↓
CONATIVE	Action	Purchase	Trial ↓ Adoption	Behaviour

These models emphasising three stages place in perspective the tasks of the marketing communicator in reaching the stage of behaviour change. Whilst potential users of energy-saving products and equipment will be at different stages the hypothesis is advanced that in the case of highly technical equipment, the cognitive stage embracing awareness and knowledge is the main barrier.

The innovation adoption model is of particular relevance in connection with, for example, relatively high cost technical equipment such as heat pumps. Whilst the principles embodied in heat pumps and other heat recovery devices are not new they are often considered to be so since it is only relatively recently that attention has been focussed on them as a result of escalating fuel prices. A heat pump is to be considered as an innovation and the process by which the use of an innovation spreads, i.e. diffusion of the innovation, is a matter of extreme importance. The ability to copy and 'borrow' the technological development of others is of great relevance to organisations and economies.

BEHAVIOURAL CHARACTERISTICS

Diffusion requires information exchange and the pattern of adoption over time by users generally exhibits an S or logistic shape. In the non-cumulative form, the distribution of types of users approximates to the 'normal' and a classification has been adopted describing users by their time of first adoption.

TIME OF ADOPTION OF INNOVATIONS

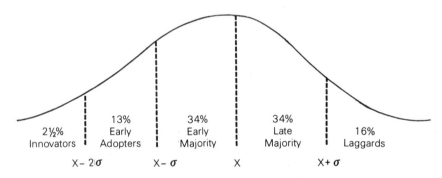

	13%	34%	34%	
2½%	Early	Early	Late	16%
Innovators	Adopters	Majority	Majority	Laggards

$$X - 2\sigma \qquad X - \sigma \qquad X \qquad X + \sigma$$

Source: Rogers E.M., Diffusion of Innovation (New York: Free Press, 1962).

Knowledge of the behavioural characteristics of early adopters may help speed the marketing of innovatory products and processes but other factors play an important part. Major determinants of the speed at which adopters first begin to use an innovation are

- the expected profitability (or 'Payback' time)
- the size of the investment involved
- the proportion of companies which have adopted
- compatability with existing systems

and • the industry concerned.

To these factors may be added communicability, divisibility and perceived risk.

DIVISIBILITY

Divisibility – the ease with which the innovation can be tested – is a particular problem in connection with energy saving. A motor car or sewing machine can be tried out by the potential buyer, but this is not so for equipment which must be installed and connected to other equipment followed by a lengthy period of measurement in order to evaluate its performance. For similar reasons perceived risk presents a problem in the early days of adoption by some organisations. The characteristics of individual organisations relevant to diffusion will include size, financial strength, managerial dynamism and the need to achieve objectives, profit expectations, rates of growth and competitive pressure. The rate at which an innovation displaces existing equipment will also be highly dependent on the profitability of the innovation.

Apart from the general characteristics of organisations or industries that determine the rate of adoption of innovatory equipment there are specific technical features that require careful study in considering the market, for example, for energy saving equipment. In initially segmenting the market for energy saving equipment it is NOT sufficient, indeed it is misleading, to segment the market in terms of energy usage. Currie (5) has pointed out that much of the industrial demand for energy is for heat but a high proportion of this is needed only at modest temperatures. This heat is usually provided by high grade fuel, i.e. gas, electricity and oil products. "Few industrial processes actually consume heat energy: most processes only degrade heat, ultimately rejecting it to the environment . . . . where the (residual) heat has no economic value. A characteristic of high grade fuels is their capacity to provide energy as work, which is usually hardly utilized. The most effective way of using high grade fuels is through a heat pump, by drawing on heat which would otherwise be rejected."

This key area and the fact that the heat pump may, for maximum effectiveness, needs to be incorporated in a 'package' of measures which will determine payback time and thus the speed of adoption.

THE INTERACTION APPROACH

The above comments have dealt mainly with marketing to the industrial (organisational) sector where it is considered vital that marketers of equipment adopt the **interaction approach** to marketing in formulating their strategy. Industrial marketing is characterised by intensive personal interaction between many functions in both the selling and buying companies. For example, in industries and organisations where energy costs are high as a percentage of total variable costs it is often vital to both parties that an interactive approach be developed. An example of this approach is given by the work carried out by the Energy Technology Support Unit (ETSU) of the Department of Energy in collaboration with the malting industry. This work summarised by Currie demonstrates the role of government in the promotion of heat pumps in industry and provides useful pointers to how other industrial sectors may make use of heat pump technology. The maltsters' requirements match very well with the conditions for economic heat pump operation since they operate continuously throughout the year, need only modest drying temperatures, are well equipped with ducting which makes for ease of installation, and currently use premium fuels. A 'bonus' for this industry arises because, for technical reasons, direct firing is undesirable. Without the heat pump they need to expend money on a system of providing indirect heat; the heat pump does this as well as reducing energy consumption.

SOURCES OF 'FREE' HELP

The Department of Energy has supported demonstration projects based or maltings which provide an elegant solution to the energy cost problems of this industry. There are many other industrial applications which, through close collaboration between manufacturer and end user, are capable of substantial energy cost reductions for example and which through intelligent use of heat pump types will yield 'bonuses' previously unconsidered. It could be that equipment suppliers have not yet fully understood the needs of the market, having concentrated overmuch on the more conventional approach to providing heat, not realising that there is a vast market for heating (and cooling) at moderate temperatures – an area in which the heat pump has particular application.

Many suppliers of complex equipment will need to reconsider, for specific user companies (and industries), their marketing strategy in order to interact more effectively with the potential user(s) in order to satisfy their joint needs. It is suggested that many supplier firms in taking a "shotgun" approach to marketing, ignore the needs of the customer and take little account of the purchaser's strategy. In this sense the supplier company demonstrates his lack of understanding of the basic marketing concept.

THE BUYER'S DECISION MAKING UNIT

In dealing with organisations where several individuals, the Decision-Making Unit (DMU), are involved, buyer behaviour can be complex and dependent not only on individual's experience, education and status but on the needs of the organisation, which in turn is influenced by external environmental events. Organisational buying behaviour is of particular relevance to industrial marketing because it will be rare that marketing communications effort is directed at one individual; rather will it be directed at a DMU consisting of buyer, user, sanctioner and other internal and external influencers. For detailed discussion on Buyer Behaviour the reader is referred to the classical marketing texts where there is considerable comment. This subject is further commented on under 'Personal Selling'.

SUMMARY

This section has summarised the basics of communication and drawn attention to the importance of communication to marketers. The communication process and several models have been discussed and the role of opinion leaders, who stand between the marketing function and the consumer mass. The information flow between the mass media and potential buyers is a two-step process requiring the selling company to provide information whilst the prospect obtains additional information which it receives from neutral sources, influences and friends. Attention is drawn to Marketer, Consumer and neutral sources of information in playing a part in the audience response to a firm's offerings. The interaction approach and low cost sources of help for the customer are noted.

REFERENCES

1. Bartles, R., Journal of Marketing, Vol. 32, July 1968.
2. Lasswell, D.W., Power and Personality, Norten & Co., New York. pp. 37-51.
3. Strong, E.K., The Psychology of Selling, McGraw-Hill, 1925, p.9.
4. Lavidge, R.J., and Steiner, G.A., A Model for Predictive Measurement of Advertising Effectiveness, Journal of Marketing, October 1961, p.61.
5. Currie, W.M., Heat Pumps in Industry, Energy Tech. Support Unit, Harwell, June 1982.
6. GTE Marketing Services Ltd., Old Trafford, Manchester M16 0PQ.
7. Business 'phone Awards, QBO House, 18 Tower Street, London WC2 HNN. Tel. 01 240 8751.
8. Pauline Marks, The Telephone Marketing Book, Hutchinson Publishing, OR, Pembroke House, Campsbourne Road, London N8 7PT.
9. Publishing, OR, Pembroke House, Campsbourne Road, London N8 7PT.
10. British Telecom, Telephone Marketing Section, London. Tel. 01 583 4444.
11. The Guide to Effective Direct Mail, Post Office Direct Mail Dept, P.O. Headquarters, 33 Grosvenor Place, London SW1X 1PX.
12. Winning Customers, Stonehart Publications Ltd., 57-61 Mortimer Street, London W1N 7TD.

QUESTIONS

1. Give some of the reasons why the amount of information generated by business is expanding. How does this affect businesses attempting to communicate with potential customers?
2. What is meant by "buyer-readiness" and how does this influence a firm's approach to communicating with potential buyers?

3. What is meant by:
   - Marketer dominated channels of communication?
   - Consumer dominated channels of communication?

   and - Neutral sources of communication?

   Give two examples of each.
4. Discuss the two-step (or multi-step) concept of the flow of information. Give some examples and illustrate the role of opinion leaders.

COMMUNICATION METHOD

COMMUNICATION METHODS

The many methods available for communicating with the potential customer cover:

- The use of directories
- Mail shots
- Door to door distribution
- Advertising
- The telephone   and

- Personal selling
- Direct mail
- Exhibitions
- Packaging
- Miscellaneous methods

These topics are discussed separately and reference material is given at the end of the chapter.

DIRECTORIES

Directories provide a good and cost effective method for promoting the firm's name and offerings. Readers are good prospects because they are looking for something specific. When they look up 'security services' in Yellow Pages, they usually have a problem and are looking for help in solving it – NOW. Unlike the newspaper advert or trade journal, the directory carries a firm's name/products every day for 365 days per year – and many directories are consulted by prospects even when the directory is several years old.

A firm will be listed in the ordinary telephone book but needs to check that it is listed correctly and without misprints which can damage its image. Is the company name ambiguous? Could a prospective customer have problems because the name has a strange spelling or is preceded by initials? To get a second entry in the next edition is very cheap; the first entry is free. If the name is JONES or SMITH it may be picked out in bold lettering; the cost of this is £15 flat fee plus £2 per quarter. A specially large type face costs only a little more and may save the prospect time in looking up the firm.

If the firm's catchment area is wider than the area covered by the local telephone book, the firm will need to be listed in other regions' directories. This is cheap (£2 per quarter currently). The U.K. is covered by 106 directories. Enquiries about telephone listings are dealt with by the Directory Entry Section of the local British Telecom Area Office.

The THOMSON LOCAL DIRECTORY is particularly useful for reaching local customers; 149 directories cover 85% of the U.K. population. A firm is given free entries in both the classified section and the alphabetic sections. Full information is obtained by simply completing the form at the back of the local directory or writing to Thomson at the address given. If the firm sells a production/service mainly to consumers, advertising in Thomson directories can pay good dividends as many firms will testify. Business obtained by the directory can be quantified if the telephone number used is unique to the advert. Advertising costs vary with the region, its population and income levels. In London, an advert of modest size will cost between £40 and £80 depending on the use of bold capitals/individual boxing etc.

Once again, listing the firm more than once may pay dividends in terms of response if the potential customer is assisted in locating the firm and its products with ease. If the firm sells an extensive list of gardening equipment but advertises only under 'Garden Centres' it may miss the prospect of selling some equipment or implement to a gardener who has a specific need but who will look under some other category.

Although Thomson is aimed at consumers/householders there are classifications used by many commercial customers, e.g. for choosing office cleaners, security services.

The most popular directory is Yellow Pages. A 1983 survey showed that on average the advertisers obtained 30% more business, an impressive statistic. Other impressive figures relating to Yellow Pages show that:-

96% of telephone subscribers refer to Yellow Pages
42% of people moving to a new location use Yellow Pages to obtain information about local businesses
Of those who use Yellow Pages 76% make a telephone call,
8% make a personal visit
and 56% purchase

Every firm is entitled to one free listing for every business telephone rented.

Information on listing/advertising is given by GTE Directories (1).
65 directories cover the U.K. and advertising rates vary with the directory.

Again it is necessary to consider the classifications under which the firm needs listing and in which regions the firm is to be promoted.

Business Pages a relatively recent publication ranks second to Yellow Pages alongside Thomson. Independent research indicates that:
64% of businesses use it each month and
47% use it weekly
Many other directories that can promote products/services exist and are listed in the reference section. Yellow Pages and the above are commonly used since they are widely known.

A 1985 survey on awareness of directories other than Yellow Pages gives:

Thomson Directories	91%
Ordinary Telephone Book	71%
Business Pages	60%
Kelly's Manufacturers and Merchants	19%

UK Kompass Register   10%

A simple method of discovering the directories which help generate business is to ASK new customers how they found the firm.

Information on specialist directories is available at the public library. Listing is usually free although there will be a charge for display advertising.

Detail of directories available to promote the firm's own specialist interest may be obtained from:– The Secretary, Association of British Directory Publishers, Telephone 01-650 7745.

TELEPHONE SELLING

This method is increasingly used in the U.K. to enhance customer relations, save time and money and speed up processing systems and make sales. At the time of writing, British Telecom and The Sunday Times are collecting entries to their Business Phone Awards Competition. The awards will be presented to those companies who "have used the telephone in the most EFFECTIVE and CREATIVE manner – however sophisticated or simple their entry – to achieve success in their own business."

EXAMPLES

Specific examples illustrating success through creative and effective use of the phone are given in the leaflets accompanying details of the awards which can presumably be obtained from the address below. These examples with summarising benefits obtained are listed under the headings:

- Making more of your people and resources
- Improving efficiency and reducing costs
- Improving credit and customer relations
- Selling more
- Offices on the road

No doubt further examples will be published when the competition entries have been digested.

Advances in telephone technology and the introduction of a digital network have transformed the telephone into a powerful instrument as a sales/marketing tool. The publications referred to above highlight some of the ways in which the telephone can work for any business and deal with:

- Cell phones
- Link line/Freefone
- Pagers
- Remote call forwarding
- Telecom telemarketing and
- Video conferencing
- Telex
- Electronic mail
- On-line information
- Facsimile

More about these products or services can be obtained by telephoning free on 0800-800 800 and asking for Creative and Effective Use of the Phone, Department ADK 153.

COSTS

Because of the high costs associated with sales representatives more firms are making use of telephone selling to carry out the common sense tasks of:

- Servicing small accounts by talking video and dealing with queries on price/delivery/new products
- Stimulating lapsed accounts
- Making appointments for field staff to call
- Following up mail shots
- Dealing with enquiries from exhibitions
- Carrying out market research
- Conducting campaigns to sell off surplus stocks

For a relatively small outlay an agency can conduct a test telephone marketing campaign. Pauline Marks UK Ltd., a telephone marketing agency (2) or B.T.'s Telemarketing Section will call 100, 1000 etc., prospects using an agreed script.

Pauline Marks has produced a book dealing with telephone marketing, 'The Telephone Marketing Book', Hutchinson Publishing. The book is practical, easy to read and firms considering using the telephone to assist their marketing, would benefit from it. The author advises that "a test of 100 contacts is adequate to validate the success of each script and that, providing sufficient communicators are available, educated assessments are possible in just one day. No other medium can equal this test facility in terms of both speed and low cost. That is not to say that telephone marketing is cheap; in terms of cost per contact made it is of the order of ten times more expensive than direct mail and a hundred or thousand times more expensive than press advertising." ADS Telephone Marketing (3) have published useful information on their own work in this field and literature describing their first computer supported facility can be obtained by contacting the ADS Group Telephone Marketing group in Manchester or London offices.

The telephone however tends to be more insistent and persuasive so that the cost per order per successful contact is often in line with the less direct media. Firms planning to set up an in-house telephone marketing operation would still be advised to pay for a test campaign by a good agency before proceeding.

AGENCIES

Choosing a telephone agency from about 150 agencies in the U.K. may be a problem and a short list can be provided by The British Direct Marketing Association, 1 New Oxford Street, London WC1.

The cost of telephone marketing varies considerably "but on average you can be expected to pay £30 per communicator hour or approximately £3 per successful completed contact." A fixed initial fee is normally charged to cover the cost of script and campaign planning.

The important cost is not the cost per call but the cost of the successful call that sells the service/product.

Telemarketing expenditure has grown enormously in recent years. If the experience of this technique in the U.S.A. is a guide, considerable further growth in the U.K. is to be expected.

B.T.'s Telemarketing operating can be contacted at – British Telecom, London, telephone 01-583 444.

Those firms wishing to try telephone selling are reminded of some of the things NOT TO DO if the trial is to be successful. Some DONTS are summarised below:

1. Do not telephone anybody without planning and preparation. A SCRIPT is a must. Some prior knowledge of the prospect's business needs and methods of buying is important.
2. It is fatal to have a long debate with the buyer's secretary. Tell as little as possible to the person guarding the decision maker.
3. If the prospect is engaged, do not hang on. Save telephone costs and ring again.
4. Do not believe the recipient when he advises that "we will call you back." They usually do not. In any case, if the prospect does call back, the telephone seller loses control over the direct aim of the telephone call.
5. In discussion with the prospect, be careful not to interrupt him; a sale can be lost this way by an over-enthusiastic salesman.
6. Do not pressurise the prospect; supply some motivation instead. Blunt questions about the prospect's current supplier/prices paid need to be softened and maybe posed in the past sense, e.g. "if I could show you how to reduce costs of . . . would you be interested? Good sales people try to get the prospect 'nodding agreement' preparatory to the final important questions.
7. Do not smoke or eat whilst telephoning, the noise travels down the line. **Smile** whilst talking, this also travels to the listener!
8. Do not make rash promises on delivery times/prices.
9. Do not talk too much. Learn to be a good listener.
10. Use a rhythmical pattern to the conversation. Make a statement, then ask a question and listen carefully to the reply.

A video titled "Successful Telephone Selling" is available from Aspen House, 1 Gayford Road, London W12 9BY. Tapes cover

- cold calling by telephone
- qualifying leads
- making appointments
- taking orders
- closing sales

DOOR TO DOOR DISTRIBUTION

This basic method has established itself as an important advertising medium for many firms as an independent method which can be targeted for a selected customer base at a relatively low cost per item delivered. Many large companies use Royal Mail Household Delivery to:

- advertise specific products
- produce sales leads
- provide market research information
- maintain regular customer contact
- test new products/various packaging formats etc. –

as well as complimenting their press, T.V./radio advertising. The use of a reply device can yield valuable information on customer needs and as a measure of the effectiveness of an advertising campaign, is quickly achieved.

Good targeting is again important and this method compares favourably with its counterparts in delivering advertising messages. For approximately £30 per 1000 the Post Office will distribute the firm's literature to households or businesses in prescribed areas. The literature will not be delivered to a named person but the envelope can specify the job holder, i.e. Office Manager, Managing Director etc.

The local Postal Services representative will give further detail and help. The use of a reply device can provide a means of building up a list of prospects for use at a later date.

MAIL SHOTS/SALES LETTERS

There is considerable literature available on this subject in the marketing texts and from the Royal Mail and other agencies. Useful free advice is available from Royal Mail in publications such as "The Guide to Effective Direct Mail" (4) which provides a guide to the process of:

- planning a campaign
- list selection
- designing/writing the mail shot
- printing
- mailing
- response and fulfilment
- analysis

Useful practical articles and advice is given to subscribers of the magazine "Winning Customers" (5). Since mail shots/sales letters provide an important means of generating sales to all companies including the small, it is suggested that the small firms, whether selling to the consumer or business markets, should attempt their own mail shot, since this will focus their attention on major matters such as:-

- precisely who to address in their target market segment(s)
- how will their product/service fulfil the needs of these prospects?
- how will they analyse the results?

and   - what must they do to increase response rate?

Reference 5 gives a case study relating to a firm whose mail shot received a 0.3% response. Using advice from a direct marketing consultant the firm tried a 'Mark II' mail shot which produced a 0.7% response; still not huge, but double the initial figure. Several simple alterations were made in order to produce the higher response rate.

Copy length was increased; long copy often outsells short copy. The more expensive the item, the longer the copy needs to be to persuade the prospect.

An emphasis on BENEFITS to the potential buyer was stressed. If the mail shot saves the reader time and effort by spelling out benefits rather than concentrating on the seller's image and other ireelevances, response and sales will increase.

IMPROVING EFFECTIVENESS

Other recommended aids in producing effective mail shots include:
1. The need to pose questions in such a form that elicits the desired answer – YES.
2. The need to put greater emphasis on the offer – free gift, brochure, free survey, discount for a speedy reply etc. and the use of a response aid.

Other advice given by the consultant involved in the above case study related to the printing type. The mail shot needs to look like a letter – not a 'flyer' – by laying out the copy more like a letter, a higher response rate can be obtained. The original writer was advised to have the copy typeset in a "typewriter" type face. The letter should begin with a salutation since it can help to address the target individual by name; alternatively his title may be used, e.g. Dear Purchasing Manager etc.

Compiling sound up-to-date lists of addresses of those prospects most likely to benefit from, and thus buy the product or service, cannot be emphasised enough. There are many sources of mailing lists. Many firms already possess their own mailing lists or the substance for compiling them in the form of customer records, warranty cards, salesmen's reports, enquiries and responses to other forms of advertising. This is a good basis for an effective list if it is remembered that very often the best customers are to be found amongst present or past (satisfied) customers. For many firms, most of their current sales come from old customers, e.g. accountancy and consultancy firms.

Modifying records can be simple and many require ensuring that different types of customer can be identified as discrete groups and cross referencing so that duplication is avoided. Changes and information that need to be recorded would include:
- addresses
- spending patterns
- job status

Addresses that can be drawn off in the order to qualify for Post Office discounts can be important.

An in-house list under the firm's control can be used repeatedly and expanded; it is also a valuable commodity (see under list brokers). Simple ways of expanding the list would include:

- asking recipients of mail shots to name friends and others who would be interested in the firm's offerings and provide space in the reply card for them to do so.

In mailing to large companies with many managers, departments or divisions, others could be interested in your product(s) and the recipient should be asked for appropriate names.

LIST BROKERS

Rented lists and List Brokers. Many specialist mailing houses compile lists covering many categories; The Direct Mail Databook and Benn's Direct Marketing Year contain a list of lists. The price of renting lists depends on the degree of selectivity and how up to date they are. Some Direct Mail Houses will provide a sample list from any of the lists whose accuracy can be checked by telephoning the names to confirm them, or by using the sample in a test mailing.

List Brokers act as intermediaries between those who own lists and potential users, charging a fee for this service. The names of list broking firms are included in the Gower Press Databook and the address of The British List Broker's Association is: Premier House, 150 Southampton Row, London WC1 5AL. Telephone 01-278 0236.

Before renting or buying lists a number of pertinent questions should be addressed to the broker, e.g.

- What is the source of the list? What appears to be appropriate for your firm, may not be so. The number of useful names may be less than required if it contains a high proportion of competitors or contacts outside your area of operation.
- How long have the names been on file? If the list is regularly updated its nominal "age" is not relevant.
- How often is the list updated? The more frequently it is updated, the more useful it will be. Those lists which are used will be better value in terms of accuracy than one which is not.
- It is worthwhile asking the list supplier when it was last used and by whom. Was the list used for a competitive product?

Testing a list is further discussed in literature available from the Royal Mail.

TRADE AND OTHER ASSOCIATIONS

These Associations can often provide a complete or part membership list of relevance. Likewise, Chambers of Commerce and professional institutions may be used and supply the information sought, free or at a nominal charge.

Directories already discussed, can be an inexpensive source of information for business mailing.

STORAGE/MAINTENANCE OF INFORMATION

Attention should be given to list storage and maintenance. When an address responds to the firm's mailing, the information supplied becomes the firm's property even if the initial list was rented. This detail is important and should be analysed and stored with care.

Storage systems of three types are available and depending on the extent of the firm's activity may be stored by:-
COMPUTER: Most mailing houses and list owners store lists in this way. With the availability of micros, your firm may have its own direct access. An advantage of computerised systems is that they can produce the mail letters as well as store information.
MECHANICAL SYSTEMS are available in many forms and can be very sophisticated and effective for storing shorter lists.
or MANUAL METHODS such as record cards in a suitable filing box can be used for storing plenty of data. They can be valuable for the smaller business with less voluminous customer records.

FURTHER HELP

A good deal of information including terminology and names of list suppliers, can be obtained by writing to the British List Brokers Association Ltd (BLBA) whose address is given on page 50.

The Consumer Location System, a new media data base is discussed by Royal Mail (4). A technique now exists whereby individual consumers can be identified even where traditional lists are not available. The technique called Consumer Location System (LCS) is based on research data from BMRB's Target Group Index and CACIACORN, a system already referred to. Further information on CLS can be obtained from the Direct Mail Sales Bureau (4). This information can provide named consumer lists by specifying which ACORN type(s) and the geographic areas at which the firm wishes to direct its product/service.

THE PACKAGE

In designing the mail package, unless an external agency is used, requires the firm to consider the usual four components:

- the envelope
- the letter
- the insert material

and
- the reply device

The envelope can be used as a selling aid since it has adequate space for messages to be read before the prospect even opens it. A postal sales representative can usefully advise on methods of preparing a well designed envelope, its size and type, so that it will stand out from other mail and please the recipient with its graphic devices and good taste. An envelope of good quality and one that is suitably sized for its contents, is important, and information without charge is available from the Post Office.

The letter is an individual communication from the advertiser to the potential customer in which illustrations support this message. The letter is the salesman, the leaflet/brochure is the sample kit.

A successful letter will direct attention to the potential buyer's NEEDS – what's in it for him? The letter must give clearly the advantages/benefits to the prospect if he buys the firm's product/service – and how his problem will be solved. How will your firm's offering(s) make the prospect's life/business easier or more profitable? The letter needs to:

1. Get the reader's attention by identifying one or more of his problems and offering to solve them.
2. Give enough detail about the offering and explain how it will solve the reader's problem.
3. Arouse the desire to buy or try and evaluate your offering. Give testimonials or names of opinion leaders.
4. Encourage the reader to act quickly by offering an incentive and including a reply-paid card or envelope.

The salutation is important; the use of his/her own name ideal. The use of Dear Sir/Madam is bad. If you do not have a name, a title can be used, e.g. Dear Marketing Director, Dear Wine Lover etc.

The letter should be carefully broken into easy-to-read paragraphs with sub-headings and underlining to emphasise key points.

Many texts and the Post Office Publications stress the main requirements of an effective mailing letter/packaging. The length of copy is an important consideration depending on the writer's product/service. If the product is expensive, high risk and has social significance, a long letter may be needed (with brochures etc.); in which case do not hesitate to use long copy. On the other hand, writers should avoid extending an adequate simple one page letter with unnecessary verbiage.

The Reply Device aids the reader to take the action the letter has hopefully stimulated. By providing a reply element with the mailing increases the chances of receiving a large number of replies.

The methods available, costs and detail concerning Business Reply and Freepost services, often with introductory offers, can be obtained from Post Office Publications designed to assist users of direct mail.

Useful advice in **inserts** to the firm's mailings, printing and production is available also from many Post Office Publications dealing with direct mail. (4)

The letter, preferably personalised, is the main vehicle for the direct mail campaign but it will usually be necessary to include other printed materials; it is necessary that the inserts should be relevant, adding information additional to that contained in the letter and "singing the same tune." Too many leaflets can confuse the reader – and can be costly. The weight of mailings should be considered; a few extra (unnecessary) grams could also put it into the next weight category – and further expense.

TESTING

Testing the mailing by sending out a representative sample and analysing the result is a commonsense approach prior to a full-scale mailing. It is important that the sample be truly representative or the exercise will be wasted. It is difficult to test small mailings since the test will need to be a high proportion of the mailing list. The Post Office advise that a mailing of less than 5000 addresses is not worth testing. A test would be directed as discovering:

- If the list(s) used have too many errors and produce many "returned-undelivered." If the list, possibly rented, gets the same responses as an in-house list.
- If the product pricing is sound. Is your price too much or too low – giving a "cheap and hasty impression"?
- Does the inclusion of some offer/incentive really improve sales/ enquiries?
- Is the package creatively constructed, the letter sensibly short/ long with full colour brochures versus two-colour?
- What proportion of enquiries are converted to sales? Is this response level sufficient to meet planned profit targets?

In many cases it becomes necessary to test by mailing two or more sample packs; one acting as control with the other(s) testing a variable against that control.

The Analysis of both test and full-mailing should not be skimped. A full analysis of all mailing will permit subsequent mailings to be improved by the detailed lessons learned from the last. The analysis will determine:

- Which are the best geographic locations for the offering
- Which segments of the total market provide the most valuable customers

- The range of order values
- The relationships between sale and cost per sale
- What cash flow patterns are to be expected in terms of payment.

Direct Mail is a major force in the media market. In terms of national advertising expenditure it is approaching the size of display advertising in regional newspapers, much greater than consumer magazines and bigger than radio, cinema and outdoor advertising.

SOME FACTS ABOUT DIRECT MAIL

1. .... advertising expenditure is shifting away from fast moving consumer goods and towards services and consumer durables. In other words, towards discrete target markets as against undifferentiated mass markets . . . Direct Mail flourishes because the mechanisms exist whereby potential customers can be located and identified.
2. Direct Mail has always been regarded as a prime business-to-business medium. However, its growth as a consumer medium has far out-stripped its growth as a business-to-business medium. In terms of numbers of items sent, the latter grew by 45% between 1975 and 1989, the former by a massive 230% . . . Direct Mail works well in relation to many of the target audiences for consumer goods and services which can now be identified.
3. The average exposure to Direct Mail is currently (1985) three times every four weeks per household . . . compared with the several hundred exposures per day to which the public is subjected by other media which may be an explanation of the extraordinary impact of Direct Mail. It is a private medium and the audiences are not exactly saturated or satiated with it. There is plainly room for more.

PUBLIC RELATIONS

Effective Public Relations (PR) for any size of business pays dividends. Many large, well-known companies spend time and considerable sums of money in promoting their image. If the public perceives a good image of the firm it develops a trustworthiness and when the public, customers, suppliers, bankers, and the community understand the scope, capabilities and soundness of the firm, they develop a greater confidence in doing business with it. A firm with a good image also attracts good employees.

Many small firms are daunted by PR believing it to be the province of big firms only – who get good PR free whilst paying for its advertising. This misconception confuses the roles of PR and advertising. The latter is one method of stimulating sales through buying space in newspapers and technical journals and through the use of TV, radio and exhibitions etc. PR is no substitute for and should not conflict with advertising since it works over a longer period and it can achieve an understanding of the company, its scope and products, creating a climate to assist the business to propagate itself. Advertising and PR both cost money but the latter can be a very cost effective way of getting the company noticed and remembered.

THE SMALL FIRM

Before seeking to promote its image and make closer contact with the appropriate media, the small firm is advised to set down clearly the reasons why it is special or unique. This analysis itself may throw light on changes in management style, products/services and methods of operation that may become necessary.

Honest opinions by management and supervision together with its professional advisers, and possibly from suppliers and buyers, will seek answers to the basic questions:

- What are the company's main strengths?
- What are its weaknesses?
- What future opportunities are expected to increase the profitability of the enterprise?
- What major threats/dangers lie ahead and how can they be turned into opportunities?

The results of this exercise need to be summarised and given to all managers, supervisors and the workforce.

SOURCES OF CONTACT

The next step may be to list those people/organisations who can favourably influence the opinions and attitudes of others. This list, which can be surprisingly lengthy, will include:-

- Past and present customers
- Potential customers
- Key suppliers
- Opinion leaders
- Local Authority officers
- Educational establishments
- Local/regional newspapers
- Trade journalists
- Local radio/TV

These, and others properly informed can be valuable assets in any PR effort. Local press including the "free sheets" can be useful allies and receptive to a good story about the firm. Firms anxious to improve their PR need not be slow in approaching the press who will be keen to publish articles concerning for example:

- A visit by a prestigious person
- A new/large order from a well-known and large concern, or the supply of goods/services to a foreign country
- An innovative new product/service

- An achievement by a member of the firm that is of particular interest and draws attention to the enterprise.

The job of contacting the media may be dealt with by the Chief Executive or possibly passed to a lively person from the sales/marketing function. After making contact with the local/regional newspaper or an appropriate broadcaster from local radio, a firm's representative should be prepared for questions from his contact who may help not only in preparing a suitable story, but by introducing other matters, not previously considered, to improve the impact. Often a good photograph can be of value when it is advisable to employ a professional to carry out this work.

Initial efforts to obtain good PR will require building up good relations with the media and planning both short term and long term objectives. Seeking opportunities to give talks/seminars relating to the business and its activities provides another source of PR.

SPONSORSHIP

Sponsoring special events, establishing links with local schools/colleges and entering for a design award are other sources of improving PR.

SOURCES OF HELP

David Morgan Rees who acts as Educational Officer with the Institute of Public Relations is the author of the book 'Getting Publicity' directed at small businesses (7) covers this subject in more detail. The National Westminster Bank's Small Business Digest carries an article by this author (6) which concludes with the comment that "Good PR gets results and not surprisingly, results get good PR."

The marketing literature provides many examples of successful results obtained by firms through the employment of PR agencies. PR consultants are currently enjoying a boom and in 1986, greater than £500m was spent by UK companies in boosting their corporate images. Assisting with press releases and obtaining editorial coverage from the trade press and from local/national newspapers is one of the basic tasks of the PR consultants; they also help in promoting a business by designing better brochures and literature and organising presentations and special events, producing in-house newspapers and lobbying local and national government on behalf of a company when legislative changes are likely to adversely affect its progress.

CONSULTANTS

The argument in favour of employing a PR consultant is that they have specialist skills, knowledge and special contacts within many business areas. They can devote the time to presenting their client's name and products to sectors that direct advertising may not reach.

Good PR can be of particular value to professional firms who are restricted from advertising. It is important to accept that PR by itself achieves little; successful PR depends on hard work and knowing well the specific market or industry and by working closely with the other parts of the client's marketing function. The principal of one PR consulting firm suggests that good PR uses a good deal of commonsense and a knowledge of where to get information and put efforts and resources into the right areas.

PREPARATORY WORK

Before engaging a PR consultant the firm needs to know what it wishes to achieve and precisely who it is attempting to reach. For a long term PR campaign it is necessary to consider the cost and how PR will best match with other marketing efforts; they all need to "sing the same tune." Help in selecting a PR consultant can be obtained using The Hollis Press and Public Relations Annual (obtainable from a reference or business library) which lists PR consultancies and the type of work they specialise in. The Institute of Public Relations, St. John's Square, London, will supply information on member companies and advise on choosing one. The cost of employing consultants depends on the amount of work commissioned and skills and resources used. A day's work can cost from £100 to £400 depending on the firm used and on whether it is London based or a regional firm with a smaller overhead structure. Many large agencies will expect to charge fees for their work in excess of £10,000 although good PR work can be obtained in a local area for fees of the order of £5,000 per year.

Before making a final choice, a booklet, "Choosing and Using a PR Consultancy", obtainable from Director Publications Ltd., Institute of Directors, London, may prove useful.

EXHIBITIONS

Whilst there are many stories about the small business exhibiting its product(s) at the right time and place and in this way starting on the path to making a fortune, there are many who query the benefits to be derived from this method of contacting customers. Cost comparisons of the various media for contacting customers reveal that exhibitions can be very costly – and very much higher than personal selling. Many exhibitors have found that the cost and time would have been better spent in pursuing the more traditional methods. Cunningham and White comment with examples on the cost effectiveness in industrial marketing in their publication 'Role of Exhibitions in Industrial Marketing' (8). Nevertheless exhibitions are growing at a considerable rate and can provide a good method of generating sales provided that some fundamental thinking is applied.

Amongst the reasons given by many companies for exhibiting regularly include the proposition that "they must be there" or they need to "fly the flag"; they may be mistaken. Those members of the Sales/Marketing function who regard exhibitions as providing an annual outing for sales staff made more enjoyable by entertaining old customers should be advised that there are alternative methods, less costly and more productive.

A firm's basic objective in organising an exhibition should be to show its offerings to the largest number of potential buyers and meet prospects to later follow-up. If a new or modified product or range can be shown, so much the better. Choosing the location and type of exhibition is the first consideration and there is a considerable choice. Amongst the literature that can provide help are the publications, Exhibition Bulletin (9), Exhibitors and Conferences (10) and Exhibition and Conference Fact Finder (11). Such publications may help by providing information on exhibitions which the firm may wish or need to attend purely as a visitor.

In evaluating an exhibition it is important to study the visitor type, a more important fact than the numbers of people attending. It is the quality of visitor that is important and the exhibition organiser, unless he publishes this information, should be asked to supply as much detail as possible. Exhibitions run by the publishers of trade magazines can be successful in terms of attracting the right type of buyer at a relatively low cost and help by publishing details of the exhibitor's product in their magazine as well as in their exhibition literature.

LOCATIONS

The exhibition venue can be important. For many shows, London, with its easy access and other attractions, may head the list. For certain shows, tradition dictates, Harrogate or Brighton etc., the latter providing, at the right time of the year, the opportunity to enjoy some relaxation during or after the exhibition. Road and rail connections and adequate car parking are other factors to consider and the National Exhibition Centre in Birmingham, for example, satisfies these criteria.

In deciding when and where to exhibit it would be sensible to attend the exhibition initially as a visitor. In this way, down-to-earth observations of the type of visitor and facilities can be made – as well as obtaining a visitor list. Talking to exhibitors will also provide clues as to the effectiveness, particularly if some exhibitors have a history of regular attendance and are prepared to comment on the quality and number of sales leads obtained. The number of re-bookings is a good indication of a viable exhibition. It is important to find out from the organiser their means of attracting visitors, to whom and how they are advertising and whether seminars or conferences form part of the exhibition. Moreover, what are the organisers doing specifically to attract and entertain decision-makers, and is their exhibition literature and 'after sales service' of high calibre?

PREPARATION

Having decided to exhibit, the firm needs to spend time in the months leading up to the event on the important basics. The size of the stand, determined by the nature of the product, its position in the exhibition hall, are matters on which some professional advice may be usefully sought from companies specialising in this field. Cotterell and Unibrand Training comment on stand size, position, manning and basic consideration in articles in 'Winning Customers' (12). This writer advises that since visitors have a good deal to see it is important that the individual exhibitor's message should be simple and clear to catch and hold attention. A large portion of visitors come looking for something new, so a new product/service labelled "NEW" in large letters will stop a good proportion. As in advertising, the word "FREE" also stimulates interest and visitors will stop to see what is being given away.

Other ways of attracting visitors is to address them directly. "A NEW DEAL FOR MARKETING DIRECTORS" or "DOUBLE YOUR INCOME RETAILING..." will attract attention.

The preparation of an attractive stand, manned by sufficient and experienced sales staff and showing new products, well presented, will be better attended if current and potential customers are informed in advance. Help will normally be given by the organising firm in mailing invitations which can be followed up by telephone calls immediately prior to the exhibition; it is worthwhile mailing customers/prospects who cannot attend the show. Well in advance of the exhibition date it is important to issue press releases and advise all relevant media stressing how the firm's product/service will benefit the visitors. Benefits need to be spelled out boldly but succinctly. Advanced publicity needs to stress benefits for the target segments, omitting detail about the exhibiting firm's history and matters which the prospect will find irrelevant. Instant impact before and during the exhibition will draw and hold visitors.

The number of exhibitions in the UK is growing and more firms are using them as an important method of generating sales. The basic considerations for a cost-effective exhibition requiring both research and creative effort, are:–

- Selection of the most appropriate show and location
- Stand design, position and staffing
- The publicity before, during and after the exhibition
- The need to stress benefits available to decision-makers in target companies/markets, before and during the exhibition.

A useful section on 'Business Tourism' is published in North West Business Monthly (13) which covers conferences, trade fairs and exhibitions and discusses centres, organisations and locations, mainly in the North West. The subject of pricing as the key to success is discussed and in giving details of many sites draws attention to the G-Mex Centre which provides good facilities and is very conveniently situated.

The book, 'Be Your Own PR Man,' by Bland (14) details ways of publicising a company and suggests methods of generating free publicity. This text tells firms how to avoid the expense of a Public Relations Consultant in:
- getting the press to write about the company or product
- getting a press release
- getting TV and radio coverage
- speech writing

and
- conducting and publicising a survey

ADVERTISING

Advertising is a non-personal form of communication through a paid media under clear sponsorship and, as indicated in the last section, to be distinguished from PR. Its objective is to make potential buyers respond more favourably to a firm's offerings and seeks to do this by providing information and attempting to modify desire by supplying reasons for preferring the firm's particular product(s). The constructive function of advertising is to explain the products/services and their availability, its combative function is to undermine the prospect's loyalty to other products/services.

MEDIA

Advertising media in the UK includes (1990):
- 10 TV Areas
- 16 National Daily Papers
- 62 Provincial Weekly Papers
- 400+ Consumer Magazines
- 40 Commercial Radio Stations
- 9 Sunday Papers
- 120 Provincial Daily Papers
- 2000+ Business and Trade Journals

– as well as directories, posters and the many other methods summarised at the end of this section. British Rate and Data, 'BRAD', provides information on sources of advertising media and lists them under area, price and potential audience as well as listing local 'free' publications.

SPECIALIST SOURCES

There are very many specialist journals covering, for example, fishing, animals, cars, aviation etc. The Radio Times provides a first-class source for advertisers, being seen on average by four people per household and may be present in the house for ten days or more.

Firms that have a clearly defined advertising objective have a marked competitive advantage.

BUDGETING/OBJECTIVES

Methods of determining the firm's advertising budget vary much; some recent published data for the UK engineering industry showed that:

29% had no known basis
39% employed a fixed sum method

28% based expenditure on a % of the previous year's sales
and   4% used other methods

This approach consigns advertising to a non-entity. Most firms have a trade cycle; when income drops some firms reduce advertising expenditure which tends to exaggerate the trade cycle, relegating advertising to be an effect rather than a cause. If this is the case, why advertise at all?

One of the problems in measuring the effectiveness of advertising arises because a firm's goals, quantified objectives are not made explicit. What are we attempting to achieve with our advertising campaign? The answer to this question needs to be clearly understood and stated by the advertiser. Is the campaign designed to accent one or more or all of the objectives indicated by the simple diagram?

Unawareness ➝ Awareness ➝ Comprehension ➝ Conviction ➝ Action

Some well known companies advertise in "bursts", i.e. advertising their product by building up to a level considered suitable and then stopping. After a period the process is repeated; others use a "drip" method by using a constant and steady level over the year. Whichever is the correct approach is debateable, possibly nobody knows. A paper worthwhile reading for background information on measuring advertising response was written by McDonald (15) who suggests that advertising is so interlaced with the rest of the marketing mix that it cannot be measured independently.

The methods of advertising and background to the American advertising industry is given in the well-known book by Vance Packard in his Hidden Persuaders (16) and well-worth reading.

COSTS

The high cost of salesmen is referred to in the next section and some firms whose customers are irregular buyers have found it more cost effective by reducing salesmen's calls and spending more on effective advertising; thus the use of indirect communication with some customers to reduce overall selling costs, although the salesman may be ultimately necessary to close the sale.

Those firms wanting their business to grow, or just survive, need to promote themselves. In these competitive times, buyers have plenty of choice and need frequently reminding WHO and where the firm is and WHAT it is offering. Advertising can be a good investment not just an expense and needs to be part of the firm's budget and not something to be done when it can be afforded.

DO IT YOURSELF?

A firm can increase the effectiveness of its advertising by employing an agency. By considering the basics, the smaller firms may experiment themselves so that later they will have some yardsticks against which to judge an agency which they may engage. Setting advertising objectives is the first important consideration; is the objective to:

a) sell the firm's product/service quickly and efficiently?
b) get new customers?
c) persuade regular customers to buy more?
d) get new sales leads?
e) attract dealer support?
f) inform more buyers WHO you are and WHAT you do?

The next stage is to clearly set down the target audience or audiences in detail. Who is most likely **to buy** the firm's offering? For domestic consumers, are they men, women or children? Which socio-economic group or income bracket? If marketing to other firms, which type, what size? To whom in the business will the offerings be made and where are these customers located?

BENEFITS

The other major consideration concerns BENEFITS to be advertised; the buyer wants to know "What's in it for me?" Those adverts which properly stress benefits will have a greater pulling power than those which do not. In this connection the selling company needs to research those factors which will motivate prospects. Is the firm's product and service unique? Do prospects seek convenience, beauty, good health, happiness, status and so on? Instead of listing technical features of the product, the advertiser is advised to translate most of these features into easily understood benefits.

Qualcast, a large producer of lawnmowers of the cylinder type, suffered competition from Flymo who manufacture the hover mower. As a result of research, Qualcast reacted with aggressive advertising using the slogan "A lot less bover than a hover", and similar adverts. Qualcast's market share increased but since their competitors quickly responded, total sales of mowers rose by 18%. The story of Birmid Qualcast is available in an interesting book, 20 Advertising Case Histories, and well worthwhile reading.

The steps in the advertising (persuasion) process can be summarised as:

PRESENTATION
↓
ATTENTION GETTING
↓
COMPREHENSION
↓
GETTING THE RECEIVER TO YIELD (comply)
↓
ENSURING RETENTION OF THE MESSAGE
↓
INDUCING DESIRED BEHAVIOUR

A good advertising agency will professionally assist in reinforcing all these stages and be able to measure and monitor them by well-known techniques, making changes where necessary to increase the effectiveness of one or more stages.

AGENCIES

Firms contemplating hiring an agency or changing their existing agency, need to devote some time and thought to the main factors involved since it can cost a good deal of money and a poor decision may even create problems for the other marketing functions. Choosing one of the big name agencies may not be appropriate for some firms, rather should they seek assistance from an agency who can demonstrate a good knowledge, understanding and contact within the seller's particular industry. There are thousands of advertising agencies in the UK. A firm wishing to employ a local agency could consult Yellow Pages unless based in London. The quarterly Brad Advertiser and Agency List gives details of agencies and some of their clients as well as listing clients under agency headings and offers a section on regional advertising. The publishers of Campaign produce a directory of the larger agencies called Portfolio. This publication gives detail about the agency's billings, clients and personnel and an indication of the agency's expertise in any particular medium. Another reference book available at many libraries is The Advertisers Annual which lists agencies by client and companies by agency. The UK Marketing Handbook also lists advertising agencies and specialist agencies. Other organisations will provide help in short listing; The Advertising Agency Register for a fee, and a suitable brief will shortlist agencies from the many on their books. They also offer a short video on each of the shortlisted agencies and detailed information about them including a sample of press advertisements. The same organisation also runs a Public Relations Register offering a service to companies trying to select a PR agent.

ASSISTANCE/COSTS

Further help is available from the Institute of Practitioners in Advertising (17); a firm supplying detail about their needs can obtain from this source a shortlist free of charge under their Confidential Agency Recommendation Service. The recommendations are obtained through the IPA's 260 member agencies responsible for 80% of total advertising by value. Firms seeking an agency should have in mind the following factors:

a) Agencies range in size and scope from the "one-man band" copy writer to the large "full service" agencies which deal with everything from market research to expert media-buying, but they can be expensive. The size of an agency is usually quoted in terms of its total billings, the total of all the agency's clients costs in advertising, most of which goes to the media where the clients advertise. The small client may not receive the close attention and help that is given to the bigger and more lucrative client. It is necessary for a firm seeking an agency to set down clearly the skills required to fulfil its particular needs.

b) The major cost in advertising is the cost of advertising space whether it be on TV, the press, posters and so on. Obtaining a good media price negotiator is therefore well worth finding. Agencies specialising in particular geographical locations or industrial sectors may be able to provide more buying power with local and regional newspapers or specialist magazines.

c) Many agencies take 15% of the client's payment to the media plus a fee related to production costs. It is in the agency's interest, because of this commission arrangement, to have the client pay the maximum for its media space. Before committing itself to an agency the client must enquire about the method of payment in detail. It may be in the client's interest if the commission method could be altered to a straight fee approach if the quality of service provided meets its requirements.

d) An examination of agency listings will give details of which organisations officially "recognise" each agency. Recognition is important because it gives an indication of the financial strength and credit-worthiness of agencies. Further, it may mean that the agency is eligible for discounts from the media that an advertiser would not be able to obtain by buying direct.

e) The location of the agency can be important in terms of the time that can be saved by the client's staff in travelling to meetings with the agency staff. A small regional agency which may be cheaper can be more convenient for meetings and will better understand local buyers and have good connections with local media.

f) It is worthwhile noting the other clients of a shortlisted agency since this will give an indication of their expertise in any sector. Agencies may specialise in specific areas such as consumer, industrial and financial advertising etc.

g) It is important for the company seeking help from an agency to work with people with whom they can work both professionally and personally. In this respect the client company should meet with the agency's technical staff with whom they will work and not deal only with a director, however charming, with whom it will later have little contact.

SUMMARY

The many methods of communicating with the customers are summarised and separately commented on with further references to guide firms in using all methods appropriate to their offerings, prior to dealing with advertising, promotion and personal selling.

REFERENCES

1. GTE Marketing Services Ltd., Old Trafford, Manchester M16 0PG.
2. Marks, Pauline. The Telephone Marketing Book, Hutchinson Publishing, 1986.
3. The ADS Group, 70/72 Sackville Street, Manchester M13NJ.
4. The Guide to Effective Direct Mail, Post Office Direct Mail Dept., P.O. Headquarters, 33 Grosvenor Place, London SW1X 1PX.
5. Winning Customers, Stonehart Publication Ltd., 57-61 Mortimer Street, London W1N 7TD.
6. National Westminster Bank, Small Business Digest No.22, July 1986.
7. Rees, D.M., Getting Publicity, David and Charles, 1986.
8. Cunningham, M., White, J., Role of Exhibitions in Industrial Marketing, Institute of Marketing Management, Summer 1974.
9. Exhibition Bulletin Infopack, 73 Mill Lane, London NW6 1YF.
10. Exhibitions and Conferences Fact Finder, Association of British Directory Publishers, London. Tel. 01-650 7745.
11. Exhibitions and Conferences, Unibrand Training, 25 Denmark Street, London WC2H 8NJ.
12. Winning Customers, Issue 18, April 1986, Issue 19, May 1986.
13. N.W. Business Monthly, July 1987, Promoter House, Heaton Mersey, Stockport.
14. Bland, M., Be Your Own P.R. Man, Wyvern Press Library, Ely, Cambs.
15. Mcdonald, G.M., Measuring Advertising Response, ADMAP, March 1980.
16. Packhard, V., The Hidden Persuaders, Penguin Books, 1981.
17. Institute of Practitioners in Advertising, 44 Belgrave Square, London. Tel. 01-235 7020.

QUESTIONS

1. List and briefly comment on methods available for communicating with customer/clients.
2. Why do directories provide an important source of communication to customers? What directories are used by your company and why?
3. List the main uses of the telephone in business.
4. What methods are available to small firms for improving their PR?
5. Why is direct mail marketing expanding? What types of product or service are most suited to direct mail?
6. List the advantages and disadvantages of exhibitions.

ADVERTISING, PROMOTION AND PERSONAL SELLING

Advertising is an important part of a firm's selling effort and needs to be planned and conducted professionally. The campaign should be kept under constant review and various media tried to elucidate that which is most effective in terms of cost and effort. Whilst the foremost task will be to promote a product or service, create a favourable impression of the firm and counter competition, there are many other tasks that advertising can accomplish. To conclude this section it is worthwhile listing what other things advertising can do.

1. Tell potential buyers about a new product and encourage them to buy it.
2. Maintain sales by keeping the product in the public eye.
3. Create new markets or revolutionise existing ones.
4. Stimulate new interest in an existing product by announcing a modification/improvement.
5. Boost sales by promoting a special offer.
6. Sell direct. "Off-the-page" selling is found in most newspapers and magazines and covers a vast range of offerings.
7. Get people to send for information, samples or a brochure.
8. Encourage stockists.
9. Create goodwill and company IMAGE through corporate advertising.
10. Educate. The Government is the main advertiser in the field of educational and public interest matters in their road safety campaigns, Health Education Councils' efforts to get people to take more exercise, give up smoking etc.
11. Invite job applicants.
12. Sell to the trade by advertising not to the general public but to members of specific trades or professions.

Reference has been made to using a mix of advertising media to ensure that the market-place is covered effectively. The following methods, not in any order of preference, are summarised with a note on some of the advantages and disadvantages of these methods.

CINEMA

Although cinema audiences are declining, the advertiser has a captive audience. This method is inexpensive and relevant to local shops, businesses, hotels and restaurants.

PARKING METERS

There are 35,000 parking meters in the UK used by more than 5 million motorists each week. For firms wishing to reach the motorist, here advertising could be effective. The local authority will supply details, and costs can be low.

POINT OF SALE

Having attracted customers to a retail shop or store it is sensible to remind them about a firm's product and why they should buy it. Reprints of advertisements made into counter cards and the use of posters, signs, and attractively presented samples can stimulate sales. Suppliers will often provide indoor point of sale displays.

PROMOTIONAL GIFTS

Carrying the firm's name in the form of pens, carrier bags, key-rings and book-matches are a method used by many big firms.

SANDWICH BOARDS

This can be a useful method of advertising a shop or business located in a side street. It is necessary to check with the local authority first in case permission is required.

TRANSPORT ADVERTISING

Taxis, buses and tube trains carry advertising. The message on the outside of moving vehicles will be short but more detail can be included on adverts placed inside tubes and buses. For local businesses this method can provide a low cost means of communicating with prospects.

THEATRE PROGRAMMES

Theatre programmes can be effectively used in promoting a firm and its offerings.

TELEPHONE KIOSKS

Telephone kiosks provide another source for local businesses; taxi firms could find this source particularly useful at some sites.

BOOK MARKS

Book marks may be sensibly used and can possibly be given to a local library.

OTHER METHODS

Amongst the "high-flying" methods of promoting a firm's image, product or for promoting a sale may be included HOT AIR BALLOONS, TETHERED BALLOONS and AERIAL ADVERTISING by using a plane to tow a message over a seaside resort or area providing a large audience.

RADIO

This can provide a cost effective method for communicating with customers. There are more than 40 commercial radio stations in the UK. The use of radio in the UK is much lower than in the US and Canada and its use here will inevitably grow over the next few years.

Amongst the benefits of radio advertising can be included IMMEDIACY, one of its strongest aspects. ECONOMY is another benefit; a 30 second broadcast can be bought for as little as £10 although prices rise significantly for peak-time transmissions. Production costs are generally low and the total costs are favourable when compared with television. Radio audiences can be very receptive and advertisers can capitalise on this fact; the well-known and friendly voice of a broadcaster can be very persuasive. Radio is LOCAL and a recent survey noted that radio can develop a good "community feeling" which provides another reason why the small business can benefit from appearing on local radio. Stations claim considerable LISTENER LOYALTY, a high proportion of listeners follow one station and many of them have direct contact through 'phone-ins', charity events and outside broadcasts. A good attitude to their favourite station provides a good advantage to advertisers.

One of the drawbacks of radio is the absence of visual stimuli by taking from the advertiser the advantage of exploiting the major sense of sight. Unlike press or direct mail advertisements, the listener receives nothing tangible to remind him. It cannot be assumed that listeners have a pen and paper handy to write down an advertiser's name and telephone number. In considering the use of radio it is worthwhile accepting that whilst radio can offer significant help in promoting a firm, it should be supported by other media, for example, the press.

TELEVISION

It is not appropriate for the small firm, mainly on account of the high cost and large area covered. Using a particular TV Region may help achieve sales and although production costs can be high, most regional TV Stations will offer special rates and discounts for first time advertisers.

PERSONAL SELLING

For many firms this method provides an important communication channel especially where:–

- The number of customers served is small.
- A flexible presentation is necessary.
- There is a need for immediate feedback of information from the potential buying company.
- Where the exchange between seller and buyer(s) has a technical content, i.e. when the selling company is adopting the 'interactive'

approach and developing/adapting a product to assist the buying company to solve a problem.

and ● When complaints are to be handled.

INTEGRATION WITH OTHER METHODS

Sometimes impersonal communication will not satisfy the needs of the customer when goods or services have a high perceived risk. Personal communication is often needed to play its part after advertising has stimulated awareness. Often the launch of a new product/service can be facilitated by the use of a sales force, after which other lower cost methods may be sensibly used.

COSTS

In recent years many firms have reduced their sales force because they have found that other means of communication are at least effective and cheaper.

Data from many sources confirms that over the past years the cost per salesperson, and the average cost per call, has been escalating. In 1980 The Financial Times published annual total costs per salesperson giving:

Year	1969	1973	1976	1979	1980	1988
£ Cost	4120	6300	10600	12046	15620	30,000[1]

Thus a critical look by many firms at the cost of their sales force. Costs are often high because the salesperson's time is spent carrying out duties which do not require particular skill and further amplified by the costs associated with travelling, waiting, product 'chasing' and administration.

A survey in one industry, carried out by a university business school gave the following breakdown of a salesman's time and similar values are available from other sources in multi-industry surveys.

ACTIVITY	% of Salesman's Time
Travelling	25
Waiting	20
Administration	16
Production 'chasing'	16
Contact with customer	23

Nevertheless despite high costs the most beneficial communication for many firms is provided by the two-way process involving a salesperson who can modify a presentation in response to the needs of the buying company. Technological changes in user and supplier industries and the increasing complexity and specialization of products, tends to increase the total communication requirements, of which the two-way communication method provides one important channel. The need to be selective in using sales staff is stressed as is the need to use the many other methods of communicating with prospects thus making the overall task more cost effective.

[1]Estimated

FUNCTIONS OF THE SALESFORCE

It is worthwhile summarising the main functions of the salesforce in the essential marketing tasks of the selling company. They are:–

1. Market research by providing information/feedback from potential buyers.
2. Market planning/budgeting by advising on product/service addition, deletion or modification.
3. Negotiation of contracts; price and terms.
4. Advising on the development of new product applications.
5. Problem solving for the customer.

and 6. Advising on new product possibilities.

PURCHASING

There are many sources of information which comment on the bases on which purchasing decisions are made and the reader may find it illuminating to consult texts which deal specifically with purchasing (1, 2). Much of this information is conflicting but draws attention to the differences in approach between large companies and the small. The large companies generally have specialist buyers who use 'professional' sources and tend to make greater use of trade and technical publications and attend exhibitions; the small company generally obtains information more frequently by accepting a greater number of visits from salesmen.

THE INDUSTRIAL SECTOR

In marketing to the industrial sector, where the selling company often has only a few buyers, there is an increasing need to focus on the efficient use of the salesforce, the oldest form of selling. It is necessary to distinguish between effective selling techniques on the one hand and how the salesforce is to best play its part in the 'promotional mix', i.e. how is the salesman to be involved in the situations of first-time buying as distinct from repeat purchasing etc.?

Personal selling is the major method of communication with the buyer(s) in industrial selling but publicity and advertising can be of great importance to the salesperson in creating awareness and building credibility so that he is more able to obtain a hearing through good source credibility. The sales staff from a little-known company have to work harder to get a hearing and try harder to make a good presentation. Allocation of communication resources will depend on the type of market and the stage in 'readiness to buy' stages.

Kotler (3) gives two simple diagrams to illustrate these points:

FIG. 1

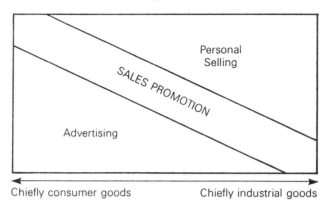

Chiefly consumer goods   Chiefly industrial goods

THE PROMOTIONAL MIX RELATED TO CONSUMER AND INDUSTRIAL GOODS.

Source: Robinson and Stidsen, Personal Selling in Modern Perspective. (Boston: Allyn and Bacon, 1967).

PERSONAL SELLING/ADVERTISING

The assumption that advertising is unimportant in industrial marketing and personal selling unimportant in consumer marketing is erroneous in terms of commonsense and many studies have confirmed this.

In industrial selling of complex and heavy machinery and commodities bought on price, delivery and reliability considerations, it would seem that personal selling would have a greater impact than advertising. Yet even for complex industrial products, advertising can play a major part in:

1. Building awareness. If the buyer is not aware of the company/ product he may refuse to see a salesperson.
2. Comprehension building. If the product(s) are new and technical, some of the explanation about them can be carried through advertising literature or the trade press.
3. Reminding prospects. If the buyer has knowledge of the product(s) but is not yet ready to buy, advertisements which constantly remind him and provide a more economical method than a sales call.

Advertisements can also be used to generate leads through carrying coupons which request further information and they can also be used to remind buyers how to use the products and provide them with reassurance.

Results of experiments in communicating show that advertising/publicity play the most important role in the awareness stage. Comprehension is affected by the education of the buyer and advertising with personal selling play equal but secondary roles. Customer conviction is influenced most by

FIG. 2

AWARENESS, COMPREHENSION, CONVICTION, ORDERING.

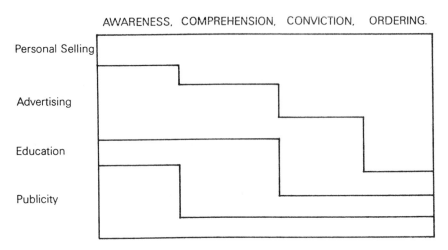

Kotler: Contribution of different promotion methods over the sales transaction cycle.
Source: Cash and Crissy, Comparison of Advertising and Selling; The Psychology of Selling, Flushing, N.Y. Personnel Development Associates, 1965.

personal selling closely followed by advertising. Closing the sale is predominantly a function of the salesperson's visit.

These findings are of practical importance in that the selling company can obtain economies by reducing sales calls in the early stages whilst concentrating on the vital final stage of closing the sale. By relying on advertising to play a greater part, the campaign can use different advertisements directed at building awareness, comprehension and conviction.

Studies reported by Theodore Levitt deal with the role of a company's reputation (built by advertising) and personal selling presentations in producing sales. This work, well worthwhile reading, is detailed in the chapter on 'Communications and Industrial Selling' in the text by Kurtz and Hubbard, The Sales Function and its Management (4).

This reference provides answers to the questions:

Does corporate or institutional advertising by industrial-product companies pay?

Do salesmen of well-known companies have an automatic edge over salesmen of little-known companies?

Is it better for an industrial product company to spend its limited funds on aggressive advertising of its general competence or more on careful selection and training of its salesmen?

Are the decisions of prospective buyers of new industrial products affected by the amount of personal risk these decisions expose them to?

Are the buying decisions of practical purchasing agents affected more by the reputation of a vendor-company than are the decisions of practicing engineers and scientists?

Does the effect of a company's reputation on a customer's buying decision hold up over time, or does it erode as time passes?

The credibility of the message source helps determine the persuasive effectiveness of the message itself. The greater the prestige or the more believable the message source, the more likely will it influence the audience in the direction advocated by the message. The less prestigious or believable the source, the less likely that it will influence the audience.

ASSISTING THE SALESPERSON

This phenomenon is referred to as the "source effect". McGraw-Hill takes the view that source effect works strongly in industrial selling and its famous advertisement shows a stern-looking buyer facing the salesman from behind his desk and saying:

"I don't know who you are.
I don't know your company.
I don't know your company's product.
I don't know what your company stands for.
I don't know your company's customers.
I don't know your company's record.
I don't know your company's reputation.
Now – what was it you wanted to sell me?"

The moral is: Sales start before the salesman calls – with corporate and business publication advertising.

Research findings provide the answers to the early questions posed. Corporate or institutional advertising does pay.

Generally speaking, the better a company's reputation, the better are its chances of

    a) getting a favourable first hearing for a new product amongst customer prospects,

and b) of getting early adoption of the product.

Vendor reputation influences buyers, decision makers and the decision-making process.

SELLING COMPANY REPUTATION

Since industrial products, particularly new products, generally require direct calls from salesmen, does the value of company reputation automatically give an edge to the salesman over the salesman from a less well-known or anonymous firm? The answer to this question is 'yes' but with reservations. In fact, customers expect more in the way of presentation from the well-known company and judge their performance rather differently from other salesmen. There is some indication that the audience at a sales presentation tends to "help" the salesman from the lesser-known firm by lowering their expectations in order to encourage competition between selling companies. Because a good presentation is always better than a mediocre one, irrespective of company reputation, there arises the further question, is it better for an industrial products company to spend its funds on aggressively advertising its competence or on more careful selection and training of its salesmen? When the influences of source effect and presentation effect are combined, research suggests that when a little-known company makes a good sales presention, it may be just as effective in getting a good first hearing for a complex product as a well-known company making a poor presentation. A little-known company concentrating on training its salesmen to make good presentations may make considerable progress towards overcoming the liability of its relative anonymity. Fuller answers to such questions and others dealing with the durability of the vendor reputation are dealt with by Levitt.

CONSUMER MARKETS — PERSONAL SELLING

The role of personal selling in consumer marketing appears to be small. Many consumer companies see their salesforce as "order collectors" and also to see that sufficient stocks are held and displayed. Nevertheless a well trained salesforce can make valuable contributions to:

1. Increasing stock position by influencing retailers to take more stock or devoting more shelf space to the company's brand.
2. Building retailer enthusiasm for a new product by a good presentation of the planned advertising and sales promotion back-up.
3. Persuading more retailers and stockists to carry the company's products through missionary selling.

PERSONAL SELLING AND THE COMPANY'S STRATEGY

The role and size of a firm's salesforce will be determined by the firm's marketing strategy. A market orientated company will take account of those INTERNAL factors which determine role and size, namely the:

- Resources of the company
- Nature of the products/services
- Price of the offerings
- Preferred methods of distribution available for serving the target markets

and those **EXTERNAL** factors such as:

- The strategy and resources of competitors
- The target market segment
- Existing industry codes of practice
- Relevant government legislation
- The existence of non-competitive conduct by firms acting together
- The type of buyers; their attitude to personal selling and the frequency with which they purchase.

ROLE/SIZE OF THE SALESFORCE

The role and size of the salesforce will also be determined by the basic marketing task, which may be:

conversional	re-marketing
stimulational	synchro-marketing
developmental	maintenance marketing
	de-marketing

and dependent on current demand which may range from negative to overfull.

There is considerable literature on the role of the salesforce. One writer on the subject comments that, "no definition can capture either the variety of tasks that can be involved or the many different selling situations which can be conducted." Types of selling can cover cold calling, developmental, missionary, new product or service selling and systems and team selling.

VARIED ROLES OF THE SALESPERSON

The salesperson is often required to service and cultivate existing customers as well as preserve and expand the value of sales to them. The salesperson is expected to find new customers (sales development) and has to communicate with prospects who may not view his company favourably and who may be resistant to change.

Thus the salesperson may be involved with a simple product which is in demand and requires little expert knowledge from him and communication skills of a low order. At the other end of the scale, the salesperson needs to be a talented business person needing to know a good deal about the product/service and also have a deep understanding of the customer's business. He may also need to act as one of a team serving an industry or individual company.

Further considerations on role and size of the personal-selling team, needs to be based on the selling company's strategy and objectives; the role of the sales team needs to be carefully defined in relation to the other components for communicating and at this point, its size and cost quantified.

INTEGRATING WITH OTHER METHODS
OF COMMUNICATION

The channels of communication available to complement the activities of a salesforce – and thus define its role and size – may be advertising, direct mail, publicity, sales promotions, product packaging and exhibitions. In this connection a published table below indicates the relative perceived importance of elements in the communications mix.

	Industrial Products	Consumer Durables	f.m.c.g.
personal selling	69	48	38
mass media, selective advertising	13	27	36
promotions	10	16	16
packaging	4	10	10
others	3	1	1

AN EXAMPLE

A large well-known company marketing pharmaceuticals provides a good example to illustrate the use of unique communication methods which reinforce the efforts of the salesforce whilst reducing their costs to a minimum.

The company's products are complex, many have a relatively short life-cycle, and are marketed to:

- Doctors in general practice (G.P's)
- Doctors resident in hospitals
- Wholesalers

The industry Code of Practice gives detailed guidance on acceptable forms of advertising and promotion and even includes suggested frequencies for sales staff to call on each of the above groups. It is not considered sufficient to simply calculate the size of the salesforce from a knowledge of potential 'customers' and recommended call frequencies. The company in question employs 3 distinct salesforces to service the above sectors. The salesforce dealing with hospitals markets products which are of little interest to G.P.'s and the salesforce serving local chemists through wholesalers, sell products which are both prescribable but may also be sold without prescription. Since chemists often recommend these latter products the allocation of the different channels of communication to this sales team will differ markedly from those of the other sectors.

In determining the role and size of the salesforce this company makes effective use of two unique supporting channels of communication. To obviate the need for lengthy and frequent meetings with doctors, and bearing in mind the code of practice, an information department, staffed by medical experts, is available at the company headquarters. One task of the salesforce is to direct attention to this function and thus doctors can address technical queries at any time on a variety of topics, including the progress of "field trials," and receive an immediate personal answer. This can be supplemented by sending information on micro-film where appropriate.

REGULAR NON-PERSONAL COMMUNICATION

The company also sends out a monthly magazine to its clients which contains technical articles, generally written by distinguished doctors or academics. Clients requesting further information on technical topics can be sent a cassette recording for which a small charge is made. The cassette injects "commercials" which subtly draw attention to the high reputation of the company and its products; this is very effective in reinforcing the work of the sales staff.

The use of a magazine further assists the sales/marketing function by publishing a client "feedback" section where recipients of cassettes comment on the content – and for doing so are paid a small fee on publication of their letter.

The company has attempted to integrate its advertising and other channels with the personal-selling activity, thereby conditioning the role of sales staff. Adverts directing attention to specific drugs having a high technical content are published in the medical journals where the company is given little prominence. At the same time sales staff are given extended training in the applications of specific products. The salesforce who arrange meetings with appropriate buyers are instructed to spend the majority of the available time discussing the single product. After this, sales staff may spend a limited time drawing attention to the previously promoted product and possibly a little "door knob" time on the product prior to this.

INTEGRATING COMMUNICATION EFFORT

The technique of integrating the efforts of sales staff and advertising, supported by an information service and providing cassettes is applied to the other sectors but with different emphasis.

The company referred to has a multi million £ turnover and a good profit record vigorously pursues market expansion and penetration as well as market development. Its message emphasis through its integrated channels is therefore:

- Reputation for product quality
- Flexibility
- Product capability and advantages
- Company image

The sales force cannot independently convey all these messages.

ROLE AND SIZE OF SALESFORCE — INERTIA

Several observers have commented on the effect of 'inertia' on the size and role of the salesforce which at a given time is often influenced by its **past** role and size. Previously an appropriate role may have been assigned to personal selling in the light of conditions then pertaining. In times of recession, falling company profits and the changing needs of the today's market, many companies have had to re-appraise their marketing communications strategy.

There are many sources of guidance on selling techniques and in salesforce management. The classic marketing texts and The Chartered Institute of Marketing (5) provide sources and the reader should refer to these for detail. Some pointers to help the personal salesperson can be usefully summarised here as well as some basic comment on their management.

THE EFFECTIVE SALESPERSON

A good salesperson must clearly know the company product(s) well, know the market and show a confident manner. A sales executive with a dull and boring manner, cannot create the vital "bond" in any interview with the buyer.

The salesperson must be a good **listener,** a fact already referred to under telephone selling, but worth accenting. Good selling does not require the salesperson to talk at length about themselves rather should they LISTEN to the customer and by questions find out about his NEEDS. The salesperson needs to be sensitive to the customer's situation and know exactly when to SHUT UP and listen.

A salesperson must philosophically accept rejection, this is part of the job. If the sales executive is concerned about his ability to deal with certain situations or technical questions and is thus somewhat afraid of some prospects he is probably short of product knowledge and training. The sales executive whose ambition is to be **liked** by the customer needs to be reminded and trained to seek **respect** from the customer through his knowledge and confidence.

CLOSING THE SALE

Persistence rather than aggression is important and the salesmen often need patience. Closing the sale requires a little push but the timing must be correct. Being in too much of a hurry and getting the timing wrong has lost many sales.

RATING THE SALESPERSON

The above points may be used in rating a sales executive and will reveal the need for help and training when he is rated low in the areas of:

- Creating confidence and making the customer feel at ease in doing business with him.
- Thinking about the customers needs rather than his own need to sell.
- Accepting rejection as part of the job and not avoiding difficult situations.
- Seeking to gain the customer's respect rather than seeking to be liked.
- Being patient and persistent as distinct from aggressive and too pushing.

THE MANUAL

A survey by the National Sales Executive Association of America shows that in most people the strength of the five senses falls in the order:

Sight	87%
Hearing	7%
Smell	3.5%
Touch	1.5%
Taste	1.0%

The eyes are way in front, a fact of some importance to the sales executive. The use of a well-designed manual can have an enormous impact in getting the prospect's attention at the initial stage leading to a sale. The proper use of a manual is often neglected and sometimes used only to show a picture of the product to the prospect. A well-planned manual designed to capture ATTENTION, INTEREST, DESIRE and ACTION (AIDA model) will guide the sales executive and prospect through the process and effectively lead to a successful closure of the sale.

The first stage in getting attention is assisted by good pictures of the product(s) preferably on the premises of a similar user. Many prospects will ask for pictures and since these are relatively inexpensive, should be given, since they leave something tangible which the recipient, with encouragement, will show to other members of the potential buying company. "Photo-testimonials" help any presentation and most satisfied customers are happy to permit photos to be taken of equipment/products in use on their premises and obtain some publicity by appending their name. A Presentation using a manual that begins with pictures needs to be followed by sheets that list BENEFITS briefly which provide a guide for the sales executive and arrest the attention of the prospect especially if the previously offered pictures show the product(s) in use on a well-known customer's premises.

CONTENT OF THE MANUAL

The size of the manual will depend on the product/service offered and to assist in closing the sale, may show some pictures of the selling company's premises, fleet of service vans, specialist members of staff and maybe the local salesman. The final sheet may include a special offer, a note of impending price increases, tax changes or special reason for buying at that time. When manuals become dirty and dog-eared they should be thrown away and replaced to include any new pictures/benefits and impending events to assist in closing the sale.

THE DECISION MAKING UNIT (D.M.U.)

Industrial marketing is characterised by the need to make contact with several individuals in the buying company's decision making unit (DMU). The subject of organisational buying behaviour is complex and there is a good deal of literature detailing the many possible buyer-behaviour 'models' (6, 7). In terms of the DMU the sales executive will recognise that participants include not only the purchasing manager but the product/service USER, SPECIFIER and SANCTIONER(S).

The purchasing process may involve 'politics' and therefore not be entirely logical. The author Pettigrew (8) discusses the role of the 'gate-keeper' who can impose himself between buyer and user to the detriment of the supplier. Such buyer-behaviour models and many others proposed serve to stress the complexity of the industrial buying process since it takes place in the context of a formal organisation influenced by budget, profit and cost considerations. Webster and Wind in offering a "General Model for Understanding Buyer-Behaviour" (9) comment that " . . . buying usually involves many people in the decision-making process and individual and organisational goals." Superimposed on the organisation are several forces in the environment and thus, variables which determine buyer-behaviour are:

- individual
- social
- organisational

and
- environmental

In designing a marketing strategy the supplier will need to be selective in approaching organisations and understand the nature of the buying-decision process, including the information sources relied on by the DMU and their methods of selecting and choosing suppliers.

PLANNING

There is no more important task in planning marketing strategy than identifying those individuals who share· responsibility and authority for buying decisions. They become the target for all marketing effort.

INVESTMENT APPRAISAL BY THE BUYING COMPANY

Because the rate of adoption of new ideas and equipment in industry is determined by their ultimate profitability the subject of investment appraisal can be an important element in communication with members of the DMU. Many buying companies necessarily preserve available funds to support the core business and require funds for new business development activities. Reference has been made to the problems of marketing/selling expensive technical equipment for energy saving and a problem arises when expenditure on such equipment and systems can be relegated to second place despite the fact that application of a sound method of investment appraisal may show worthwhile savings and generate greater profit than other projects competing for funds. The subject of investment criteria in connection with energy saving was dealt with at the National Energy Management Conference in 1982 (10) and many other commentators have stressed that the attractiveness of a project can depend on the appraisal method adopted. Such literature can help in marketing many complex and expensive pieces of equipment and systems.

METHODS

Several methods of investment appraisal are available and require some study by marketers if they are to succeed in the final stage of a sale. Further, the adoption of an innovation by one enterprise in a given industry will speed the adoption by the industry as a whole – such is the tempo of competition in industry at the present time.

The advantages and disadvantages of the main methods for investment appraisal are given below.

Payback Time

Advantages

1. Simple to calculate.
2. Gives a measure of time that capital is at risk.
3. Can usefully be used as an initial filtering device to rule out projects which are not worth more detailed consideration.

Disadvantages

1. Ignores all proceeds after payback date.
2. Completely ignores the timing of cash flows before payback is reached.
3. Gives no indication of profitability.

4. Overwhelmingly biased in favour of short term projects.
5. Useless for comparing projects of vastly different time spans.

Annual Rate of Return

1. Gives an indication of profitability.

1. Ignores the timing of cash flows.
2. May be affected by tax considerations.
3. Generally discriminates against projects of short duration.
4. Concept of profit, rather than cash flow is misleading.

Net Present Value (NPV)

1. Gives an absolute measure of profit in £ terms.

2. Takes into account the timing of cash flows.
3. Particularly useful for choosing between mutually exclusive projects.

1. Does not give a measure of profitability (in % terms) unless combined with a receipt/cost ratio.
2. Need to select a discount rate in advance.

3. In practice less easy than DCF to allow for risk.
4. Less easy than DCF to use in capital rationing situation.

Discounted Cash Flow (DCF)

1. Gives a measure of profitability (in % terms) which is easy to interpret.

1. The measure of profitability may mislead in the absence of information on the absolute amount of the investment when finance is not limited.

Advantages	Disadvantages
2. Summarises profitability into a single % regardless of size of project.	2. Not appropriate when the surplus cash generated is not reinvested at the same rate of interest, unless Dual Rate DCF is used.
3. Easier than NPV to allow for risk.	3. A possibility of multiple solutions – more theoretical than real.
4. Particularly useful for choosing between projects when finance is limited.	

TAKEN FROM: National Energy Management Conference, October 1982, Presenting a Case for Energy Conservation Investment.

Firms marketing expensive innovation equipment/methods have a formidable task if they are to properly answer the questions, WHO is to say WHAT . . . in WHAT CHANNEL . . . TO WHOM and with WHAT EFFECT?

In the final analysis the marketing function has to show how their product/service provides the best solution to the problems of the buying company. Research will elucidate the main message required and the market segment(s). Effective communication for organisational markets requires information about buyers and their response to marketing effort and this will determine the appropriate channels for communication.

MEMBERS OF THE D.M.U. — THE 'BUYER'

The problem of WHO to address can be difficult; it is individuals who act on behalf of a company and not organisations as such. The buying centre may be made up of all individuals who influence the buying decision process, including users, deciders, influencers and 'gate-keepers.' Simply recognising this, serves to remind sales executives that they must identify those individuals. In multi-location organisations the problem of identification can be complex.

Profitability has been stressed as a major factor in the diffusion of innovation and thus the necessity of employing sales personnel who can sensibly discuss investment criteria in a given situation. Marketing texts raise the key question of the power and influence of the executive designated 'buyer'. Articles on organisational buying are unanimous in their warning that the 'buyer' does not have sole responsibility, but the sales executive who assumes that he has little or no authority is often operating on a false premise.

Information flows between members of the buying organisation and it may only be possible to reach some members through others in the organisation.

IMPORTANCE OF INTEGRATING METHODS

The integrated approach to communicating with potential buyers should be stressed as an important marketing tool. Many firms arrive at a total communications budget by little more than "guesswork." Sometimes a sum of money based on a % of last year's sales income is used or what the Finance

Director decides is "affordable." Some firms use a value based on an estimated competitor's budget or on the "collective wisdom" of the industry. The larger firms with a sophisticated marketing function regard such "guesses" as nonsense and direct their communication efforts by setting clear objectives for each channel, cost each programme and then monitor results, so that when objectives planned are not achieved, corrective action can be taken.

MOVING THE BUYER(S) — WHICH CHANNEL?

No single method of communication – personal selling, advertising/ promotion, technical literature, the use of trade press or exhibitions – can move potential buyers from awareness of the firm and its offerings, to purchase. All sources need to "sing the same tune" but at different times during the buying process. Reference has already been made to the need to direct somewhat different efforts to various members of the Decision Making Unit in industrial marketing. The individuals in the DMU will have specific interests which will include:

- Technical Data
- Quality
- Cost
- Prompt delivery
- Helping the user with particular problems
- Good stock control/production
- After sales service

A planned approach to a communications strategy requires the firm to:
1. Define the target group(s) that the firm seeks to influence.
2. Study how these groups make purchasing decisions (literature read, is T.V. or radio appropriate?)
3. Determine the type and amount of information needed by the prospects and the nature of the appeals to be made.
4. Define the objectives for communicating. Without OBJECTIVES it will not be possible to measure the results achieved.
5. Allocate **SPECIFIC TASKS** to **SPECIFIC CHANNELS,** e.g. personal selling, advertising, technical literature, exhibitions etc.
6. Estimate the allocation and cost to each channel and then sum to get the total communications budget.
7. Integrate the communications strategy into the general marketing strategy.
8. Monitor results against objectives for use in adaptive control.

SUMMARY

Advertising and other means of communicating with the customer are discussed in this section as is the importance in many situations of personal selling. It is important that all the means of communication are integrated so that they all "sing the same tune" at the appropriate stage in the selling process. The cost of personal salesmen is very high and many firms have found that other means are often as effective and a great deal cheaper. The proportion of a salesperson's time actually in contact with the customer is often only of the order of 20%.

Despite the high cost however the most beneficial communication for many firms, particularly to 'close' the sale is provided by the two-way process involving a person who can modify a presentation in response to the needs of the customer.

The requirements of a salesperson are listed as is the need for the firm to expend resources on advertising, promotion and good public relations.

The role and size of a firm's salesforce is discussed and an example summarised of the sensible use of other methods of selling to reinforce the work of the salesforce and minimise the total costs of selling.

A salesman needs to be a good listener and seek to be respected by the customer as distinct from being liked.

A properly presented sales manual which is updated regularly is an essential aid to the salesperson as is the need to be well informed on the methods of investment appraisal by the buying company.

The chapter concludes with the importance of integrating all the methods of communicating with the customer and offers a simple checklist.

REFERENCES

1. Fox, H.W., Rink, D.R., Coordinating Purchasing with Sales Trends, Journ. of Purch. & M.M., Winter 1977.
2. Farmer, D., Developing Purchasing Strategies, Journ. of Purch. & M.M., Vol.14, No.3, Fall 1978.
3. Kotler, P., Marketing Management Analysis, Planning and Control, Prentice-Hall Int. Editions.
4. Kurtz and Hubbard, The Sales Function and its Management.
5. The Chartered Institute of Marketing, Moor Hall, Cookham, Maidenhead, Berks. SL6 9QH.
6. Webster, F., Modelling The Industrial Buying Process, Journ. Mark. Res. NW. 1965.
7. Brand, G., The Industrial Buying Decision, Chapter 6.
8. Pettigrew, A., The Industrial Purchasing Decision as a Political Process, Eur. Journ. Markg., Spring 1975.
9. Webster, F., Wind, Y., A General Model for Understanding Organisational Buying Behaviour, Journ. Markg., April 1972.
10. National Energy Management Conference, Oct. 1982. Presenting a Case for Energy Conservation Investment.

QUESTIONS

1. Give some of the reasons why the amount of information by business is expanding. How does this affect businesses attempting to communicate with potential customers?
2. What is meant by "buyer-readiness" and how does this influence a firm's approach to communicating with potential buyers?
3. List and briefly comment on methods available for communicating with customers/clients.
4. Why do directories provide an important source of communication to customers? What directories are used by your company and why?
5. List the main uses of the telephone in business.
6. Why is direct mail marketing expanding? What types of product or service are most suited to direct mail?
7. List the situations when personal selling is a particularly important channel of communication. What are the main qualities of a good salesperson?
8. What is meant by the 'integrated approach' to communicating with potential customers? What is its main purpose?

PRICING

ROLE OF PRICE IN THE 'MIX'

Of the four components that constitute the marketing mix (often referred to as Product, Place, Price and Promotion), pricing clearly has an important bearing on purchasing behaviour. Pricing is a complex subject which has received a good deal of attention by economists and many marketers, yet many business managers including those associated with marketing, have treated pricing as one of the less important factors in effective marketing. It is not uncommon for a firm to have carried out a good deal of product research, have a sound range, a good promotional strategy together with sound methods of distribution, yet treat pricing as a "residual variable" to be left to relatively junior staff who may use a simple cost-plus method. In some industries, often where there is poor control of labour and material costs, pricing is left to the work study practitioner who evaluates the cost of production, and an accountant who produces an overhead recovery cost (based on the previous year's information?) to which a 15% or 20% mark-up for profit is added to give the selling price.

THE IMPORTANCE OF PRICING

In a survey amongst managers, many of those questioned did not select pricing as one of the most important areas in their firm's marketing success. In recent years, however, pricing has received greater attention because of:

- Inflation
- Over capacity and competition
- Government interest in price competition.

The large successful companies take pricing seriously and top management are involved in directing research into those aspects relating to the firm's pricing policies.

BASIC FACTORS IN PRICING

Pricing is concerned with COST, DEMAND, and COMPETITION and important in at least four situations when:-

- Setting a price for the first time.
- There is an indication that price is incorrect; when demand changes, there is an inflation in costs or where there are shortages of the product.
- Competitors change price up or down and careful analysis is required in dealing with this situation.
- A firm produces a range of products with linked demand, the optimum price for the time needs consideration, i.e. when there is interrelated demand.

Some texts dealing with price, consider a single product and treat the pricing objective simply as a means of maximising profit; business however is often not quite so simple and other objectives might be applicable and relate to:

MARKET PENETRATION

Is aimed at stimulating market growth to capture a larger share of the market and likely to be used if the market is highly price sensitive. Higher output can result in greatly reduced costs and a lower price will discourage actual or potential competition.

MARKET SKIMMING

Takes advantage of the fact that some buyers are ready to pay a higher price than others since the product/service has a high present value to them. This situation can be advantageous if there are enough buyers whose demand is relatively inelastic, smaller volume production is not unduly expensive and there is little danger of entry by rival firms.

The firm needing rapid cash return if liquidity is a problem or if the future market is uncertain.

SATISFICING

Where the company is satisfied with a rate of return that is conventional for a given level of investment and risk, despite the possibility of an increased return.

PRODUCT LINE PROMOTION

When the objective is to maximise revenue on a range, rather than a specific line. A "loss leader" of very low return may be included to stimulate sales of others in the range. Alternatively, a "fair" rate of return may be considered preferable to individual optimum prices.

POLICIES

Pricing policies have to consider other parties involved as well as the end consumer, since the former can affect the profitability of a decision on pricing because:-

- The margins required by retailers, wholesalers and agents is relevant and these intermediaries will also be conscious of the reaction of their competitors.
- Of legislation by Governments relating to retail prices and competition. Price co-ordination between firms may attract attention from the Monopolies Commission.
- Supplies of labour and finance may need to be borne in mind. If profits are too high, unions may react by demanding higher pay and if too low, the bank or other sources of finance become concerned.

● The reactions of competitors to price changes may need to be predicted and since price is only one factor in the marketing mix, decisions on pricing need to be related to the other components so that executives responsible for these areas can be involved in commenting on proposed changes in price.

Pricing methods in practice tend to emphasize one of the factors such as cost, demand or competition to the neglect of other factors and it is necessary to comment on cost-orientated, demand-orientated and competition-orientated pricing.

COST-ORIENTATED PRICING

Is used by many firms to set prices mainly on the basis of costs. All costs are included together with an allocation of overheads based on expected production levels. Cost-plus pricing and mark-up pricing are similar in that price is set by adding a fixed percentage to the unit cost. Mark-up pricing is used in the retail trades where predetermined but different mark-ups to different goods are added. Cost-plus pricing is often used to price products/jobs that are non-routine and difficult to "cost" in advance, e.g. construction and development work. Mark-ups vary much for goods sold by retailers and dependent on the bases of:

● Cost of goods
● Retailing costs
● Prices charged by specialist retailers

● Prices of main competitors
● Prices in local markets
● Prices charged in the past

PRICE DIFFERENTIALS

Depend on geographical location; a retailer with many outlets across the country may divide stores into 3 categories depending on location, size and turnover where 3 different gross margin percentages apply to the 3 groups. Some very large retailers with a wide geographical spread often have a greater number of price bands.

Internal differentials provide ways of spreading prices over all product groups. Because some items cost more to sell (in terms of stocking costs, space requirement and selling cost, i.e. labour cost per items sold), some products attract higher margins. Items such as shoes may have different mark-ups depending on price bracket, expensive shoes may have a mark-up of 60% whilst cheaper lines only 25%. Such pricing policies apply to grocery and other items.

TEMPORAL (TIME) DIFFERENTIATION OF PRICING

Occurs when retailers are promoting products and some retailers at any one time can have hundreds of promotional events. Price cuts by retailers can be implemented as a result of:

● Support from the manufacturer, increasingly pressured by the retailer to reduce prices.

- Competitor price cuts.
- Seasonal lines.
- Items in a major audit by a consumer protection agency, since the retailer may wish to promote his image as a good value low cost outlet.
- A 'segmentation' approach to items considered essential to a particular organisation.

Several large retailers cleverly concentrate on maintaining low prices for a key range of goods to improve their 'image' and to assist this are often strong enough in terms of buying power to dictate the price required from the supplier.

RETAIL PRICING

For further detail on the many pricing methods adopted by different sectors of the retail trade, the reader is referred to specialist literature on this subject noted at the end of this chapter.

A good deal is also written by academics on consumer price awareness/sensitivity (1) (2). Price awareness in purchasing groceries and other products can be easy to measure through a survey over a period. In industrial purchasing, many companies stick to the same supplier or obtain only two or three quotations from others. Buyers in this sector are often more concerned with the reputation and performance of the supplier than price and for infrequently purchased items refer only to the last price paid. **Service providers** have difficulty often in defining precisely what they are offering for a given price and there is a low price awareness in this area.

PRICE AWARENESS

The implications of this are that when price awareness is high for a firm's offering, it should not be out of line with its competitors. If the firm has high production cost it must concentrate on creatively differentiating its product to blur price awareness. When price awareness is low, price can be increased but with caution and some firms take advantage of this fact by drawing attention to their product compared with competitors. Competitors may reply, and in this situation, stimulate a price awareness where previously none existed! 'Improved' marketing by banks in recent years has provided an example of this situation.

SENSITIVITY

The levels of consumer's price awareness and sensitivity to price have important implications for a firm's pricing policy, matters dealt with in a good deal of literature (3) (4). Early studies on consumer goods by survey revealed a remarkable dispersion of price awareness amongst different products and respondents questioned about prices of grocery items purchased over the previous week gave a variety of answers unrelated to actual prices.

Consumers have a greater awareness in times of low inflation but a high inflation rate leaves consumers confused. Valuable information to guide pricing policy is available from published work by research agencies and manufacturers can profit by taking account of work in this area (5).

Many writers like Gabor, Livesey, Riesz and others deal with the subject of price as an indication of quality in the market place. Traditional demand theory is wedded to the idea that price is the main factor which determines the consumer's choice and assumes that consumers:-

- have a good and accurate knowledge of prices.
- are able to distinguish the bundle of attributes being purchased from competitive products.

and - perceive quality.

DEMAND, PRICE/QUALITY

The laws of normal demand based on historical data consider the long-run only, short-run demand is neglected and governed by factors not fully explored. The significance of price in economic theory is often over-rated. Price serves as an indicator of quality with great frequency.

Early research in this field showed that a consumer intent on purchasing an item has two price limits in mind. Beyond the upper limit the item is considered to be too expensive, below the lower limit quality is considered suspect. For detail of the methods used, the reader should refer to published work on this subject (1) and how buy-response curves are constructed to help price setters fix a price which maximises profit. Curves of the type:

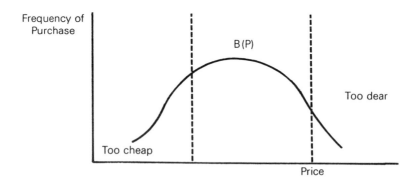

- can be useful in price setting and show that the manufacturer of a new brand can make as great an error in fixing a price which is too low as by setting it too high. Research in this area directed at short-run demand and based on the idea that customers enter the market with a price 'bracket' in mind, gives rise to the phenomenon of the market demand curve. The important findings are that:-

- The concept of price limits is realistic and an effective tool of research into consumer behaviour.
- It confirms the hypothesis concerning the logarithmetic nature of the subjective price scale.

and
- Results clearly show that the typical short-run demand curve for competitive brands has a backward sloping portion.

PRICING BY THE SELLER

The importance of these studies is that it enables suppliers to explore some of the ways in which price acts as an indicator of quality and discredits some of the convenient simplifying assumptions of traditional demand theory.

PRICE CONSCIOUSNESS

A knowledge of consumer price consciousness for firms setting a new product price will assist the decision on whether to pursue market penetration pricing or market skimming. The pricing decision requires the supplier to:-

1. Determine the degree of price consciousness of the new product in relation to different factors.
2. Weight the different factors according to their degree of importance.
3. Rate each factor and sum up the total rating.

A POSITIVE rating suggests market penetration pricing.
A NEGATIVE rating suggests skimming pricing.

FIG. 1

	RELATIVE WEIGHT	DEGREE OF P.C. −2 −1 0 +1 +2					RATING
1. Competitiveness 2. Price/product relation 3. Price/quality relation 4. Brand loyalty/popularity 5. Awareness 6. Availability 7. Market segment							

FIG. 2

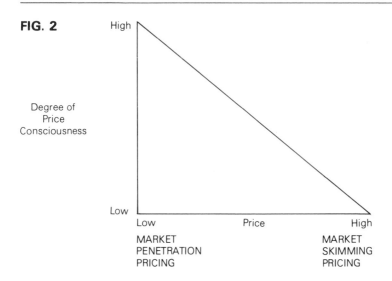

TARGET PRICING

Another cost-orientated approach to pricing is target pricing where the manufacturer decides the price that will give a rate of return on total costs at budgeted volume in line with the financial objectives set by the company board. This method is used by a number of prominent firms and state agencies who have large investments, have a monopoly position and need to demonstrate a fair rate of return on costs. Cost-orientated pricing policies rely on an addition to costs and/or a conventional level of profits. The demand-orientated approach considers the level of demand where a high price can be charged when demand is high and a low price when demand is low, an approach appearing simply to be profit-maximising pricing.

The strategy of the demand-orientated company provides an approach to the simultaneous achievement of both short and long run profit maximisation by adopting differential pricing. Companies, particularly in the consumer products field, establish prices in each significant market segment but to be practical this can only be achieved when:

- The market can be clearly segmented.
- The segments show different demand characteristics. (elasticity of demand)

and
- Where the low price segments cannot readily sell the product to the higher priced segments or competitors sell to the latter at significantly lower prices.

There are some difficulties with differential pricing since separation of markets, including those overseas, is becoming difficult because:

- Competition is becoming more international.
- Communications are improving and distributors and others meet frequently when prices are inevitably compared.

and ● Regional economic groupings provide increasing pressure to move towards price uniformity.

PRICE DISCRIMINATION

May increase income and profits in the short-term can damage the firm's image in the longer term.

COMPETITION PRICING

The pricing policy of firms who set prices on the basis of what their competitors are charging adopt a competition-orientated approach. In this situation there is no strict relation between production cost or demand and the firm decides prices which may be a little below or above its main competitors. Going-rate pricing is common when the firm sets prices at the average level charged by the industry and where setting prices on this basis will preserve harmony with the other firms who supply homogeneous markets. Firms selling to homogeneous markets which are highly competitive have little choice about setting prices and the main concern will be to control production and distribution costs if profits are to be maximised. The extreme example of competitor-pricing is found in the commodity markets, e.g. wheat, tea, coffee etc., where world prices are known and established by the collective interaction of many buyers and sellers. A producer quoting a price above that prevailing will suffer a loss of orders and to quote below it would be pointless.

DIFFERENTIATION

For markets where product differentiation can be accented firms can be more flexible in their approach to pricing and suppliers of petrol, oil and many basic raw materials provide examples of this approach.

MODELS

Marketing texts and journals contain many 'models' and theories about the complex problems of determining what is an acceptable price for a product. The application of sequential analysis in pricing research is discussed by Anderton, Gorton, Hammersley and Tudor (10) whose researches were aimed at investigating the relationship between price and customer preference for consumer durable articles. The differential method of pricing, and approach recommended by Oxenfeldt (5) provides an illuminating way of dealing with pricing which focuses attention on crucial relationships and issues of concern to price setters. This method arrives at price by adding "appropriate" amounts to specific "bases" and the amounts added represent differentials of which several are relevant to every price decision.

DIRECT MARKETING AND PRICING

Firms involved in direct marketing have specific problems in arriving at selling prices and amongst the useful literature on this topic are the practical booklets issued by Royal Mail such as 'Pricing Strategies in Direct Marketing' (9) in a series of papers on aspects of mail order and small freight distribution. The sensitivity of direct marketing allows a flexibility unlike any other marketing method since firms are able to react immediately to meet consumer demand or changing market conditions. Within days of making a pilot offer to the public the firm knows whether its decisions, including prices, have been right or wrong. The important price component is virtually unknown until after the product has been offered. If a £10,000 advertisement generates 5,000 orders the sales cost is £2 per order, but if it only produces 500, the sales cost per order will be £20. The break-even price cannot thus be identified before the product is sold. Some firms guess the price that consumers will be prepared to pay or employ an agency to carry out the necessary research based on its past experiences and/or through a survey directed at past clients who have purchased similar goods. The variable and hidden costs of this form of selling are often under-estimated by newcomers to direct marketing. Depending on the marketing tactics employed e.g. –

- Cash with order where the customer sends cash with the order form supplied.
- Free-examination offer when the customer takes the product without sending payment.
- Selling in stages when the potential customer first requests information to be later followed up by the supplier to convert the enquiry to a sale.

Costs will vary depending on the method used to attract buyers and the "arithmetic" of arriving at selling prices, testing and retesting methods for the product to maximise profit are succinctly dealt with in the Royal Mail publications referred to. As well as tailoring prices dependent on selling method there are other elements to be considered. Charging for post and handling in addition to the advertised selling price, offering discounts for the purchase of more than one item, offering a number of different products in the same campaign and offering personalised or de-luxe versions at higher prices are important. Advertisers who offer a credit card facility usually increase sales income significantly.

VALUE ADDED PRICING

Pricing by a "Production value added" method as a way of avoiding errors of conventional methods and contributing to establishing the "right price" is advocated by Hapgood in the text, "The Sales Function and its Management". Production value added is defined as sales value less the outside purchases of materials, supplies, power and similar items that are used in, or are necessary adjuncts to manufacture or processing. The actual contribution to the total economy of a company or economic unit is obtained by subtracting from its sales the outside purchases of materials and supplies to obtain the figure for production value which the company adds to its raw materials so that after converting to a new article it can sell the product for more than the cost of the materials themselves. On the same assumption that hourly pay-rolls tend to be stable and a consistent percentage of this Production Value Added, incentive pay plans, productivity measures and a pricing method, as well as top management controls can be developed.

The theory underlining the Production Value Added method of pricing is that all the company's income return should come as a mark-up on labour to Production Value Added and that material and supply cost is merely brokered for the customer and should only enter into the price structure on the basis of cost without mark-up. This approach therefore does not use any price mark-up for pricing purposes on material cost per se. Two similar products may have approximately the same processing costs but have widely varying material costs depending on specification and customer needs. Thus some products will have high or low material costs in relation to labour costs. In conventional pricing the high material cost product may give a price that is higher than necessary resulting from the mark-up on material; for a low material cost product the price may not be high enough to produce sufficient Production Value Added per £ of labour cost. When the mark-up is taken on labour only and material cost merely added to the Production Value Added the danger of pricing the product out of the market with a high material cost product or selling at too low a price with a low material cost product is avoided. For further comparison of conventional costing with this approach and equations for pricing methods the reader is referred to the original text.

MARKET PLANNING/ORGANISATION

A customer costing approach to pricing can have important implications for market planning and if adopted requires changes in a firm's organisation. A useful paper by Yorke (7) which discusses customer costing in the development of marketing strategy suggests that a system using the market – or an individual customer if large enough – provides a useful basis. The marketing concept requires firms to regard customer needs as paramount and conventional systems of product costing and profit centres do not entirely support this aim. In the 1960's products and brands were the key variables and organisations were structured on a product basis and costing systems produced all the necessary information for marketing managers to manipulate brands to maximise profit. Brands were cost/profit centres and sales staff pressurised to "push" their particular products. The traditional organisation structure appeared as in (1) with more or less tiers depending on company size.

(1)

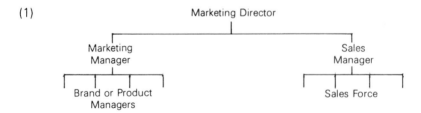

This type of structure has difficulties in terms of relationships with the two parts of the marketing effort partly from centering cost/profits on products or brands each of which the sales force is expected to sell. Industrial or capital goods companies have organised their activities according to type and/or size of customer as in figure (2) but the product has remained the profit centre.

(2)

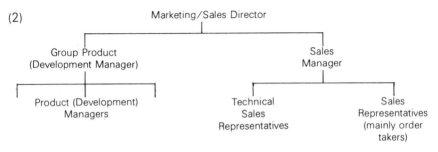

It has thus not been possible to establish profit targets other than by product group whilst the marketing strategy should be aimed at developing those market segments that represent prime targets. Yorke's paper suggests that there is now a good opportunity for firms to alter their strategy and attempt to operate in line with the marketing concept. Customer profitability statements, if available, could be used as a basis for future market planning and major customers treated as individual market segments with a profit objective for each. Historical costing information would be vital to such planning from the point of view of the product and the individual customer or market segment. Traditional costing methods would highlight those products which yielded high or low returns to the company. Those offering a high return would require pushing. Customer costing however might show an unacceptable loss on products sold to particular accounts. In this case although the product(s) may be important to the customer, attempts to change price may cause substantial resistance. A manufacturer selling to a major customer and wishing to set profit objectives will find it difficult when those of the customer do not coincide. The supplier nevertheless, on the basis of information about profitability has to decide whether (and when) to use it or reject it.

Two interlinked changes in the consumer goods markets have occured in recent years:-

- The increased concentration of purchasing power, e.g. a few major multiples now have over 30% of the total grocery turnover.

and ● The growth of 'own label' products.

The effect of such changes and trends and the need for a change of approach to marketing/pricing are further discussed in the thought-provoking paper by Yorke.

MARGINAL COST PRICING

A firm who can find an isolated market segment at home, or more likely abroad, may adopt marginal cost-pricing. In simple terms manufacturing costs may be divided into fixed and variable costs; the former being rent, rates etc. which remain unchanged regardless of level of activity and the latter being those costs such as materials and labour that vary according to output. When output produces sufficient revenue to cover all fixed and variable costs it is said to have reached break-even point. At break-even total revenue equals total cost and above this level fixed costs have been recovered so that any price which is above the variable costs per unit will produce a profit. If prices remain the same to its existing customers the price may be lowered for new segments to gain extra sales and profit. If the firm can find an isolated market or segment without jeopardising price levels in its established market but above the variable cost per unit it can quote prices based on marginal cost; additional sales will increase the firm's total profit although the percentage profit per unit would obviously be lower. A typical situation here would be that of a firm who sells at high prices in his domestic market and periodically sells surplus capacity to an appropriate country abroad at marginal prices. The use of marginal-cost pricing will only be worthwhile when:-

- It is unlikely that there will be rapid intervention by the government of an importing country, such as the imposition of dumping duties.
- There is no more profitable use of resources for a market where a higher price would be acceptable.
- Markets can be clearly segmented so that prices in the principal markets are not depressed.
- Marginal business is controlled so that it does not form an unduly high proportion of total sales.

International pricing decisions and pricing strategies in countries abroad are discussed in the text 'International Marketing' by Walsh (8) where pricing methods applicable to domestic and international markets are reviewed as well as sections dealing with:

- Build-up of export price.
- Advantages of quoting in a foreign currency.
- Marginal costing.

     ● Dumping

and   ● Devaluation and the exporter.

An interesting section deals with Barter Trading. A further note on factors to be considered in costing and pricing for export markets is given in the text by Neilands and Deschampsneufs, 'Exporting, a Basic Guide to Selling Abroad,' published by Pan Books Ltd.

Pricing remains an important element in marketing and presents difficulties in certain situations. The increased role of non-price factors in marketing however provides firms with opportunities to market their products by placing accent on matters of equal or greater importance than price alone such as:

     ● Quality/reliability
     ● Prompt delivery
     ● Good after-sales service
     ● Interacting with buying companies to help them solve problems.

ELASTICITY

Price elasticity of demand. This term refers to the % change in demand (quantity sold per period) caused by a % change in price. A price elasticity of -1 means that sales rise (fall) by the same % as price falls (rises). In this case the total revenue is unaffected.

A price elasticity of -1 means that sales rise (fall) in % terms, by more than price falls (rises). A value of -1 means that sales rise (fall) by less than price falls (rises) in % age terms. In this case total revenue falls.

To maximise revenue, price is too high if demand is elastic and too low if demand is inelastic. This may not apply to maximising profit.

Elasticity can be written as:

$$\text{Elasticity } E \quad = \quad \frac{\text{relative change in quantity}}{\text{relative change in price}}$$

$$= \quad \frac{\dfrac{Q_1 - Q_0}{Q_0}}{\dfrac{P_1 - P_0}{P_0}}$$

SOME LEGAL ASPECTS RELATING TO PRICING

When goods are offered at reduced prices, e.g. in special events, the previous price must have been charged for a continuous period of 28 days within the past six months. This "28 day clause" (Trade Descriptions Act

1968) makes it illegal to pretend that goods have been reduced in price when they have been bought in specially for a sales event.

The government has power under the Price Commission Act of 1977 to take action against the use of recommended prices. The Trade Descriptions Act lays down that a recommended price is presumed to be that of the manufacturer or other supplier and not that of the retailer. If it is the retailer's list price, this must be stated to avoid committing an offence. Special price cuts advertised on printed packages must conform to the price requirements given above and further there should be no confusion relating to the actual price to be paid. The practice of using 'loss leaders' by retailers is an issue that can cause friction with manufacturers who may be concerned at the idea that this practice degrades his product and is unfair to other retailers. The Resale Price Act of 1976 allows suppliers to cut off supplies to a dealer who uses the same or similar goods for loss leaders. According to the act a loss leader is a resale of goods, not for the purpose of making profit, but to act as an advertisement for the dealer. The Consumer Credit Act of 1975 insists that certain information must be included in advertisements for goods offered on hire purchase or credit sale. The information must include the full cash price and the total amount on instalments, the length of the period covered by each payment and the number of instalments which may be required before delivery of the goods. This Act also deals with matters relating to the deposit and interest rates. Further information on legal aspects is available in texts from Wyvern Business Library (11), Institute of Trading Administration and many County Councils, e.g. Cheshire (12).

There are many methods of dealing with the price component in discussion with buyers and below are summarised some relevant considerations.

QUANTIFYING BENEFITS

When a machine/work aid etc. can be shown to save £x per week/month such that its cost can be recovered in a relatively short time, e.g. six months and thereafter will generate additional profit without cost, the potential buyers must be impressed. Thus such benefits need to be heavily stressed.

PSYCHOLOGICAL PRICING

The retailer increases sales by bringing the price down to a level just below a supposed barrier price, e.g. £9.95 is more attractive than £10. This approach can be used for higher priced items; buyers cannot be fooled by 'charm' pricing but many buyers have limits on their expenditure. If research indicates that a particular buyer is limited to £1500 he may accept a product priced at £1495.

INFLATION

It is simple to plot a graph showing how inflation has progressed and if a firm's product prices have been less than the general rate of inflation, possibly using a shrewd base line, a buyer may agree that price is reasonable. Graphs showing the escalating cost of fuel compared with the inflation of other prices have been helpful to companies marketing energy-saving equipment.

SALESMEN

Salesmen, whose customers usually complain about price, sometimes initially offer a product of higher cost and specification than actually needed. When the customer complains about price the cheaper model can be offered.

A KNOWLEDGE OF COMPETITOR PRICES IS IMPORTANT

In this way a list of products priced lower than that of the seller can be made. If at least one benefit of the product on offer can be listed against that of the competitive item a sale will be assisted despite the higher price.

Some goods/equipment are eligible for a:
State grant or subsidy and some buying companies may be unaware of these. A selling company well briefed in this area can succeed in selling a product if they can offer financial help in this way to a buyer.

QUOTATIONS

Wordy quotations giving specification detail, price, delivery dates and payment terms will be less confusing to potential buyers if the document starts by stating the buyer's objectives and needs and how they can be dealt with by the product/supply company before dealing with other matters which will normally be followed by guarantees and after-sales assistance.

(A salesman may not need to raise the issue of price at a sales meeting but let the prospect do it; the prospect may not in fact do so.)

PRICING IN A NEW BUSINESS

Price is an important factor often in developing a business. Sometimes a natural inclination is to set a low price to get a good share of the market for a new product. This can be the first mistake and possibly the last. The right price is one which the buyer is prepared to pay and one that gives a satisfactory profit to the supplier. Price-cutting can invite failure; rather should the selling process stress benefits to the buyer, quality, reliability, good after-sales service and speedy delivery. Effective advertising and promotion should reinforce these points in communicating with potential buyers.

REFERENCES

1. Gabor, A., Granger, C.W.J., On the Price Consciousness of Consumers, App. Statistics, 10 (3) 1961 pp.170-180.
2. French, N.D., Williams, J.J., Chance, W.A., A Shopping Experiment or Price-Quality Relations, Journal of Retailing, Vol.48, 1972.
3. Riesz, Price Quality in the Market Place, Journal of Retailing, Vol.54, No.4, Winter 1978.
4. Gabor, A., Grange, C.W.J., Price as an Indication of Quality; Report of an Enquiry, Economica, February 1966.
5. Oxenfeldt, A.R., The Differential Method of Pricing, Eur. Journ. Mark. 13,4.
6. Oxenfeldt, A.R., Consumer Knowledge; its measurement and extent, Rec. Economics & Statistics, Vol.32, 1950.
7. Yorke, D.A., Customer Costing in the Development of Marketing Strategy, Management Accounting, May 1980.
8. Walsh, International Marketing 2nd Edn. M & E Handbook Series, MacDonald & Evans Ltd., 1981.
9. Curtis, P. and Associates, London, Commissioned by Royal Mail, London EC2A 1PH, Pricing Strategy in Direct Mailing.
10. Anderton, Gorton, Hammersley & Tudor, An Application of Sequential Analysis Pricing in Research, Eur. Journ. Mark. 12,6.
11. Wyvern Business Library, Ely, Cambs. CB7 4BR.
12. Cheshire Trading Standards, County Hall, Hunter Street, Chester.

OTHER READINGS

1. Harper, W.M., Fixing the Right Price, Accountancy 1972.
2. Hapgood, R.L., A New Approach to Profitable Pricing, from the text The Sales Function and its Management, 1971.
3. Neillands R., Deschampsneufs H., Exporting, Pan Books Ltd., London 1969.
4. Kotler, P., Marketing Management Planning & Control, 2nd Ed. Prentice Hall 1972.
5. Walker, Q.F., Some Principles of Department Store Pricing, Journ. Mark. Vol.14, April 1950.
6. Dean, J., How to Price during Inflation, Eur.Journ.Marketing.
7. Gabor, A., Pricing Principles and Practices, Heinemann Educational Books, London 1977.
8. Winkler, J., Pricing for Results, published on behalf of the Institute of Marketing, Heinemann, London, 1986.
9. Livermore, J.L., Legal Aspects of Marketing, Heinemann, London.
10. McDonald, M., How to Sell a Service, Wyvern Business Library, Ely, Cambs. CB7 4BR.

QUESTIONS

1. What is cost-orientated pricing, demand-orientated and competition-orientated pricing? Give examples to illustrate.
2. What is price elasticity?
3. Why is the separation of markets for differential pricing purposes difficult, even in international markets?
4. What is marginal costing and under what circumstances would it be used?
5. What is penetration pricing in connection with launching a new product?
6. What methods are available for researching acceptable prices?
7. What is the "28 day clause"?
8. Comment briefly on customer costing.
9. How do you deal with pricing in:
   a) times of inflation
   b) at each stage of the product life cycle
10. Describe the pricing strategy for one of your firm's major products. How does it compare with that of your major competitor?

THE PRODUCT LIFE CYCLE

Most Marketing Managers are familiar with the concept of the Product Life Cycle (PLC) particularly where they are employed in industries where PLC's are relatively short as in the pesticide, pharmaceutical and other sectors. A study of the PLC concept and the detailed history of many well-known products can highlight those methods available to firms for extending the life and profitability of their product by planning at the earlier stages of new product development a series of actions to be implemented at subsequent stages in its life.

VIEWS ON THE PLC

The literature on PLC is voluminous and the reference section to this chapter lists some of the many papers by academics and others available on this topic. The literature directed at different audiences has, on the one hand, recommended a study of PLC theory as a useful guide to recommending different strategies at different stages in the life cycle of a product to its use as a 'managerial instrument of competitive power.' (1).

A review of a typical product life cycle is given as background to further discussion on practical lessons to be learned. Successful products pass through the following recognisable stages in the order:

MARKET DEVELOPMENT

When a new product is first brought to the market and before there is a proven demand for it, sales are low and creep along slowly. Introducing a new product is for most companies a costly and difficult exercise and demand must be created at this stage. The time taken to introduce a new product will depend on its complexity, cost, competing products and the promotion effort made by the manufacturer. The early problems, pitfalls and costs of launching new products have convinced some innovators that they should let another firm endure the pain and instead of taking "the first bite of the apple" be content with the second bite! Factors to be considered at this stage include:

- containing development costs
- deciding pricing policy
- determining advertising and promotion budgets
- organising product distribution channels

and
- organising production levels to meet forecasts of demand

MARKET GROWTH

Is the second stage of the cycle where demand begins to grow and the size of the total market expands quickly – the product has "taken off." At this stage competitors who have been watching stage 1 join in and some enter the market with "carbon copies" (me-too products) whilst others make design improvements/modifications. Brand differentiation starts to develop.

Competition forces the original producer to consider a new set of problems which require changes in marketing strategies and tactics. The presence of competitors dictates price testing and an appraisal of the best channels of distribution. As demand accelerates it becomes easier to open new distribution channels or retail outlets. The filling of distribution channels and retail outlets causes the industry factory sales to rise more rapidly than retail sales and the evident possibility of increasing total sales attracts more competition. Some competitors will reduce price as a result of cost reductions through improving manufacturing methods and because they wish to capture a bigger share of the market to further reduce manufacturing costs and increase profits. At this stage the industry moves towards a different competitive situation.

THE MATURITY STAGE

At this stage there is evidence of market saturation when most buying companies or individual consumers own or use the product and further sales grow roughly on a par with population. Price competition will intensify and firms attempt to preserve brand preference by adding finer differentiations to the product, improving customer service, communicating more effectively with the end user, improving packaging and extending promotions. When market maturity tapers off the product enters the final:

DECLINE STAGE

Transforms the market and some producers take steps to withdraw from the competitive struggle. Other firms survive and concentrate on aggressive measures to force competitors to quit through mergers, company buy-outs and other means of depressing competition. Production becomes concentrated to fewer products and prices and margins may suffer.

The lives of successful products follow such a pattern, illustrated by the simple diagram 1.

EXAMPLES OF PLC SHAPES

1.

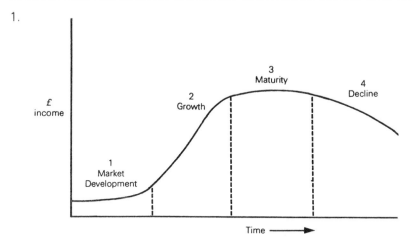

The shape of PLC curves and time scales from stage 1 to 4 vary considerably. In terms of shape there are many variations of the classic curve shown in I; sometimes the curve has one or more 'kinks' as illustrated below:

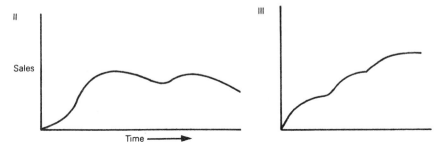

II illustrates the progress of a product where a second cycle appears possibly due to the product receiving aggressive promotional push during its life or a major competitor withdrawing from the market.

The 'scalloped' progress of the product illustrated in III suggests that the product life has been extended in stages as a result of new users being discovered or new markets (possibly abroad) being entered; curves of this type relate to many well-known products whose life has been extended over many years as a result of new user markets having been discovered; sales of nylon provide a good example here.

Products with a high fashion element which go in and out of vogue can exhibit a curve of the type shown in IV and 'fad' items which show rapid growth and decline characteristics could be illustrated by the curve V.

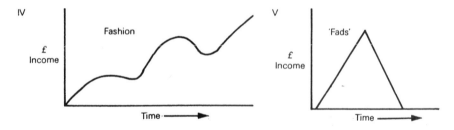

PLC AND THE PORTFOLIO

Portfolio theories (2) have the PLC concept as one of the bases in discussing the rise and fall of products in a given company and the cash flow implications. New products, the "question marks," at an early stage in their development become "stars" during the growth stage developing into "cash cows" at maturity and described as "dogs" at the decline stage at which point companies need to consider whether to drop the product or take action aimed at revival.

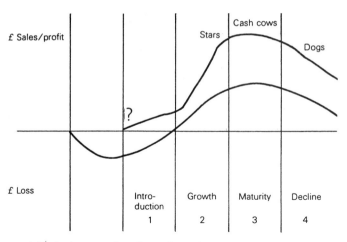

In terms of PLC time scales from introduction to decline, life times vary enormously dependent on product type. For some fashion items, medical products, pesticides etc. the cycle can be short and for 'fads' very brief indeed. Products like cars, bicycles, aspirin have very long lives, extended by new styling, additions/modifications to the basic concept, extended uses and improved reliability. The PLC concept becomes less relevant as the basic product gives way to form and brand:

e.g.	cigarette	**Product** (class)	e.g.	Car
e.g.	Filter type	**Form**	e.g.	Sports
e.g.	Players	**Brand**	e.g.	Ford

PLANNING

When a company develops a new product/service it should plan at an early stage a series of actions to be employed at the various stages in its life cycle in order that sales/profit curves are constantly sustained rather than follow the classic patterns of decline. Advanced planning should be directed at extending or stretching out the life of the product. It is this idea of planning in advance of the actual launch to take specific actions later in the life cycle that provides important instruments for long term strategy.

The history of nylon provides a model of the kind of actions needed to systematically extend product life. Nylon was first used in military applications for parachutes, ropes and thread. This was followed by nylon's entry into the circular knitting market and its dominance of the women's hosiery business. When PLC curves began to flatten the producers took measures to revitalise sales and profits to produce the extended curve shown below:

EXTENDING THE PLC

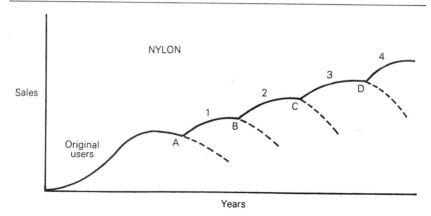

At point A the curve, dominated by hosiery sales, began to flatten; instead of allowing the curve to follow the classic (dotted) line efforts were exerted to extend its life by increasing sales. Similarly at points B, C and D new sales and profit expansion was pursued through:

    1. PROMOTING more frequent use of the product amongst current users.
    2. DEVELOPING MORE USES of the product amongst current users.
    3. CREATING NEW USERS by expanding the market.
and   4. FINDING NEW USES for the basic material.

In the case of Item 1, research indicated an increase in "bareleggedness" amongst women and this was approached by mounting an aggressive campaign to stress the social necessity of wearing stockings at all times. This difficult and costly campaign extended the PLC.

In the case of Item 4, nylon had many triumphs in developing new uses such as:

- stretch stockings/socks
- rugs
- tyres
- bearings for machinery

The story of nylon provides many examples of an approach to the methods of "stretching" PLC's.

The manufacturers and marketers of such products as "Jell-O" and "Scotch tape" provide further examples of methods adopted to extend the life of their products. Jell-O enjoys a long life through the introduction of an extended range of flavours and the creation of many other uses amongst desert users. The promotion of Jell-O as a base for salads and vegetable flavoured Jell-O's were other measures adopted. 3M increased sales amongst current users by marketing a range of scotch tape dispensers to make the product easier to use; in addition they produced coloured, patterned, invisible and write-on-tapes for sealing and decorating items for gift wrapping. To broaden the use in commercial and industrial markets 3M introduced "rocket" tape, a similar product but lower in price together with a range of commercial tapes in many widths, lengths and strengths.

These two companies actively sought new uses for their basic products and using effective and continuing promotion/advertising campaigns have planned and succeeded in prolonging the lives of their products.

The existence of a life cycle for any product suggests that there are considerable advantages for companies who need to develop new offerings through planning to extend the lives of their products before the new product is launched and very shortly after it has been found to be acceptable by the consumer. In terms of product policy the company will be forced to take an active rather than a reactivate approach by thinking and planning ahead. In this way the company will breathe new life into a product at the proper time using the appropriate effort.

EXTENDING INCOME/PROFIT

Companies ambitious to see continuing growth in sales/profits from new products need to understand the PLC concept and plan before the product launch to take actions throughout the life cycle to extend the life of their product. A marketing plan may aim to achieve, for example:

- In year 1 to increase sales by x% to users through new designs, creative communication with the customer and the creation of new uses.
- In year 2 to expand the market to new user sectors at home and abroad.
- In year 3 find new uses for the basic product or its derivatives.

EXPORTING

In analysing opportunities for exporting it is often worth considering how the life cycle of a given product in one country relates to that in other, possibly less developed countries. Whilst a U.K. marketed product may be approaching the stage of decline the market elsewhere may be exhibiting growth characteristics (3). The manufacturer experiencing a decline in sales at home may consider aiming at the market in a less developed country after making appropriate (but minimal) changes required by the foreign buyers. Because product manufacture tends to move from country to country in a kind of "pecking order" the home-based manufacturer may have to accept that the less developed country to whom he exports will eventually take over the manufacturing.

Most products (and many organisations) are born, grow, mature and finally die. When a product has outlived its usefulness there is little to be done about it but sometimes the reason for its premature death is the fault of its producer who is guilty of inefficiency, inadequacy or failing to take early and creative action to prolong the life of its offspring; the PLC concept simply provides an excuse for its death. British Telecom has lost its monopoly for supplying telephones and must now compete with other suppliers in the UK, Europe and the US. Solicitors no longer have a monopoly on conveyancing and there are many examples of products/services that are increasingly being offered by organisations who normally kept out of the market for such products/services. In these instances, the telephone, conveyancing and many other items cannot be said to have reached maturity and heading for decline. The 'normal' suppliers must face the new competition through improving their marketing/selling methods and expending more on better communication with buyers. Changes can be made in many ways such as:-

- Developing an entirely new product based on some new technology.
- Discovering a new use for an existing product, quite common for some basic materials like plastics, synthetic fibres, energy saving devices etc.
- Entering a new market sector or exporting.
- Increasing the level of consumption; campaigns urging consumers to eat more bread, drink more milk and install extension telephones/answer phones etc., provide examples.

EXISTING MARKETS

It is often more profitable for the marketing function to pursue increased consumption in existing markets than aim for greater penetration although attempting both may be desirable. Extending product life, income and profit may require committing more resources to research and development work, a bigger marketing input for new product launches and continuing a creative marketing effort during the growth stage of the new product. Anticipating competitor entry and planning to counter attack it will require effort by both the research/development, and marketing functions. When efforts succeed in getting a sizeable market share for its product a company can enjoy the benefits to be derived from large-scale production through improvements that come from experience and either lower price to deter competitors, or keep its price and improve profitability.

Throughout the life of the product continuous effort will need to be aimed at finding new product/market opportunities.

REFERENCES

1. Levitt, T., Exploit The Product Life Cycle, Harvard Business Review, Nov/Dec 1965.
2. Hedley, B., A Fundamental Approach to Strategy Development, Long Range Planning, Feb. 1977.
3. Wells, L.T., A Product Life Cycle for International Trade? Journal of Marketing, Vol.32, July 1968.

ADDITIONAL REFERENCES

1. Doyle, P., The Realities of the PLC, Quart Rev of Marketing, Summer 1976.
2. Cunningham, M.T., The Application of the PLC to Corporate Strategy, Brit.Journ. of Marketing, Spring 1969.
3. Shalla, N.K., Yusper, S., Forget the PLC, Harvard Bus. Rev., Jan/Feb 1976.
4. Polli, R., and Cook, V., Validity of the PLC, Journ. of Business, Oct. 1969.
5. Cox, W., Product Life Cycles as Marketing Models, Journ. of Business 40, Oct. 1967.
6. Harrell, S.G., and Taylor, E.D., Modelling the Product Life Cycle for Consumer Durables, Journ. of Marketing, 45, Fall 1981.
7. Day, G.S., The Product Life Cycle; Analaysis and Applications Issues, Journ. of Marketing, Fall 1981, Vol.45 (includes 42 references related to the PLC concept).

QUESTIONS

1. Cider is a product that is in the mature phase of its PLC. Is this true and if so what steps can cider producers take to increase sales?
2. Summarize a long-range plan for marketing a new range of electric heaters, showing for each stage of the PLC how policy on quality, price, advertising/promotion and channels of distribution should be handled.

LAUNCHING NEW PRODUCTS, PRODUCT DELETION

A major task for the top management of any company is to continually review its products with the aid of technical, marketing and financial managers in the task of:

- deleting products
- modifying existing products

and ● adding new products to its range

PLANNING

Effective product planning is aimed at obtaining optimum profit over a defined time-scale from the range. This chapter deals with launching new products, a vital task for the market-orientated company and one which is costly and presents many pitfalls; the task of deleting products/services, another difficult area, is reviewed.

INNOVATION

Many firms need to innovate to survive in the long term through continuing to satisfy customer needs, which change with time, and many firms whose business becomes vulnerable because of increasing competition and changes in fashion/technology seek to become less dependent on some of their core products which no longer yield the returns the firm has set as its financial objectives.

NEW PRODUCT SUCCESS RATE

The literature dealing with the generation and launch of new products reveals that many firms in technologically-based industries have marketed products which have failed to satisfy the criteria for commercial success and the cost of their failures has been high. One successful international company producing semi-technical products reports that for every 100 new products concepts investigated only one third are found to be technically feasible and only 3% are commercially successful. A U.S. based aggressive food manufacturer reports that of 600 products vetted, 90 are finally test-marketed but only 30 reach commercial success, a 5% success rate.

Developing/launching new products is possibly the most difficult task confronting firms who must innovate to survive, particularly in those sectors where product life cycles are short.

SOURCES

Sources of new product ideas are numerous and range from in-house research, brain storming and value analysis methods, search for externally published ideas and inventions to a close working with customer companies with special needs and who stimulate innovation, often through developing an interactive relationship with their suppliers. Methods of generating ideas may be summarised as coming from:

- The firm's own R and D function
- Direct search and exploration outside the firm
- Technological information and forecasting
- Exploratory consumer studies using 'focus groups' to evaluate concepts of new products when such meetings are recorded for analysis

The reasons for new product failure are reported by many authorities and the British Institute of Management offers the following acceptable list in decreasing order of importance (1).

- inadequate market analysis
- product defects
- higher costs than anticipated
- poor timing of product launch
- competition
- insufficient marketing effort
- inadequate salesforce
- distribution weaknesses
- initial and continuing marketing and RD costs

Competing innovations at this point are ranked in order of cost/benefit versus risk in the selection process. Since benefits can occur over a lengthy time period it is advisable to use discounted cash flow methods. For detailed discussion of the factors relevant to this stage the reader is referred to specialised literature on this subject (2),(3),(4),(5).

BASICS FOR SUCCESS

Some new products fail because insufficient time is spent at the planning stage and the British Institute of Management has published two useful checklists which draw attention to the many key factors that need to be taken into account (1). These checklists ask pertinent questions of the type: Have you evaluated the new product in broad terms?
1. Is there a market for it?
2. Is it within the terms of your Articles of Association and is it patentable? Does it infringe other patented products?
3. Does it fit in with present production lines?
4. Have you facilities to produce it?

Do you know enough about the market you want to enter?
1. Who and where are your potential customers?
2. How big is the estimated market (home and abroad)?
3. What is your share of the market for similar products?
4. Who are your competitors and do the products compare with your own in terms of price?

5. What is the advantage of your product compared with those of competitors and what is their share of the market?
6. Will the new product affect sales of your existing products?
7. What are the seasonal fluctuations demand, if any?
8. What are the present and future demand for the products?
9. What is the best time of the year to introduce it?

Have you carried out adequate research into the product and its design?
1. Is the product easy to use? Easy to learn how to use?
2. What are the best materials to use? Have you combined functional efficiency with attractiveness in shape, texture, finish and colour?
3. Is the design adapted to facilitate repairs and replacement?
    – and so on.

Other questions deal with the sales organisation, e.g.
1. Can your existing salesforce handle the new product or will you need a separate salesforce or additions to the existing one?
2. Will you need to reorganise salesmen's territories and will they need special training?
3. Will you need additional warehousing facilities?
4. What type of distribution will you use?
5. Would it be advantageous, for an initial period, to restrict distribution to a few selected regions of the country?
    – and so on.

These checklists assist by directing questions at those involved in launching a new product from the aspects of:
1. Manufacturing the new product in terms of labour, machinery and equipment requirements, planning production to cope with expected demand, product testing and quality control.
2. Materials purchasing in terms of where they can be obtained, maximum and minimum stock levels and storage space needed.
3. Product costing and pricing policy (subjects considered in Chapter 5).
4. Promotion and advertising new products.
5. Packaging and labelling the products.
6. Policies regarding servicing.

In appraising the product mix, management will identify those products which are 'weak' and can be a burden in terms of financial resources and management time. Alexander (4) commented, "The old product that is a 'football' of competition or has lost much of its market appeal is likely to generate more than its share of small unprofitable orders; to make necessary short, costly production runs; to demand an exorbitant amount of executive attention and to tie up capital that could be used profitably in other ventures." There is, nevertheless, often a reluctance to make the hard decisions to eliminate products from the mix. Some of the reasons offered will include:
1. Sales could be increased by modifying the product.
2. Economic and marketing factors could change in the future thereby resulting in improved sales.

3. The product is contributing to overheads. If this is the case, then until a product which contributes more is found the original product should not be deleted.
4. If the product is removed some customers could go elsewhere for it and where they might buy other products currently supplied by our firm.

PRODUCT DELETION/RETENTION

The major reason for retaining a product may not be economically rational and it may be that management feels it has committed the product and does not want to affect change and face the consequences of implementing change.

Where a firm is manufacturing a large number of products, a formal and simple screening process is required to minimize the managerial resources required. Kotler (5) has suggested a product review committee, a management team consisting of marketing, manufacturing, R and D and personnel executives be appointed. It should be responsible for product pruning. A product deletion process would then consist of:
1. Gathering data on each product's profitability and market share trends.
2. Evaluating products using a computer programme to identify dubious products.

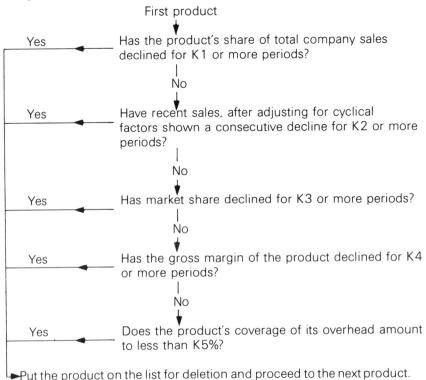

First product

Yes ← Has the product's share of total company sales declined for K1 or more periods?

No

Yes ← Have recent sales, after adjusting for cyclical factors shown a consecutive decline for K2 or more periods?

No

Yes ← Has market share declined for K3 or more periods?

No

Yes ← Has the gross margin of the product declined for K4 or more periods?

No

Yes ← Does the product's coverage of its overhead amount to less than K5%?

→ Put the product on the list for deletion and proceed to the next product.

When the candidates for deletion have been identified more detailed analysis is required. Hamelman and Mazze (6) suggest a simple measure:

$$r_i = \frac{C_i/\Sigma C_i}{F_i/\Sigma F_i} \times C_i/\Sigma C_i$$

where r_i = selection index number for product
       C_i = total contribution from product
       F_i = facilities cost associated with product
       Σ = Sum of

RANKING

The text by Kotler (7) reproduces an evaluation matrix to illustrate one method of ranking products where the rating obtained by extending the relative weight allocated for a set of factors to give a total rating used in comparing different products.

PRODUCT COMPATIBILITY VALUES B

Sphere of Performance	Relative weight A	0.0	0.1	0.2	0.3	0.4	0.5	0.6	0.7	0.8	0.9	10	Rating A × B
Company personality and goodwill	0.2												0.120
Marketing	0.2												0.180
Research & Development	0.2												0.140
Personnel	0.15												0.090
Finance	0.10												0.090
Production	0.05												0.040
Location & facilities	0.05												0.015
Purchasing & supplies	0.05												0.045
	1.00												0.720

From: "A Rating Scale for Product Innovation", Richmond, B.M., Business Horizons, Summer 1962, pp. 37-44.
Rating scale: 0-0.4 poor, 0.41-.75 fair, 0.76-1.00 good. Present acceptable rate 0.70.

REVIEW

The review committee has to decide on the retention index threshold below which the product will be eliminated.

In phasing out a product the following considerations are important:

1. Obligations to existing customers need to be taken into account. It will be necessary to ensure that there are sufficient spares/replacements to last over the expected life of the most recently sold units. Customer dissatisfaction could affect sales of other company products.

2. Timing of withdrawal is important since deletion of a product will release resources and to ensure that their release coincides with the need for them in other developments is important.

3. A product deletion plan needs to provide for the clearing out of stocks, again a matter for careful timing.

4. Industrial relations can suffer where product deletion results in redundancies and changes in skills required and careful handling of this area is necessary.

5. As already indicated particular attention needs to be given to the possible implications of a product withdrawal on the sales of other products. What sales may be lost by the decision to withdraw one product and what will be the effect on cost structures?

The marketing function should carefully consider the possible alternatives to product deletion, including the effects of changes in the elements of the marketing mix.

The profitability of an individual product in a multi-product firm is sometimes not easy to evaluate since often several items in the product mix are made of common materials and use the same equipment and labour. Further, the firm's marketing efforts and costs are devoted to selling and distributing a range rather than an individual item.

THE NEED FOR CHANGE

Marketing is concerned with looking outside the firm to discover changing needs and often it is necessary to be active in stimulating change rather than become a victim of it. New product development and product modification/deletion are difficult areas for any company but the dangers of failing to grasp them are greater than the dangers and difficulties of tackling them in a competitive world where the need to innovate to survive and grow profitably becomes increasingly necessary.

REFERENCES

1. British Institute of Management, Checklists 29 and 30, Launching New Products, Feb. 1973.
2. Marketing Society Ltd., Financial Aspects of a New Product Launch, Brentford, Middlesex, 1968.
3. University of Sussex, Centre for the Study of Industrial Innovation, Success and Failure in Industrial Innovation, 1972.
4. Alexander, R.S., The Death and Burial of Sick Products, Journ of Mktg., 28 April 1964.
5. Kotler, P., Phasing Out Weak Products, Harvard Business Rev., March/April 1965, pp. 107-113.
6. Hamelman, P.W., and Mazze, E.M., Improving Product Abandonment Decisions, Journ. Marktg. 36, April 1972, pp. 20-26.
7. Marketing Management, Analysis, Planning and Control, Prentice-Hall International Editions.

OTHER LITERATURE

1. Booz, Allen & Hamilton Inc., Management of New Products, 4th Edition.
2. National Industrial Conference Board, Organisation for New Product Development; a symposium. New York, 1966, 83pp. (EM M 11).

QUESTIONS

1. What are the stages in the process of adopting a new product?
2. List some of the reasons for the high failure rate of new products.
3. A firm test markets a new product and finds that results indicate that it would possibly yield a below-average return. If the firm has expended a great deal of money in developing the product should it –
   a) Drop the product?
   b) Introduce the product?
   Give reasons or suggest what other actions it should take.
4. Introducing new products/services starts with the collection of information from within and outside the firm. List the methods of generating ideas.
5. List the main marketing considerations that guide the introduction of new products.
6. Discuss methods available for guiding decisions on product deletion.

FRANCHISING

Franchising is a marketing technique rapidly being adopted by a broad spectrum of businesses throughout the world permitting business expansion with minimum risk. Franchising and expansion go hand in hand and many kinds of businesses cannot ignore the potential of franchising when considering their expansion strategy. Franchising presents a practical way of expanding without having to expend the large amounts of capital associated with setting up new units in different geographical areas.

PRINCIPLES

The franchisor finds franchisees who provide the funding from their own sources and who become investors in the franchisor's systems to generate his own business in a safe and economical way. Information from the many specialists and advisers in this area, draw attention to the relative success rate of franchisees compared with those who start their own business in the more conventional way; Fig. 1 illustrates this point.

FIG. 1

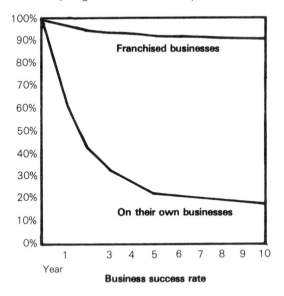

Source: Franchise Development Services Ltd., Castle House, Castle Meadow, Norwich. NR2 1PJ.

At its most basic, franchising is obtaining a licence to use a business name and idea. Reputable franchisors offer a sophisticated service and on-going help through staff training, installing control systems and assisting start-up and expansion by promotion/advertising in local and national media. The

British Franchise Association (1) provides information about its members and what they have to offer as well as literature for both franchisor and franchisee. In return for providing his name and systems, the franchisor normally asks for an initial fee from the franchisee and a continuing royalty and management fee usually based on sales or a mark-up on goods supplied.

THE FRANCHISEE

The advantage to the franchisee is that he buys a ready-made proven business and a nationally known and advertised trading name. It is similar to owning the local branch of a large multiple operation. Many franchisors have a head office that will supply help and advice at any time. Unlike the conventional employee, irrespective of his seniority in the business, the franchisee is highly motivated because his own cash is invested in the business, a fact that contributes to the recorded high success rate.

THE FRANCHISOR

The company that expands by franchising advertises and markets its own products/services on a much larger scale and is able to exploit the scale of economies of operating a large company.

REQUIREMENTS

A firm needs a number of features if it is to become a profitable franchisor and amongst the many publications available for assisting franchisors and potential franchisees is the very useful Gower Publishing's, 'The Successful Franchise,' which lists several important features that need consideration by either party to an agreement:

- The product/service must satisfy a continuing demand.
  The franchisor needs to demonstrate to the franchisee that he can recover his start-up costs and become profitable in a reasonable time if he follows the format laid down.
- The format should be simple and easy to follow.
- The business should have a simple and memorable name.
- Uniform standards of quality and appearance for all outlets.
- Suitable premises in the right positions and with proper access available within a price range that franchisees can afford.
- Administrative procedures that can be kept simple.
- A strong financial position to provide adequate training and back-up services.
- A trade 'secret' or patentable device or some characteristic that can be marketed as being virtually unique.
- Support from a clearing bank in order that potential franchisees have a reasonable assurance of financial support.

LEGAL AGREEMENT

The firm considering franchising needs a legal adviser preferably familiar with the franchising concept since the legal agreement between the parties is of extreme importance. The agreement not only needs to set down the initial and on-going fee structure, but spell out franchisee's territories to prevent future argument and ensure that franchisees properly handle company products/secrets and deal with the protection of trade names etc.

FINANCE

Financial advice on the tax implications of franchising and the fixing of financial terms and obligations between parties is important. The accounting firm Spicer and Pegler produce a useful brochure, 'Financial Aspects of Franchising,' which can be obtained free from the local office (2).

The High-Street Health Food Chain, 'Holland and Barrett' have many retail outlets of which a large proportion are franchised. One of their reasons for opting for fast expansion through franchising rather than the slower process of internal expansion, was to pre-empt the entry of a major specialist competitor; other firms have directed their expansion in this way for the same reason.

BASICS

Basic advice for firms considering franchising can be summarised as follows; Unless the firm's product/service is unique, the demand for it growing, the parent company sound and profitable and not easy to imitate, it should not pursue the franchising route to expansion. Other basic matters to be noted are that:

- The legal agreement, training and systems manuals on which the system is based, require good legal and professional help; the firm should not underestimate the time it takes to deal with these basics and employ advisers preferably with practical experience of franchising.
- Potential franchisees should be carefully vetted and selected by senior members of the firm who can enthuse and reassure them. Franchisees need to demonstrate their commitment, be physically fit and able to handle the 'arithmetic', book-keeping and administration tasks in a disciplined manner; these remarks apply particularly if the franchisees are husband and wife who will need to work closely and hard in the early stages. Providing help to a happy well-motivated franchisee team will be both easy and economic.
- Initial and ongoing training should be the task of a professional and not a job for a junior member of the firm who is not a good communicator.

- If the potential franchisee needs to approach his bank for help, the franchisor or one of the firm's senior staff should accompany him to explain the scope and nature of the business and supply financial information about other successful franchises.
- A successful franchise is one in which both parties make money, but this takes time. The franchisor should be prepared to support the business he has spawned for two or three years. Franchisors in a hurry to make large profits in too short a time can create problems for both parties.

SOURCES OF HELP

The Royal Bank of Scotland in its publication 'Buying a Franchise' (3) provides useful help for the franchisee on choosing and evaluating a franchise. A check-list on buying a franchise is included which directs pertinent questions to the potential franchisee dealing with:

- His background knowledge and past experience of management.
- The project's background, success and structure of the franchisor's organisation.
- The market place and main competitors.
- Financial requirements and repayment programme.

This publication gives sources of advice on choosing and evaluating a franchise and lists useful publications which are included with others at the conclusion of this section. Another publication from the same source, 'Expanding Your Business Through Franchising' (3) provides useful guidelines to firms having a proven profitable business with a distinct trading style suitable for franchising.

According to the British Franchise Association (1985) there are over 8,000 separate franchised businesses in the U.K., employing over 70,000 people. The franchising sector is large and growing at a high rate. The growth rate published in literature from the Franchise Development Services Ltd. (5) is reproduced below.

ANNUAL GROWTH RATE OF NEW FRANCHISORS
IN THE UNITED KINGDOM

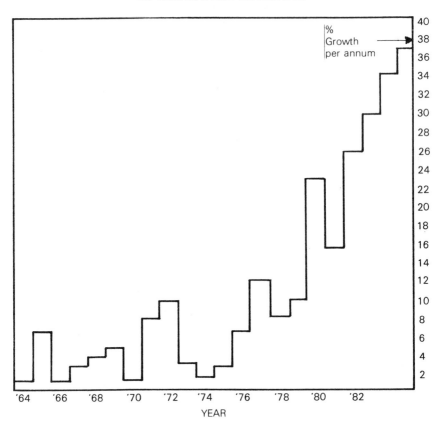

A wide variety of products/services are embraced by the franchise concept and include a very wide spectrum of business. The following list is not exhaustive:

- Video hire
- Office cleaning
- Secretarial training
- Specialist paints
- Soft drinks
- Coffee suppliers
- Nanny agencies
- Windows
- Garment cleaning
- Photographic equipment
- Display lighting
- Specialist concrete products

- Insurance brokers
- Management recruitment
- Car rental
- Kitchen supplies
- Prescription spectacles
- Hairdressing
- Photoglazing
- Car components
- Art shops
- Greetings cards
- Games
- Garden products

At the time of writing two useful and relevant articles have appeared; a short report in The Sunday Times (4th October, 1987) titled "Franchising boom provides low-risk entry to Business" advises that investing in a franchise continues to be a low-risk route into business, quoting a new report, Franchising in the United Kingdom (6). This report records a rise in sales and employment within the industry, and a fall in business failures with annual sales up 40% on the previous year to more than £3.1 billion, providing 169,000 jobs. Of 399 businesses claiming to be franchises, the report concludes that only 253 actually conform to the principles of business-format franchising, i.e. they grant a licence to use a package of all the elements that are needed to start and run a branded business. The failure rate in this group fell from 7% to 4%. The previous year's estimate that 14% of franchises failed was considered to have been caused by the inclusion of businesses that did not meet the true definition of franchising. The British Franchise Association (BFA), conscious of the need to preserve the good image of franchising introduced in 1987 a code of ethics to dispel confusion about what business-format franchising is about and what it is not.

HELP FOR FRANCHISEES

Individuals interested in taking out a franchise can make their own assessments of what is available by attending Franchise Exhibitions. At the October 1987 National Exhibition in London 100 franchises from tie shops to estate agencies will be represented. Jill Papworth, Features Editor, Accountancy Age, offers an interesting and informative article in Family Wealth (7) 'How to become your own boss.' This article advises that although franchising is not a short cut to riches it is one of the safer ways of achieving business success – and growing at 50% per year. Other figures quoted include 148,000 jobs attributed to this trading concept in the 1986 franchise survey sponsored by National Westminster Bank and commissioned by the BFA. Franchising accounted for nearly 20,000 businesses, 56% more than in the previous year, with £2.2 million sales and over £6 billion predicted in 1990. Types of franchise are discussed and attention is drawn to the fact that although buying a franchise can cost anything from £5,000 to £400,000 depending on the type and size of business, sources of financial support are available. The major clearing banks are giving increased attention to franchising and all have finance schemes worked out with established franchisors to lend up to two-thirds of the initial start-up costs.

This useful article contains a list of franchising 'Do's and Don'ts' which include the advice to:-

- read and research a good deal.
- find out the range of franchises on offer and select the type you would enjoy; but do not rush into the first one that sounds appealing.

- interview franchisors and ask the basic questions, who are the directors/shareholders? Can you meet them? Ask for plenty of detail and ensure that you can get to like and trust them.
- find out **all** cost and royalties involved.
- enquire whether a major bank offers a tailor-made franchise loan scheme for your chosen franchise. If not, why not?
- ensure that you have sufficient funds to meet living expenses for the period before you expect to live from the business.

Franchise World (8) offers regular courses for prospective franchisees and franchisors and in 1987 offered four presentations on "Buying a franchise and making the right choice" in conjunction with the business services page of The Daily Express. Using specialist speakers a programme giving impartial advice on all aspects of franchising allows potential franchisees to learn in some depth about a number of actual franchise opportunities in different types of businesses and at various price levels. Courses for the prospective franchisors are also offered and a recently published programme (8) covers the following areas:

- Franchising: is it your best route?
- Preparing your business for franchising.
- Preparing to market your franchise.
- Looking after your first 10 franchisees.
- The service sector/retail sector/converting to franchising.
- Legal considerations.
- Financial considerations.

This organisation publishes a Franchise Manual and Directory which "embraces the needs of just about all parties (actual and potential) to franchising without any of the hyping, ill-informed or misconceived content so common in franchising". (Franchise World 1987 Catalogue). This manual formerly titled, The Directory of Franchising was updated for 1987 and listings cover franchisors, BFA members, franchise trade associations in the various countries, franchise consultants, sources of franchise finance and key addresses of firms offering supporting services to the industry. This Franchise Manual and Directory or a composite introductory pack, one copy of each of the 1987 Franchise Manual, Franchise World and Franchise Reporter can be obtained from reference (8).

A further detailed work on the subject is 'Taking up a Franchise,' which deals with:

- Financing a franchise
- Evaluating a franchise proposal
- Tax and legal considerations
- Avoiding potential pitfalls
- The future of franchising
- A complete list of BFA members

This publication by The Daily Telegraph (9) is yet another valuable source of information on the subject and the section dealing with current franchise opportunities is particularly useful and detailed. This guide is comprehensive but cannot deal with every franchise opportunity since new franchisors are being 'born' every few months.

REFERENCES

1. The British Franchise Association, Francis Chambers, 75a Bell Street, Henley on Thames, Oxon, RG9 2ED. Telephone 0491 578049.
2. Spicer and Pegler, Financial Aspects of Franchising, October 1985, Friary Court, 65 Crutchfield Friars, London EC3N 2NP.
3. The Royal Bank of Scotland PLC, Expanding Your Business Through Franchising, Buying a Franchise, 36 St. Andrew Square, Edinburgh, EH2 2YB.
4. Franchise Development Services Ltd., Castle House, Castle Meadow, Norwich NR2 1PJ.
5. Franchising in the UK (Developments in Scale and Character 1987), Power Research Associates, 17 Wigmore Street, London W1H 9LA.
6. Family Wealth, October 1987. 128 Burnt Hill Road, Lower Bourne, Farnham, Surrey GU10 3LT.
7. Franchise World, James House, 37 Nottingham Road, London SW17 7EA.
8. Taking Up A Franchise, 3rd Edition, The Daily Telegraph Guide, G. Golzen and C. Barrow, Kogan Page.

Other References — Information Sources:
The Guide to Franchising, Martin Mendelsohn, Pergammon Press.
Franchising for Profit, W.A.J. Pollock and G. Golzen, Institute of Chartered Accountant Publications.
The Franchise World, James House, 37 Nottingham Road, London SW17 7EA.
Franchising, a small business Guide by Alan and Deborah Fowler, Sphere Study Aids.
The Franchise Shop deals with the buying and selling of franchises. 6 Old Hillside Road, Winchester, Hants. SO22 5LW.
International Franchising and Distribution Law, Frank Cass and Co., Gainsborough House, 11 Gainsborough Road, London E11 1RS.

QUESTIONS

1. List the main features required by a business that is considering expansion through franchising.
2. List 12 kinds of businesses that operate a franchise and comment on their success and future potential.
3. What are the main advantages offered to a franchisee? Why is the franchise route to starting a business more successful than the more conventional way of starting up a business?
4. What information is required by a potential franchisee preparing to start up a business?

MARKETING PLANNING

PLANNING — GENERAL

The cycle of events in any well-run business involves:

        1. Setting objectives
        2. Developing a plan to achieve them
        3. Organising the implementation of the plan
and then 4. Controlling performance by monitoring actual results against planned performance, taking remedial action when actual results depart from those planned.

This chapter whilst drawing attention to the plans employed by businesses deals mainly with the difficult area of marketing planning, a subject given inadequate attention by many companies.

Planning is deciding in the present what to do in the future and is a process whereby companies attempt to reconcile their resources with their objectives and opportunities. Most companies pay lip service to planning but often do little in practice; some top management take the view that their firm is too successful to spend much time on planning! Planning can be carried to excess, like other virtues, but there is sufficient evidence to suggest that those firms who develop sensible plans, tailored to the needs of the specific situation, enjoy positive benefits. In terms of market planning, studies by Cranfield (1) amongst industrial companies showed that those companies which did not have a marketing plan but which were nevertheless profitable were operating in buoyant and high growth markets. Such companies however were less successful than those comparable companies that had implemented good planning systems.

All firms need to develop planning procedures appropriate to their size and situation with the participation of all staff and management and develop a competence in carrying them out – a process which takes some practice!

The benefits of planning are that it:-

        ● Encourages systematic thinking ahead by management.
        ● Leads to better coordination of company efforts.
        ● Makes the company sharpen its objectives and policies.
        ● Results in better preparedness for sudden changes.
and   ● Makes the participating executives more aware of their interacting responsibilities.

TYPES OF PLANNING

Company planning is not a single process but several kinds of planning activity can be distinguished.

- Long range planning deals with the longer term objectives and growth plans by forecasting and an analysis of future opportunities and threats.

- Annual planning is dealt with by top and middle management whose output covers goals/budgets for the company by territory and product/service.

- Product planning much involves the marketing function in deciding product deletion/modification and additions and setting sales targets.

- Venture planning and activity planning are concerned with developing new products and possibly planning acquisitions as well as detailing project timetables.

Whilst long range plans can be prepared for a 5-year period it is sensible to revise the 5-year plan each year. Such a "rolling long-range plan" provides the needed flexibility to make a firm less vulnerable. Many large firms who have invested in long-range planning have not had impressive results from planning 5 or more years ahead. There is a clear need to estimate what is going to happen in the future if growth objectives have to be formulated but long-term plans are sometimes only forward projections, predictions, extrapolations or 'questimates'. A plan is an intention to take definite action but anything 5 or more years ahead is only a possibility. Forecasting is not planning but an attempt to establish a range of probabilities. The object of forecasting is to attempt to predict what will happen but planning is deciding what to do about it. Planning involves decision-taking and is about finding a systematic way of identifying options and then preparing a timetable of what has to be done to achieve it together with a cost of doing so.

MARKETING PLANNING

Marketing planning is concerned with setting objectives and strategies which will be used to gain and maintain the competitive position and results that the company is seeking. There is no tailor-made package for marketing planning which requires basic amendments to suit the situation – specific needs of each company. The planning procedure is the most difficult of all marketing tasks because it involves bringing together into one coherent plan all the elements of marketing and to do this requires an established procedure; it is this fact that causes difficulty in many companies and sometimes results in firms trying to do too much too quickly and without training staff in the procedures.

The starting point is a marketing audit which requires clear answers to the questions:

- Where is the company now?
- Where does it want to go?

and
- How should it organise its resources to do it?

This audit requires a systematic, critical and unbiased appraisal of the company and its operations and the environment. The marketing audit is part of a larger audit of the company and helps to define the problems and opportunities facing the company as a whole. The audit which looks at:-

- The external situation

and
- The internal strengths and weaknesses

- may be aided by the use of outside consultants working with company managers and specialists in their own areas of responsibility. The object of this exercise is to decide what the firm's marketing objectives and strategies should be and a format is needed to help organise the major finding. A Strengths, Weaknesses, Opportunities and Threats (SWOT) analysis is undertaken to permit comparison with competitors and prepare to deal with key external opportunities and threats.

Audit ──────────▶SWOT analysis ──────────▶Marketing plan

The marketing plan should detail activities for a year and outline broad plans for subsequent years as a basis for a corporate plan which will outline the longer term view of what the company wishes to become.

OBJECT SETTING

The key step in planning is to agree marketing objectives and set down strategies to achieve these objectives. Objectives/strategies should be set for all aspects of marketing.

Object setting is crucial and occupies the centre of the process; objectives must be realistic and inadequacy in object setting is the main cause of serious problems for many companies.

Marketing objectives are concerned with products and markets and strategies available to companies seeking growth will be concerned with:

- Market penetration where increased sales for current products in current markets are sought by more aggressive promotion.
- Market development where increased sales are obtained by offering current products to new markets.
- Product development through offering new/improved products to current markets.

and
- Diversification by offering new products/services to new markets.

Strategies summarised in the table below are given by Ansoff (2) who offers a classification of intensive growth strategies based on cross-classifying product/market possibilities.

FIG. 1

	Current Products	New Products
Present Markets	MARKET PENETRATION	PRODUCT DEVELOPMENT
New Markets	MARKET DEVELOPMENT	DIVERSIFICATION

Objectives which are real must be capable of measurement and the strategies for achieving these objectives will be concerned with the elements of the marketing mix. Product/service deletion, modification and addition as well as 'packaging' are prime considerations as is policy on pricing for the product/service in particular market segments. Policies on distribution channels and the level of after-sales service need re-appraisal and in terms of communicating with the customer/client, objectives in terms of:

- The role and size of personal selling activities.
- Advertising/promotion.
- P.R.
- The use of direct mail.
- The effectiveness of exhibitions.

– require quantification.

After testing the feasibility of achieving the objectives through strategies adopted in terms of expected market share, sales income, costs and profit, alternative plans may emerge. The task of the head of marketing will then need to justify all marketing expenditure preferably from a zero base against the tasks set – each year.

To repeat, market planning is a management process which involves a logical sequence of activities which lead to the setting of quantified marketing objectives and the implementation of plans to achieve them.

Effective marketing remains a difficult area for many firms and attempting to formulate a marketing plan will inevitably throw light on fundamental problems associated with a firm's current management procedures and policies and require a re-appraisal of those external activities and changes in the market for its product and services that present both current and future opportunities and threats.

Many new and existing companies currently without a practical quantified plan need to attempt this difficult process and "plan to plan" whilst accepting that even in successful companies it takes a long period to establish a sensible and practical market planning system understood by all managers involved in the process.

The excellent text, Marketing Plans by McDonald of The Cranfield School of Management, (3) deals in detail with the key areas of marketing planning and refers to practical research by Cranfield in this difficult area. This text, in discussing design and implementation, summarises the most frequently encountered problems in marketing planning as:

PROBLEMS

1. Weak support from Chief Executive and top management.
2. Lack of a plan for planning.
3. Lack of line management support.
    - hostility
    - lack of skills
    - lack of information
    - lack of resources
    - inadequate organisation structure
4. Confusion over planning terms.
5. Numbers in lieu of written objectives and strategies.
6. Too much detail, too far ahead.
7. Once-a-year ritual.
8. Separation of operational planning from strategic planning.
9. Failure to integrate marketing planning into a total corporate planning system.
10. Delegation of planning to a planner.

These areas are summarized prior to considering the detailed planning process whose stages are given in the diagram over, reproduced from this text.

FIG. 2   THE MARKET PLANNING PROCESS

From: Marketing Plans, Malcolm H.B. McDonald

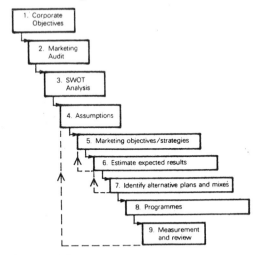

The marketing plan contains:

    SWOT analysis

    Assumptions

    Marketing objectives and strategies

    Programmes (with forecasts and budgets)

SUMMARY OF PROCESS

The internal company audit analysis of strengths and weaknesses in relation to external opportunities, threats and competition can be carried out by an outside consulting agency who will have special knowledge and, being unhindered by the normal day-to-day management problems, can be constructively critical and objective in its analysis of the internal situation and have facilities to research the external opportunities and threats. In practice this audit needs to involve closely all the company's executives who will participate in the final plans and agree a planning process and systems to be followed in subsequent years with rigorous discipline to reinforce a critical appraisal of needs and changes/training required at all levels.

The internal audit will set down in detail:

- A breakdown of sales by product/service type, customer, geographic location and attempt to quantify market shares and profit margins.
- The firms marketing structure and control systems.
- The adequacy of its market research function.
- Product policy in terms of deletions, modifications and the introduction of new items.
- Distribution methods including relations with dealers.

- Pricing policies.
- Selling methods.
- Advertising goals and public relations programme.
- Training needs in all areas.

An objective analysis of all these areas will throw light on the organisation's strengths and weaknesses and the need to alter/reinforce those areas with shortcomings to ensure that the marketing objectives aimed at are consistent with corporate objectives and finally stated clearly and understood by all participating executives and specialist staff. At this stage any differences between the marketing and other functions, e.g. production, research and development, personnel, will have to be resolved.

OPPORTUNITIES/THREATS

Opportunities/threats external to the firm embrace those complex economic, political, legal and technological areas which can affect the enterprise and need to be researched well before short or longer term plans can be implemented. Information requirements that will create opportunities and threats will include:

- Materials and labour availability, energy costs, inflation etc.
- Taxation changes and duty increases, constraints on advertising, pricing, packaging/labelling rules, product quality and changes in trade practices.
- Population distribution by age, sex, social class, location and size of ethnic groups, changes in needs and life style amongst consumers/buying organisations.
- Changes in technology relevant to methods of production, use of new materials, substitutes available, new machinery and equipment that will reduce costs etc.

Detail about market sizes, growth and trends require quantification as well as data on price competition, government regulations, trade practices and the methods available for physical distribution. Further information relating to channels of distribution, purchasing patterns and purchasing advantages/restraints as well as updating the buying methods and structures of decision-making units amongst organisational buyers is also required.

Information regarding competitors in the industry is a vital ingredient of marketing planning. Marketing methods, pricing policies, distribution arrangements, product quality and reputation as well as diversification into other areas by competitors needs digesting. New entrants to the market, mergers and acquisitions as well as the main strengths and weaknesses of all competitors will provide further information to assist in planning for the long-term and detailing marketing programmes for the coming year.

In terms of profitability in the chosen market(s) the planners should attempt to produce a 'league' table of the competition showing return on investment, sales volumes for all competing products, cost of investments etc. and the main sources of profits in the market.

INFORMATION NEEDS

The detailed analysis of the complex data summarised above will isolate those factors relevant to the company's ability to maintain and extend its competitive strength. The auditor's task will involve discarding information not relevant to the task of planning, putting relevant data in a form most usable to the company, and listing other areas for detailed research. SWOT analysis precedes the stage of marketing planning and some basic assumptions which will be key points in setting strategies and tactics. An example of a firm's strategy based on assumptions following studies of market needs, trends and competitor size/methods may be to pursue market skimming and appropriate tactics could be:

- Up-lifting product/service quality.
- Charging a higher price.
- Extending after-sales service.
- Changing the emphasis in advertising, improving P.R.
- Selective distribution.

Setting realistic marketing objectives and strategies are the next crucial steps in the planning process. Marketing objectives were summarised in the Ansoff diagram as aiming to offer:-

- Existing products to current markets.
- New products to current markets.
- Existing products to new markets.
- New products to new markets.

A company might modify this list by aiming to offer:-

- Existing products to the same market in different geographical areas.
- Modified products to the above.
- Modified products to a new market.
- Completely new products to a new market.

The audit process leading to implementation of a marketing plan embraces the products/services offered, the buyers and the markets and will include considerations of the main pillars of marketing: price, promotion and distribution. A key factor in planning is market segmentation, the subject of Chapter 2. In researching needs the marketeer will be conscious of the distinction to be made between customers and end-users, a subject discussed in Chapter 3, and be clear precisely WHO the customers are and what factors need constant study if changes that will determine current and future needs are to be satisfied by the product/service on offer.

MARKET SHARE

A company's share of the market for its offerings has important implications and is a major factor in mapping its marketing strategy (4). Attention has already been drawn to the need to distinguish between product class, form and brand when measuring market share in order to be clear that what is being measured is the actual share of the market for its specific product compared with competing products, e.g. a specialized car manufacturer will not be interested in its share of the total car market but only in the particular sector(s) for which its offering has been designed.

The well-known Pareto rule, sometimes called the 80/20 rule, applies in most markets. In essence it is common to find 20% of customers, or thereabouts, account for 80% of sales. When analysis of product/service sales to a sector reveal this, it is often possible to deal with the 80% who only buy 20% in another way in terms of organising selling, distribution, pricing and promotion to reduce the cost of dealing with the latter group whilst directing more effort to the more lucrative sector and developing extra business from it. One simple example here would be to maintain sales to small and infrequent buyers through the use of telephone selling with a change in promotional literature to them and reduce or eliminate personal visits by sales executives.

SEGMENTATION AND PRODUCT LIFE CYCLES (PLC's)

The criteria for effective market segmentation, discussed in Chapter 2, must be observed or planning aimed at improving profitability and growth will not succeed because the selling company will be offering something that can be bought easily elsewhere to the detriment of margins unless the company has particularly good control on production costs.

The product life cycle was the subject of Chapter 7 and relevant in completing a marketing audit in that plans need to include all those actions required to stretch the life cycle of each product before launching and during its life by manipulating all components of the marketing mix. By adhering to a premium pricing policy at the mature stage in the PLC of its product(s), at a time when the market has high competition, price wars could ensue with a loss of market share. Planned changes to advertising and promotion will similarly be necessary because different themes during:-

- product launch
- market growth
- maturity

and ● decline

will require re-appraisal if sales growth and market share are to be maintained.

Plotting PLC curves is not easy nor is market share measurement which is to do with the proportion in terms of volume and value of the ACTUAL market and not the POTENTIAL market for the precise product on offer. A cigarette manufacturer with a brand of filter cigarettes will be concerned with his share of the total market for products that satisfy the same customer needs and not with the total cigarette market. This manufacturer will still need to be aware of smoking trends and habits, particularly at this time when smoking is increasingly 'taboo' since this may affect the total market and his share of a part of this. For methods of determining where a company's product/service is at the stage of its life cycle references to the literature on PLC given can prove useful. When measurement of sales growth and external information indicate that a company's product or products have reached a stage where there is a need to launch one or more products the market plan will include the steps to be taken if overall sales/growth are to meet company objectives and its product portfolio will change.

THE BOSTON MATRIX

The Boston Consulting Group (BCG) and others have directed attention to this subject and caused company management to think afresh about product/market strategy. A company's product/service portfolio changes over time as market needs change and in order to maintain growth, cash flow, profit and minimise the risk of not achieving its objectives this portfolio must be constantly reviewed. New product development, new product/service launch, product modification and deletion follow from this and are relevant to the planning process.

The BCG and other strategy consultants offered a set of simple concepts readily understood by businesses which nevertheless hired the consultants to implement them to get full benefit. The three key concepts were, firstly, that a company's various activities in the market place should be understood in terms of, and segmented into, strategic business units (SBU's). An SBU could be regarded as a free-standing business, selling a product or a set of related products, to a definable market. Such units were strategic because they required a company to identify competitors in a particular business precisely and to evaluate how it stood relative to those competitors. The second concept was the 'experience' curve. If a company is making a standardised product and if the process is being properly managed, every significant increment in the cumulative amount of product manufactured brings with it a predictable decrase in unit cost of the product. Doubling cumulative volume (doubling "experience") produces a unit cost decrease of 20–30%. This exciting fact was the link BCG posited between the experience curve and market share. If a company is a market-share leader, the consultants suggested that it could follow the curve faster than the competition, reduce prices and stay top of the league forever. A competitor only in sixth of seventh place should probably think of quitting the business. Such logic gave rise to the third concept. The growth and market share matrix of BCG gave a grid upon which a company's business, or more properly business units, could be judged according to two criteria as shown in the diagram below.

FIG.3

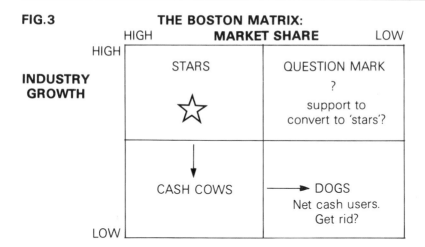

THE BOSTON MATRIX:

The horizontal axis indicates relative market share, from high to low and the vertical dimension indicates total market growth from slow below to fast above. A business in the upper-left quadrant with high share of a fast growing market was a 'star', throwing off enough cash to sustain itself. A lower-left hand quadrant business had a high share in a mature industry – a 'cash cow' that provided cash. An upper-right hand quadrant business – low share in a fast growing market was a 'question mark'. Low right-hand quadrant businesses in a slow growth market were 'dogs' – cash traps.

At the very least, BCG advised that a company should manage its portfolio of business to balance cash flows and when the 'dogs' consumed too much cash they should be discarded. Armed with this package the experts went to many large companies and segmented them into business units and carried out cost analysis. Frequently the consultants discovered that their clients did not truly know what it cost to make their tractor for example, and that costs from different product lines were jumbled under an organisational umbrella, e.g. "farm machinery division".

Over many hours, consultants and client staff recalculated costs on the proper basis of business unit segmentation. The client company could then look again at market prospects and the competition that every company faces. Thus the strategy appeared with recommendations to cut price to gain market share or remove from certain areas of business. The experts, much richer from the high fees charged, then went home.

For detail about the techniques and concepts employed, the 'Corporate Strategist', papers by Hedley are useful, references (4) (5).

CRITICISMS

Much criticism followed the period when consulting firms were selling strategy-consulting and an article by Kiechel gives a useful summary in his paper "Corporate Strategist Under Fire" (6). Critics both inside and outside consulting firms nibbled at the key strategic concepts from their invention; a series of articles in Fortune (7) beginning with 'The Decline of the Experience Curve' reinforced the critics.

Criticisms of this approach can be summarised as:

1) Segmenting the business into SBU's did not clearly advise the firm how to deal with them. The experience curve proved useful mainly for products sold on the basis of price alone, but many industries did not fit this pattern. More significantly its operation was not automatic – the firm had to manage costs tightly to proceed down the curve.

2) If a firm charted its business on a growth share matrix what did it do if it found that it had only 'cash cows' and 'dogs'?

Criticism of their concepts was countered by consultants in terms of "implementation problems". The strategy was sound but the client company could not implement it. For outsiders and some consultants came the comment "does not the fact that few can carry it out say something about the value of the strategy?"

What the consultants offered was a set of concepts, simple and seemingly powerful enough to be grasped by businessmen. These concepts in fact were also difficult enough in application to require most companies to hire an outside expert to set their full benefit.

Three concepts were key matters. The first, developed by McKinsey and Co., but given more analytical treatment by BCG, was the notion that a firm's activities should be understood and segmented in strategic business units, or SBU's. An SBU worked like a freestanding business; it sold a product or a set of related products to a definable market. Such units were strategic because they required it to identify competitors in a particular business and to evaluate just how it stood relatively to those competitors. It was no longer sensible to say that, "we compete with X and Y in farm machinery and we are well in front." You had to realise that you might be winning big tractor orders, you had a modest lead over X in combines and that X and Y were very well ahead in the rotary-plough category.

The second concept was the Experience Curve, a BCG improvement on the old learning cuve. For a standardised product, doubling cumulative volume (doubling "experience") produced a 20–30% decrease in costs.

The link between the experience curve and market share was an important idea. The market-share leader would drive down the curve faster than the competition, underprice them and stay on top.

This logic produced the third concept – the big one. The BCG grid above with its two criteria, the horizontal axis indicating relative market share from high on the left and low to the right; the vertical dimension indicated total market growth. Thus the terms stars, cash cows, dogs and problem products.

The detailed marketing audit preparatory to setting marketing objectives will require drawing a product life cycle for all main products/services and a prediction, using the audit information, of its future length and shape. Portfolio matrices will also be part of the analysis.

The key step in the marketing planning process is the setting of clear, realistic objectives which can be achieved for all company products in each market. To repeat, setting objectives is the main step in planning since without them a company cannot decide the strategies needed to achieve them.

OPPORTUNITIES

Having identified opportunities and agreed on those basic assumptions about factors that will affect the setting of objectives would appear to be straightforward; it remains then to quantify results expected. Objective setting proceeds by fixing broad objectives first, followed by specific objectives. The initial statement would concern itself with the precise nature of the business the company wishes to compete in, translated into key result areas vital to the firm's success. Market penetration and growth rate of sales are such key objectives. Sub-objectives necessary to achieve these would be sales volume targets, geographical expansion, increasing product range etc.

MANAGEMENT TASKS

At board level, directors are guardians of the company and concerned with propagating the business in the long term for the benefit of customers, shareholders and employees. Part of their task is to make those fundamental decisions on risk and resource allocation to ensure the long term profitability of the company. At the lower level, managements need objectives defined in detail such as increasing market share, obtaining new markets, controlling costs and monitoring performance. Further down the structure, management/executives need objectives defined in greater detail. The overall marketing objective will only be met if sub-objectives are achieved and sub-objectives must be an integral part of the broader objectives if company resources are not to be used wastefully. Corporate objectives need to be wedded to marketing objectives so that if a marketing objective is to increase sales of a product but can only do so at a cost not consistent with the main plan, a change is required. In this case the cost may be switched to a product in an expanding and profitable market sector. Similarly objectives set for communicating with buyers need to be consistent with the wider objectives and be integrated with the other components of the marketing mix to result in a consistent, logical marketing plan.

BENEFITS

Segmenting the market provides an important component for the marketing plan and not only requires detail of what product/services and the volume currently bought but a study of why it is bought so that effective communication aimed at increasing future sales to existing and potential new buyers can detail and stress **benefits sought by buyers. Do they buy because:**

- The offering has special characteristics?
- Price is important?
- The offering is easily and conveniently obtained?
- The offering satisfies emotional needs, status?
- Or a combination of such reasons?

Individuals do not buy a product for its physical features but because it satisfies a need. The company preparing a marketing plan must analyse the benefits sought by its buyers and following some detail about its product/service, prominently list why the offering meets buyer needs. Benefit analysis will list every benefit in detail and ensure that none are taken for granted. Sometimes a double (or treble) benefit can be offered and this can be an important fact in countering competition; an electroplating compound based on fluoborates, as distinct from cyanide, may deposit a covering on components at a higher rate (and a lower cost) but since it is relatively non-poisonous have very significant advantages from a health and safety point of view.

SEGMENTATION

Effective market segmentation is a key area in market planning and concerned with:

What is bought in terms of
- volume
- price
- outlets
- location

Who buys in terms of
- demography
- class
- volume bought
- personality, life style
- brand loyalty

And why in terms of
- benefits
- preferences
- perceptions
- attitudes

PRICE FACTOR

Careful and detailed segmentation is important since for many products, price is not the major factor uppermost in the minds of buyers and segmentation supplies the way to differentiating the offerings from competition so that the planners can target their efforts more precisely to the markets most likely to buy. Planning requires identifying key segments through in-depth research before completing the audit of the product/service, sorting its portfolio along the lines discussed which involves attempting to plot accurate industry and product life cycles.

Having set market objectives, it remains to detail the strategies by which they will be achieved and these are to do with the elements of the marketing mix. **Product** policies on deletion, modification and new additions, updating designs and packaging are areas that need spelling out. Increasing product/service range performance and quality, positioning and branding are further matters that determine strategy.

Pricing policies need re-appraisal in line with the other components and whether price skimming or increasing market penetration policies must be pursued. Price changes in line with increasing material/labour costs or competitor changes will need defining.

Place. Under this heading, policies in channels will be laid down and changes to delivery, service and channels will be detailed.

Promotion policies to do with communicating with the customers through advertising, sales promotions, exhibition, direct mail and personal selling will be reviewed and agreed as will the P.R. programme.

At this stage the firm will have made an objective and critical analysis of its:

- corporate objectives
- corporate strategies
- marketing objectives
- marketing strategies

and ensured that they are compatible.

There follows from objectives/strategy formulation the detailed plans for the areas of:

COMMUNICATING WITH THE PROSPECT

Communicating with customers/prospects which will be sub-divided into the areas of advertising, promotions, and PR i.e. the impersonal methods and the personal selling through face-to-face meetings which will include exhibitions. Because no single method of communication will move the buyer from awareness to purchasing this plan will integrate all methods so that they "sing the same tune" but at appropriate stages in the buying process. Methods of communication including personal selling were discussed at length in Chapter 5. For each channel of communication, setting achievable and measurable objectives is the starting point and finally all methods must be integrated to produce a total communications budget which is the most cost effective, a subject that concluded Chapter 4.

PROMOTIONS

Sales promotions are activities designed to move customers to providing income to the company at easonally convenient times, to hasten sales of slow-moving items, induce trial purchase, pay bills speedier than normal, counter competition etc. and promotional activity clearly affects planning of associated activities to do with total communication and selling activity as well as stock-holding and cash generation. Promotions which are irregular in frequency are tactical devices distinct from advertising strategy which is to create a long term effect.

PERSONAL SELLING

The reasons when personal selling is appropriate and necessary for many companies was discussed in Chapter 6 as was the role and size of the salesforce and the advantages of this method over other elements in the communications mix. Marketing strategy will be much concerned with this aspect on account of its relatively high cost and new approaches/ techniques for communicating with customers. Many companies in recent years have had to review their salesforces and planning and programming of marketing activities altered significantly: a useful example was given under personal selling in Chapter 5.

There is a good deal of literature on the planning of selling and for companies where personal selling is an important cost element, a useful paper by Oliver on 'Sales Force Planning' (9) deals with the role and size of the salesforce and methods available for maximising its effectiveness. Amongst the literature on salesforce motivation is a useful paper by Doyle and Shapiro, 'What counts most in Motivating your Sales Force' (10), who studied the sales systems of four companies, two with a clearly defined sales task and two without. They discovered that sales people worked longer hours and more effectively when the task was clear, i.e. when they saw a positive and firm relationship between their efforts and results. It appears that the nature of the sales task has more to do with motivation than personality, compensation plan, or quality of management. McDonald in dealing with Marketing Plans (3) also comments on salesforce management and motivation and offers some guidelines for preparing the sales plan, although individual plans will not have the same headings or content.

PRICING

A pricing plan is a necessary element in the planning process despite the fact that price is generally not easily separated from the other components of the offer to customers; promotion, distribution and other components can be more easily managed and measured but pricing can be complex as discussed in Chapter 5 but nevertheless is a key determinant in influencing purchasing behaviour. Pricing can be a source of conflict between the marketer and the accountant especially when the latter regards his task simply as ensuring that prices charged are set to maximise profitability and for a given product to ensure that it yields profit in line with company targets. The ideal planning teams would include a marketing orientated accountant together with marketing executives with a sound understanding of finance. Although price is only one component of the offer to customers it nevertheless dictates to some extent how much of the product will be sold and thus its relevance to the marketing plan. Decisions on price clearly affect revenue and margins.

PRICE AND PLC

Sometimes pricing is dictated by forces outside the company as discussed in Chapter 7. On other occasions the accounting function may wish to increase price to maximise profitability whilst the marketer wishes to reduce price to capture a bigger share of the market. The decision on price might be resolved by a reasonable calculation aimed at showing which price would give the maximum profit in the long term. Lessons to be learned that throw light on this dilemma can be found in the writings of the Boston Consulting Group and others in offering explanations for the demise of the British Motor Cycle Industry. By contrast, the Japanese have shown that cutting prices to obtain an increased share of the market paid dividends for the long term despite a low profitability in the shorter term. Whilst a price reduction can sometimes increase sales and the increased volume of production lead to cost savings, profitability will decline if sales do not increase sufficiently to balance revenue and costs. Because demand curves change over time, depending on many factors, there are dangers in accepting profit decline in the short term if it is likely to carry on into long term. The planners in fixing a pricing policy designed to improve profitability or market share need to consider:

- corporate and marketing objectives
- The product/service portfolio
- Life cycles and position in the market
- Competitors
- Costs
- Channels of distribution

Corporate objectives influence marketing objectives, the former may need short term profit to be generated to facilitate growth in a particular sector and need to keep down market penetration in another. In this case pricing strategy will be influenced. A given product or range may not be selected for heavy investment, since it is required elsewhere; the aim may be to make the largest contribution to profits from a product and the pricing would be set to achieve this. Setting marketing objectives for a given product is the starting point in fixing price.

A knowledge of product life cycles has been stressed as being important in setting marketing objectives. Depending on the stage in the PLC price will change up or down. If a product has a long life ahead of it, it can be sensible to reduce price to maintain or enlarge market share. For a product with a known short life, pursuing increased market share growth would not be a sensible marketing objective.

POSITIONING

Price is relevant to product positioning (a term discussed in Chapter 3) and a high quality, exclusive product can be priced too low. The proposal, discussed in Chapter 7, that a buyer has two price levels in mind when contemplating purchase, a price below which the product is considered to

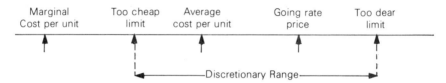

be too cheap and one above which it is regarded as too expensive. The marketer is required to set a price at the optimum point between the two.

The other factor in price planning requires a knowledge of actual and potential competitor prices and the marketing function will carefully research this area and contribute, from this standpoint, to final price setting.

Product/service production costs provide basic data for pricing and cost plus pricing and other approaches were dealt with in Chapter 7 and need to be understood by all participants setting the pricing plan. During this process, unprofitable products may need to be discarded and this will necessarily reduce the scale of operations and the product mix. This process if repeated several times can lead to the death of a company. McDonald (1) has coined the expression 'anorexia Industrialosa' for this process to describe the excessive desire to be leaner and fitter, leading to total emanciation and death! His intention is to advise caution and a broader view when using any kind of costing system as a basis for pricing decisions.

INTERMEDIARIES

Marketing intermediaries, the link between supplier and consumer, provide many necessary services to maintain the supplier's income/profit and intermediaries need help and adequate reward. The pricing plan will carefully set down the amount and method of rewarding these links covering:

- Trade discount depending on the services supplied by the intermediary in terms of bulk buying, costs of re-distribution, stock holding and servicing etc.
- Quantity discounts to encourage holding high stock levels.

- Cash discounts to encourage prompt payment in order to preserve the supplier's cash flow.
- Help with advertising and promotions.

The marketing plan will have as a basic task a detailed appraisal of all intermediaries from which the removal or improvement of inadequate intermediaries can be decided and additional/replacement intermediaries sought. The costs of intermediaries will be an important component in product/service price setting.

PRICING PLAN

Pricing policy is determined by taking account of all the factors involved in pricing decisions which can be summarised as shown in Fig.4 opposite.

FIG.4

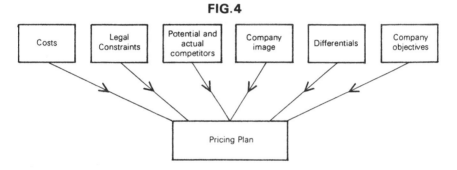

DISTRIBUTION

The marketing function must be closely involved with distribution, a major component in the marketing mix. For many companies distribution can be an involved and costly area. It is little use having a good product, sound promotion and carefully thought out pricing if the product is not available at the right place and time in sufficient quantity for actual and potential customers. Product distribution requires sound decisions on:

- How the product is to be physically moved to the buyers.
- Where the customers are geographically located and what quantities they require.
- The most appropriate marketing channels for the supplier's products.

In some companies different parts of the distribution function are allotted to different departments, the marketing function possibly only accountable for controlling the channels through which the products move. The allocation of other parts to the production or accounting areas has some disadvantages insofar as each has its own objectives and level of efficiency and it could be in the interests of the company as a whole, and the marketing function, if distribution were centralised. As a starting point to planning it can be worthwhile appraising all the parts of the distribution task with a view to reducing total costs, improving overall efficiency and customer satisfaction by appointing one individual, in marketing, to be totally accountable for the whole function. Many companies expend huge sums of money on distribution in terms of inventory costs such as storage costs, interest costs, deterioration, shrinkage, insurance as well as administration and computer costs. Transport costs can be high and embrace decisions on vehicle owning, leasing, delivery scheduling and maintenance etc.

GETTING THE RIGHT PRODUCTS TO THE RIGHT CUSTOMERS

An important marketing task which will determine where and how many production units and/or warehouses should best be located involves forecasting the nature, size and geographical spread of demand. Also necessary is the determination of levels of servicing required by customers. Having good data on the level of inventory to hold, where to hold it and in what quantities to order are important issues and serve as the means of deciding the level of service the firm can offer its customers.

The packaging of individual products and the sensible packaging of quantity for transport and storage has an important bearing on the economics of distribution. This area which includes the use of mobile racking systems has seen important changes and innovations in recent years and has had significant effects on the way many products are marketed.

Getting the right product to the right customers at the right time, requires the marketer to choose the most appropriate channels. A marketing channel can have a number of stages (selling intermediaries) between the producer and final buyer. A manufacturer can sell direct to the consumer and thus have no intermediaries. Generally firms will use one, two or three stages, e.g.

Cost and income profiles will depend on the alternatives summarised above and since the job of the intermediary is to assist the producer in obtaining the best possible market coverage at the least cost the marketer needs to play his part in the planning process by selecting not only the most appropriate channels but the specific intermediaries who can offer the best coverage at minimum cost and provide a sound after sales service. Decisions on marketing channels are of key importance as are the constant monitoring of all intermediaries so that they can be helped or discarded for alternatives when necessary.

APPRAISAL OF INTERMEDIARIES

In evaluating intermediaries the supplier's marketers will use some basic criteria such as:

- Is the intermediary set up and efficient enough to sell the products to the market segments selected?
- Is he suitably located and able to service the maximum number of buyers?
- Does he communicate effectively with prospects and is adequate finance available for task?
- What competitive products does he deal with and what are his intentions?
- Is he credit worthy?
- Does he adequately deal with after sales service?

CUSTOMER SERVICE

A supplier's production planning and control and distribution are about customer service, a subject of increasing importance and vital to effective marketing. Those firms aiming to improve customer service should be aware that small increases are often associated with sharp increases in costs. Beyond a certain level costs associated with improving customer service increase exponentially and marketers should contribute by giving careful thought to and researching acceptable customer service needs in order to seek a balance between associated costs and the benefits to be derived. Ideally, the marketing function should contribute to designing different customer service offers for each market sector.

CHANNELS

Marketing channels do not remain static but change continually, sometimes dramatically. A major contribution to marketing planning should come from marketing specialists who will design sound channels and spell out channel objectives, alternatives and likely benefits. After this the firm needs to be effective in channel management through choosing particular organisations/individuals to work with and help them through supervision and the provision of incentives. Because markets and needs change the producer through monitoring the performance of individual channel members must be prepared to revise channels, drop or add individual members and possibly with time, re-design the whole system to retain its competitive position and profitability.

Distribution planning which will be integrated into the final marketing plan should closely involve marketing managers in clearly detailing:-

- Marketing objectives
- Changes in methods of distribution
- Guiding distribution policy in terms of type and number of outlets

- Setting performance targets for intermediaries and thereafter continuously monitoring their performance
- Making changes/additions as required.

The marketing management should be able to give reasons why current channels used are the most appropriate, what advantages/disadvantages they offer and pronounce on cost effective customer service levels needed and compare them with those offered by competitors. They should also offer methods for producing savings in the firm's distribution system without reducing customer service.

Before designing and implementing the marketing planning system it is necessary to comment on the basic marketing information that provides the platform on which the planning system is based. It is also necessary to comment on the organisational needs for marketing planning. Some basic matters require answers to the questions:-

- Who should do it, WHEN and HOW OFTEN?
- Does planning depend on size and type of company?
- Is planning different depending on whether the company operates only at home or both in its own country and internationally?
- What is the role of the Chief Executive?
- How is the short term (one year) plan related to the strategic (longer term) plan?

INFORMATION AND FORECASTING

A plan is only as good as the information on which it is based. This chapter started by noting that planning was about the firm attempting to reconcile its resources with its objectives and opportunities and it must strive to match its capabilities with customer needs. The starting point is marketing research, the subject of Chapter 3 which dealt with methods of gathering and analysing data about needs in a logical and systematic way. The cost of employing research specialists, with examples of cost, were given for the guidance of firms who did not have their own research department. The importance of using professional researchers in the context of getting help in formulating the direction and content of the programme was stressed. Because of the high growth rate and sophistication of methods employed by research organisations over the past 20 years it is important for all firms, with or without their own research team, be well-informed on facilities available and how they are best used.

Chapter 3 stressed that a good deal of information is usually available from within the firm as well as that available externally and the two sources should complement each other.

SOURCES OF INFORMATION

An enormous amount of information is available from government statistics, OECD, ECC, the United Nations, technical journals, trade associations and published market surveys. Such sources of information require a good deal of desk research and senior executives should set aside regular periods when they can read these (often free) publications which, when combined with internal sales information, provide a powerful source of knowledge and background data which can contribute to the firm's marketing plan. Efforts by managers to gather useful information to further their company's aims often reveal that there is available an excess of data and information rather than too little.

Because sound information is vital to decision-making the marketing planners need to effectively organise information collection and flow, a process often referred to as a marketing intelligence system (MIS). Implementing a practical MIS requires effort and discipline if the planners are to identify the decisions that have to be taken and have available, in the right form, information to quantify these decisions. The steps to be taken in constructing a MIS are to:-

- List all data and information available
- list the decisions to be made by all participating managers and the information required for making them.
- combine the above in order that all unnecessary information can be discarded.

INTERNAL INFORMATION

Internally generated sales information may be listed in terms of product lines, product line summaries, trade categories, geographical areas, purchasing patterns, time scales etc. A monthly report listing sales volume by sector can be used to:

- identify the spread and penetration of individual products by segment.
- assess penetration of new products to particular segments.
- assess loss of sales by segment.
- assist in improving target marketing.
- compare actual sales to potential sales.

A MIS which is to do with information gathering (internally and externally), information processing (the output of information through regular reporting) and the utilization of this information requires managing. In some organisations a central company intelligence unit is accountable for a MIS but it could equally be managed by a team in the marketing function provided its leader is strong, preferably a company director, market orientated and with financial skills.

FORECASTING

Forecasting is a necessary part of marketing planning; it is difficult and whilst many managers are quick to make forecasts based on their past experience they can be wrong, with serious consequences for their company. Others show a reluctance to forecast in quantitative terms for this reason. Nevertheless, forecasting is necessary and needs to be done well. There are many forecasting techniques available to companies but outside the scope of this chapter. Simple extrapolations of past sales is rarely the answer since in time of increasing competition, changes in markets, politics, the law, and social and cultural changes etc. prevent this.

Forecasting is concerned first of all with forecasting markets in total and then with detailed unit forecasts. The macro forecasting precedes the setting of objectives and strategies, and the micro forecasts come after the firm has decided which specific market opportunities it is best equipped to tackle and how this should be done. Forecasting can be qualitative and quantitative and both will normally be used. A combination of an intuitive and mathematical approach is required. Relevant sound data provides the platform from which management has to predict the future using appropriate quantitative methods, together with qualitative methods such as expert opinions, market research and analogy to predict the possible discontinuities with time. Only by using the tools and information available will management be able to match its own capabilities with the selected market needs. Unless this is properly understood and acted on forecasting will be a useless exercise.

ORGANISATIONAL NEEDS

Before designing and implementing a marketing planning system it is necessary to comment briefly on the organisational needs. When a firm begins its life, the principal character, the entrepreneur, takes the central position and his technical knowledge and familiarity with customers ensure all decisions and communications come from this one person. In this situation formal marketing planning systems are not too relevant. As the firm grows in size and as new products and new markets are added, an organisational framework is required in which specialised jobs are allocated to people who will head specific functions. From this point the organisation can become decentralised or centralised. Decentralised organisations will have their own central services such as market research, P.R., etc. which can lead to duplication of effort and differentiation of strategies with inevitable problems unless a company-wide planning system is adopted. For companies operating abroad large sums of money can be wasted through duplication of research etc. by the different parts. In this situation a strong central coordination through a planning system is required if wastage of corporate resources is to be minimised through different parts of the business striving to succeed in their own part of the business.

A centrally controlled company will not have a strategic level of management in its subsidiary units, especially in terms of introducing new products. In this situation standardised strategies are adopted. When a new product is launched it may be aimed at as many markets as possible with market research information in one area utilized in another. It is possible that subsidiary units can become less sensitive to the detailed needs of specific markets and lose out to competitors. Marketing in this situation has a different meaning from that in the previous situation.

There is a difference between a corporation and its individual components and a problem of deciding how managers at the different levels in the organisation may best be involved in the planning process and precisely how, can only be resolved by the Chief Executive spelling out the kind of business and markets the company is pursuing.

Whilst both centralised and decentralised organisation structures have disadvantages there is some merit in the centrally organised form in that it is easier, under a strong executive, to more effectively provide a formal system to allow operating managers to have a clear view of their task and whether they are concentrating on essentials. It is fundamental that a system of planning to control business growth effectively utilises all skills to improve the reputation of the enterprise whilst avoiding waste of talent, time and money through duplicating effort.

No particular organisational form is essential for proper marketing planning; the firm's situation and its market(s) are the main determinants, supplemented by commonsense and a chief executive who demands a disciplined approach and insists on co-ordination between all functions and appoints sound managers to whom he can give clear accountability. A marketing planning system will only be truly effective if the chief executive leads the way and takes an active role.

Designing the marketing planning system will depend on size and complexity of the firm and attention has already been drawn to the difficulties and the reasons that hinder, or stifle the process. Attention has also been drawn to the fact that it can take several years, especially in large firms, to successfully introduce effective marketing planning. The potential complexities of marketing planning in large diversified groups and the requisite planning levels is discussed further by McDonald in his text, Marketing Plans (1) who offers a simple summary to illustrate how the degree of formalisation of the planning process relates to size and diversity of the company. McDonald comments that the degree of formalization must increase with size and diversity; nevertheless while the degree of formalization will change, the need for a complete marketing planning system does not.

The setting of objectives is the key element for any organisation intent on planning as are the decisions which executives should be involved in:

- situation review
- objective setting
- listing assumptions
- setting down strategies
- costing programmes
and - scheduling

FIG.5

COMPANY SIZE

		LARGE	MEDIUM	SMALL
MARKET/PRODUCT DIVERSITY	HIGH	HIGH FORMALIZATION	HIGH/MEDIUM FORMALIZATION	MEDIUM FORMALIZATION
	MEDIUM	HIGH/MEDIUM FORMALIZATION	MEDIUM FORMALIZATION	LOW FORMALIZATION
	LOW	MEDIUM FORMALIZATION	LOW FORMALIZATION	HIGH FORMALIZATION

From: Marketing Plans by Malcolm H.B. McDonald.

How they are to be involved and at what level is the important preliminary to the implementation of marketing planning and company size, type and diversity guide the answers to these questions.

Company size generally determines the type of planning system adopted. Some companies complete the steps in the planning process in a relatively informal manner; the market audit. SWOT analysis, the basic assumptions, objectives and strategies are carried out by the top management and transmitted to subordinates personally.

COMPANY SIZE

The smaller the company the more informal and personal are the procedures for marketing planning. As size and diversity increase, the need for institutionalized procedures increases.

In any system, control over the factors that determine success is a vital ingredient. In large diversified multi-nationals marketing objectives and strategies are difficult to set from a remote headquarters. A system is required that strikes a proper balance between the flexibility of the operating unit to react quickly to changes in local markets and centralized control. Companies which have a framework which through a hierarchy of bottom up/top down negotiating procedures, get a proper balance between the need for detailed control at the lowest level of operations and centralized control. The main role of headquarters is to harness the company's strengths on a worldwide basis and ensure that lower level decisions do not cause problems in other areas and lead to wasteful duplication.

The marketing planning process can now be summarized to provide the basis for designing a system suitable for any kind of business.

Every company needs to answer some fundamental questions such as 'what sales/profit should we be achieving in the current trading conditions?' The marketing plan will contain a well researched section to answer this question. The marketing plan provides the tools to decide what to do now and in the future (changing) conditions.

The process of marketing planning must involve all managers/specialists within the company at all levels from the board through subsidiary units and departments within them.

COMMUNICATION

Good communication up and down the organisation is essential as is careful research from outside the organisation. When budgets are agreed and set down all participants must be flexible enough to take corrective action by manipulating the elements of the plan when actual results depart from standards set.

The Marketing Audit is the starting point in planning and is an analysis of the firm's strengths and weaknesses in relation to external opportunities, threats and competitors. All managers involved in auditing their own area of responsibility will need help in constructing a detailed list of questions to be answered using sales data from the company information system. Market research information produced internally or by an outside agency will supply detailed information about all markets and product need and trends.

The audit checklist will be tailored to the level in the organisation so that each list is meaningful and relevant to each participant.

Additional information will be required at this stage and managers should prepare their own source book on product/services and markets, kept updated and used in discussion during planning. This data will help throughout the year in reviewing the state of affairs and if kept updated can be used by a new manager as an important reference work and help him to grasp the department's situation quickly.

The SWOT analysis should be concise and draw attention to strengths and weaknesses, highlighting the issues that head the list of priorities, and be a summary of the major issues emerging from the audit and obtained by internal discussion so that the general view emerges. The SWOT analysis will provide answers to basic questions such as:

- Who are the customers and what are their needs?
- How do they select and choose suppliers?
- What is the competition doing?

A SWOT is a group task essentially and not the view of one individual if it is to provide a sound building block for the final plan. Managers involved in producing it will find it a useful and informative discipline.

Key Assumptions on which the plan is based will be listed in the marketing plan and will normally be few in number.

Marketing Objectives, a vital task, will involve all managers at the start of the planning process. Each manager will set his objectives and discuss them with senior managers/directors who will contribute through giving a fuller picture of the firm's overall objectives and in this way not only modify and possibly change priorities but be better committed to them.

Objectives will need quantifying and measuring since without them, performance cannot be monitored. The final list will rank objectives in order of priority.

Marketing Strategies indicating the way in which objectives are to be achieved will also be included in the plan and deal with policies on product, price, distribution and promotion.

Programmes included finally in the marketing plan will detail budgets and sales forecasts to match the marketing objectives; objectives, strategies and programmes need to match the agreed budgets and forecasts. A detailed understanding of the market is necessary to highlight viable marketing objectives and strategies consistent with the firm's distinctive competence. Individual budget items will be clearly identified with the key points in the SWOT.

The Written Marketing Plan is the product of the marketing planning process based on the process:

SWOT ⟶ Objectives ⟶ Strategy ⟶ Actions over time
Decisions

A written marketing plan is the recipe for success when adhered to since it sets down proposals and courses of action commensurate with resources and skills available.

THE IMPORTANCE OF THE CHIEF EXECUTIVE

This has been commented on and his main tasks are to:-

- show to all management his commitment to sound planning
- set down the organisational structure
- play a part in the planning process

by
- define the roles of the participants and ensure that the appropriate managers/specialists are recruited
- preserve the balance between short and long term results
- act as a catalyst, stop over-planning and stop excessive bureaucracy developing

TIMING OF PLANNING

Planning for one year begins early enough in the previous year to collect market research data and clarify market trends/changing needs. The early preparation of strategies/tactics allows thinking time so that modifications can be made before final approval. It is practical to prepare a marketing plan that coincides with the firm's fiscal year.

Planning periods of one and five years are common. The five year planning permits consideration of many basic factors such as development and launch of new products/services, time required to recover capital investment costs, availability of raw materials, energy costs, life of existing equipment and manufacturing sites, movements of key customers etc. A five year cycle can be too long to be considered in certain industries operating in volatile fashion conscious markets and equally for certain industries planning for ten and fifteen years ahead is appropriate and necessary; the nuclear industries would be an example here. The bigger and more complex companies will need to plan further ahead whilst a smaller firm can be more flexible and able to react quickly to changes. The problems and disadvantages of planning more than five years ahead has already been commented on.

LEVELS OF AUDIT AND SWOT ANALYSIS

Whilst each individual involved in the marketing planning activity should produce an audit and SWOT analysis for his own area of responsibility, in practice a hierarchy of audits will be carried out – using the same format but differing in detail, e.g.

- Individual manager's audit/SWOT analysis will set down detail about internal strengths/weaknesses and opportunities/threats relating to competitors.
- The Group Manager will summarise the above.
- A Profit Centre will summarise the Group Manager's audit.
- The Head Office will summarise Profit Centre audits.

The top management of the company sets the aims and objectives of the business as a whole, deciding in this process in which parts of the enterprise will be given resources and how much and which parts will have their activities reduced or even sold off. Operating managers being less able to see the whole company and its future aims will naturally direct their interests to their own products and markets and for this reason a top/down system is necessary in offering guidance and allocating resources. The inter-dependence of the higher and lower levels of management is nevertheless vital in setting objectives and strategies.

It has already been stated that there is no universal 'package' for marketing planning and it requires direction, effort and a good deal of patience, experiment and commonsense. At the end of the day if a marketing planning system in time becomes effective, the enterprise will be equipped with a powerful tool for continuing success and profitability, with the marketing planning fitting in with the corporate plan.

REFERENCES

1. McDonald M.H.B., Marketing Plans, How to prepare them. How to use them. Heineman Ltd., 1984.
2. Ansoff, H.I., Strategies for Diversifaction, Harvard Business Rev., Sept/Oct. 1957.
3. Refer 1. See also Thesis 1982 (ref 5 under Further Reading).
4. Hedley, B., Boston Consulting Group, A Fundamental Approach to Strategy Development, Long Range Planning, Dec 1976.
5. Hedley, B., Strategy and Business Portfolio, Long Range Planning, Feb 1977.
6. Kiechel, W.K., Corporate Strategies Under Fire, Fortune, Dec 27th 1982.
7. The Decline of the Experience Curve, First of articles in a series in Fortune 1977.
8. Oliver, G., Sales Force Planning, Marketing Today, Prentice Hall, 1980.

FURTHER READING

1. Hall, W.K., Strategic Planning, product innovation and the theory of the firm, Journal of Business Policy, Vol.3, 1973.
2. Wind and Claychamp, Planning Product Line Strategy, Journal of Marketing, Vol.40, January 1976.
3. Kotler, P., Growth and Competitive Strategy, Marketing Management and Control, 2nd Edition, Prentice Hall.
4. Levitt, T., Planning and Preparation for Change in Innovation and Marketing. McGraw Hill, Chapter 7, 1972.
5. McDonald, M.H.B., The Theory & Practice of Marketing Planning for Industrial Goods in International Markets. Thesis, 1982. Cranfield School of Management Library, Cranfield Institute of Technology, Cranfield, Bedford, MK43 0AL.
6. Haley, Benefit Segmentation; a decision orientated research tool, Journal of Marketing, Vol.32, July 1968.
7. Doyle, S.X., and Shapiro, B.P., What counts most in motivating your sales force?
8. Kotler, P., Marketing Management Analysis, Planning and Control, 2nd Edition, Prentice Hall.

QUESTIONS

1. Summarise the steps in the marketing planning process and list the main problem areas that reduce the effectiveness of planning.
2. Draw the BCG grid relating Market Share and Industry Growth and explain briefly the meaning of the terms
   - Star
   - Cash Cow
   - Dogs
   - Problem children.
3. What factors are to be considered in preparing pricing plan(s) during the marketing planning process? Comment on each of the factors.
4. List sources of external and internal information available to market planners?
5. What are the major differences in planning between small, medium and large enterprises?
6. What is a SWOT analysis? Who is best qualified to carry it out?
7. Discuss marketing intermediaries and state what factors are considered by the marketing company in appraising their effectiveness and how the intermediaries can be helped.

 # INTERNATIONAL MARKETING

This chapter deals with international marketing and is aimed at stimulating businesses to extend their activities by marketing their offerings abroad. The advantages of exporting are discussed and include extending product life cycles, evening out fluctuations in sales by opening new markets, writing off R and D and other costs against a larger volume of sales as well as other methods of increasing profitability. At this time the successful UK exporter will help to cut down imports and ease the country's balance of payment problems.

Chapters 12 and 13 are very much interelated since the latter chapter concentrates on the literature and help available to UK businesses of all sizes from government sources and those other agencies now urging all enterprises to prepare for and export to the Single European Market (SEM).

Marketing was defined in chapter 1 and the basic principles are universal but international differences present some changes in emphasis arising from differences in culture, politics and the state of development of a given country.

International Marketing may therefore be described as:

- The marketing of goods/services across national frontiers and
- The marketing operations of an organisation that sells and/or produces in a given country when that organisation is part of an enterprise which also operates in other countries and
- There is some degree of influence on or control of the marketing activities from outside the country in which it sells and/or produces.

Another description of international marketing (1) is that it is to do with the marketing of multinational companies. It is sometimes wrongly assumed by the smaller company that international marketing is sensible only to multinational giants and that it has nothing to offer the many companies of more modest size. The term multinational company is loosely used and can have several definitions; the term is applied to describe so many different organisations that it may be virtually meaningless. When a firm considers marketing outside its own country it needs to set down and answer the following basic questions.

FUNDAMENTAL QUESTIONS FOR THE EXPORTER

- WHY should it venture abroad and expand its operations?
- WILL it generate good profits?

Many studies of firms who have gone through the processes leading to "internationalisation" have been reported and are given in the reference section to aid firms seriously considering exporting for the first time. The stages proceeding from zero could be:

- No regular activity
- Export via industrial agents (representatives)
- Establishing a subsidiary (of our own company) and registration as a legal entity.
- Establishing a manufacturing subsidiary.Terpstra (2) discusses the 5 stages of:
- Casual or accidental exporting
- Active exporting
- Overseas marketing
- and Foreign production

ADVANTAGES OF EXPORTING

However the firm proceeds from domestic marketing to exporting, many advantages can be listed such as:

- Profit margins are often higher abroad. Even if the margins are lower however, total sales and profits in real terms should increase.
- The Product Life cycle (chapter 8) is extended as the Product is added to new markets.
- Seasonal fluctuations in demand can be evened out by sales to new markets.
- Exporting can offer opportunities for marginal pricing if the basic rules discussed in chapter 7 are followed.
- Often obsolete products can be sold overseas without harm to the home market.
- An international, as distinct from a national image gives the firm added prestige. Further, research and development costs can then be written off against a large sales turnover.
- Sales growth may be easier, especially if domestic demand has reached a plateau or the firm is approaching a monopoly.
- It is in the country's interest to export and cut down on imports to ease balance of payment problems.

Such considerations as above provide only some of the opportunities for venturing abroad. Opportunities must be greater than those available in the home markets (and need to be to compensate for the additional cost and risk of trading abroad) because there is a lack of opportunity in the home market or there is something unique in terms of extra demand and profit.

Further basic questions would include:

- WHICH markets sector(s) should it enter? WHAT is the best method of entry?
- DOES it know enough about demand for its product(s) in the chosen country?

MARKETING RESEARCH, MARKETING METHODS

The above decisions must come back to market research and a good understanding of the detailed methods of marketing as well as the available channels of distribution in the chosen country. Whilst market research and its methodology was discussed in chapter 3, there is now on offer from the British Government, Chambers of Trade and other agencies schemes available to all firms ffor obtaining free or low cost aid for researching the markets in the SEM. In addition, and supplied freely fby the DTI and BOTB, are Country Profiles for each country in the community which are detailed and provide information on:

- Useful country maps
- The Regions
- Information on Industry, Trade and the economy
- Opportunities for British Exporters
- The importance of design and technical requirements
- Marketing Methods
- Investment
- Export conditions
- Contracts for further information
- Useful publications

Other important questions to which answers must be found for the aspiring exporter would include:

- DOES the firm have a suitable organisation structure at home and ABROAD? If not, how will it build one?
- Will the firm pursue undifferentiated, differentiated or concentrated marketing?

PRICING POLICY

This matter is dealt with in chapter 3 by defining the terms and discussing the appropriate strategy to employ. **Concentrated Marketing** devotes its whole marketing effort to one, or a very few, segments, that is the segment(s) with greatest needs and which it believes will be the most profitable; and designs its products and marketing programme accordingly. The firm will concentrate on a very limited market and this strategy will appeal to firms with limited financial resources. **Segmentation** will be based on a variety of variable such as geographic, demographic, buyer behaviour etc as discussed in Chapter 2. **Geographic segmentation** is of particular importance to international marketing strategy.

In terms of international marketing the **undifferentiated approach** implies one standard marketing mix world-wide. Only a few companies can offer the appropriate product lines or have the rersources to attack world markets. An example of such a firm is the UK Coca Cola company.

Differential marketing implies that the company has identified different market needs in various parts of the world and attempts to fix its marketing mix to satisfy the needs of each market.

The choice of strategy to adopt has to be carefully considered for each enterprise but internationally minded firms would do well to adopt a strategy of concentrating their efforts on a limited number of key markets, because the alternatives are very wide and company's resources often are limited.

Any size of firm ambitions to export will find it instructive to read those papers that debate the differences between domestic and international marketing; as an example the paper, 'Are Domestic Markets and International Markets Dissimilar?' (2) and reference (3) and (4) are relevant. The subject of pricing and pricing strategies discussed in chapter 7 are relevant to both domestic and international pricing. It is relevant to comment on the subject in terms of international applications.

PRICING

Three different approaches to pricing policy have been discussed, i.e. – the **competitor, cost** and **demand orientations.**

The extreme example of competitor pricing is to be found in the commodity markets eg wheat, tea etc. Where world market prices are known and established through the collective interaction of a large number of buyers and sellers. To quote a price above the accepted price would simply invite a fall in orders, to quote below the price accepted would not be necessary.

In commodity marketing the producer has no pricing decision to make but to concentrate efforts on cost reduction to maximise profit. Companies practicing **cost-oriented** pricing simply base price on total unit cost and add a profit element in line with company policy. Demand for the offerings have little influence on the final price. This approach is useful for industrial goods where differentiation between similar products is easy to justify to the customer.

Demand-oriented pricing needs detail about the strength of demand from the market. A high price can be obtained when demand is high and low prices when demand is weak even though unit cost may be the same for both situations.

Price setting will be flexible and alternative strategies can be followed by the selling company where price can be an effective tool for the marketer.

The long term objective of all firms is taken as profit maximisation subject to ethical and legal restraints, a subject dealt with briefly in chapter 7. In pursuing this objective a company may adopt different short-term strategies including:

● A Market-penetration strategy
● A Market-skimming strategy
● An early cash recovery

● A strategy based on achieving a satisfactory rate of return on investment

The above terms were discussed in chapter 7 and are defined in Appendix 2 to chapter 14.

The exporting company has a further matter to consider, ie the standardisation or differentiation of prices between countries. Many companies make use of **differential pricing.** In the consumer goods markets a different price can be set for significant segments and setting a price which that market will accept. The demand-oriented company in this situation can only get close to achieving both a short-term and long-term profit maximisation when:

● The market can be clearly segmented
● These segments show different elasticities of demand
● There is a fair separation between segments and
● A lower priced segment can not easily re-sell the product to the higher prices segments.

Such requirements are easier to meet by the exporting company as distinct from one attacking only the domestic market since advantage can be taken by charging different price levels in different carefully selected countries where research has shown a particular demand.

EXPORT PRICING

In arriving at the export price, regardless of the pricing policy adopted, the real cost of the offering provides the yardstick against which pricing decisions can be made on an informed basic. Sometimes the export-price is based on the domestic price plus obvious additions for carriage, duty, channel additions. The domestic price however can include costs not applicable to export prices such as the cost of the home sales force, domestic transport costs, publicity and advertising for the home market, costs of financing stock levels and so on.

On the other hand export prices attract obvious costs not applicable to the home market.

The table below indicates common export terms and what they include:

Common Export Trade Terms and what they include

Quotation	cost of goods at factory	transport to dock	loading on to vessel	ocean or air freight charges	shipping insurance	unloading foreign ports
Ex-factory	X					
Free alongside (fas)	X	X				
Free on board Name of home Port (fab)	X	X	X			
Cost of freight: Name of foreign Port (cof)	X	X	X	X		
Cost, insurance, freight, name of overseas port (cif)	X	X	X	X	X	
Ex dock	X	X	X	X	X	X

Ex-works price is the direct cost of manufacture, including the cost of any modifications required by the market. Appropriate allocation of overhead costs excluding any overhead relevant only to domestic sales (or sales to other export markets).

Allocation of part of export department overhead costs and local export costs specific to the market such as advertising. Part of the firms R and D cost associated with the offering. Agency commissions and special export packaging. Profit margin in line with company policies.

Fob price will include transport and insurance costs to the dock/airport.

Cif price will include transport to the appropriate country and insurance in transit.

Local market price will include landing charges, import duty and internal transport, storage and handling. The price will also embrace the main distributor, wholesale or retail mark-ups.

Additional costs may be included in the export overhead but if significant require special treatment.

Insurance of credit/political risks may need to be included through the Export Credit Guarantee Department.

Other additional expenses arising through small scale operations in some markets eg minimum handling charges and storage charges for small lots may have to be added.

The level of profitability of export sales is concerned not only with short-term profit but pricing policy, and it is very important that all costs be accurately calculated; for this reason the check list above will help to avoid any serious errors/omissions that detract from calculating the profitability of goods exported. It may be that an export price could be lower than that of the home market but nevertheless more profitable. It is important in calculating profitability of export items to study very carefully how overheads are allocated between home market export sales.

Marginal costing and its relevance to export pricing was discussed in chapter 7 when some basic rules concerning when and when not to practise marginal costing were noted. Several useful papers noted in the reference sections deal with international pricing and are included because they give interesting case studies (4) (5) (6) (7), (8) and (9).

PSYCHIC DISTANCE

In considering an extension to markets abroad any business should be conscious of the concept of PSYCHIC DISTANCE which can be defined as those factors which prevent or disturb the flow of information between the firm and its market. Differences in language, culture, political systems, level of education and the stage of development of the country are such factors.

In considering exporting psychic distance is relevant if the problems of "self-reference" are to be avoided. The international environment needs to be recognised since national interests give rise to conditions which influence commercial relations, such basic matters as:

- Import/export control barriers
- Documentary procedures
- Restrictions on Capital Movements
- The existence of international and free trade areas

These matters need study and information on such matters which is now easily available through the DTI, BOTB, Chambers of Commerce and others noted in chapter 13.

- Work by Johanson and Weidersheim-Paul (10) researched the processes of internationalisation using Swedish companies. The study of four successful companies concluded that the development of the firms was through an incremental approach eg by proceeding through
- Exporting via an agent or representative
- Forming a sales subsidiary
- Producing/manufacturing in the country

Each item requires an increasing involvement with the foreign market. It is likely that the marketing success of many German and Japanese firms arises through the same incremental approach to countries where market size and psychic distance have been carefully considered.

Of the many problems that can disturb the flow of information between the firm and its markets, language is the most obvious. Of greater importance is the infinitely more complex cultural factors. It has been suggested that there has been a tendency on the part of multinational marketers to lack sensitivity to cultural factors, in particular US companies may have been guilty since "the American way of life" has been so dominant and widely spread.

Many suggestions in the literature have been put forward for providing a framework for anylising world cultures. The reader is referred to suitable references by writers who have attempted to provide a framework for analysing world cultures. Such classification does not provide a sharp tool for the marketer who, without developing a classification system, may simply observe the empirical differences' in terms of the demographic variables such as:

- Population
- Rate of growth of population
- Urbanisation
- Per capita income (misleading for some countries)
- Literacy

Whilst some of the products may be marketed multinationally in one form, the diversity of world cultures is such that a very close analysis is required for the successful marketing of a company's product(s). Turnbull (11) has stressed that industrial export markets are characterised by extensive personal interaction between a wide variety of functions in both the buying and selling companies.

The need for interpersonal contact will be even greater in the early stages of internationalisation, their primary function will be to reduce psychic distance between the parties to a ralationship by facilitating understanding of difference in culture, and the technical and economic factors in the foreign country.

Trying to build a global minded company requires managers to become polycentric, ie to become aware of traits and behaviour patterns of persons of a nationality other than their own. In preparing for a first time business venture in Japan, for example, the manager would be advised to:

- Read up on Japan's historical culture and social heritage
- Be aware of the significance of the Japanese negotiation process...
- Be aware of their attitude to time . . . and how they treat each other.
- Read up on – current events – parliament's legislation schedule – the economic situation – position of the yen etc. And try to learn a little of the language.

In discussing product promotion within a culture we should note that it is a cardinal rule of marketing that it is always easier to appeal to existing cultural wants, needs and expectations than to try to change the culture or create new needs.

In conjunction with advertising/promotion references under 'further reading' suggested are (12) (13) (14) (15) (16)

SMALL FIRMS

The smaller firm ambitious to export its products, requires both knowledge and motivation. It can obtain help from the many sources now available. Further comment on small firms is given in chapter 12. The small firm can get help from:

- Government sources (DTI, BOTB, SITPRO) on methods of entry to their market, market research, distribution methods, statistics, customs procedures etc.
- Banks, Accounting Firms, Chartered Institute of Marketing, International movement of money, documentary credits, trade bulletins, overseas visits, training, the legislative impact of 1992, harmonisation of standards, legal implications of 1992.

Help is often obtained by collaboration with other firms in similar complementary markets. Germany and Japan foster joint ventures between smaller firms to encourage joint distribution methods as a preliminary to manufacturing in the chosen country. Several articles/ papers of interest to small/medium size firms are given as recommended further readings (17) (18) (19).

PIGGY-BACKING

For some firms anxious to get their offerings to the market abroad the method of piggy-backing can be employed. This method can be of great benefit to new suppliers and also smaller firms as it reduces the time period involved. A larger firm, active in marketing to many countries abroad can often carry and sell products manufactured by others. An interesting article in International Product Policy (20) discusses the role of Colgative-Palmolive in selling its marketing services to other firms. This firm used its marketing muscle to sell products manufactured by others; one of these products was Wilkinson Blades. The latter company had discovered that having the same name on shaving cream did not help them when Colgate marketed the Wilkinson name they found it easy to sell.

In the US Colgate sold several products make by European manufacturers; they used someone else's technology and their own worldwide research. Potential new products from outsiders were evaluated by their New Venture Group, a task force of seasoned executives. Once such products were accepted and successful in the New Products Group, they were taken over by the regular marketing organisation. As of 1976, Colgate management anticipated growth in similar arrangements round the world to augment its own resources in the new product area. Compared to the US market, where it faced the dominance of Proctor and Gamble, Colgate often had a distribution advantage in overseas markets.

ADVERTISING/PROMOTION

Advertising, promotion and personal selling were discussed in chapter 6. In terms of international advertising, promotions, exhibitions, the use of Radio and TV abroad, it is considered outside the scope of this chapter. With the coming of the SEM and with the help of low cost or free help from Government agencies summarised in this chapter, an in-depth study of these topics would occupy another volume. The current momentous and rapid changes taking place in East-Germany, Rumania, Poland, Hungary, Czechoslovakia and elsewhere in many other countries in Europe will need time to settle and stabilise at which time communication, by its many methods, aimed at total comminication across Europe, will need to be reappraised.

The list of suggested readings will help the reader to obtain a picture of some important areas and hopefully, through references, stimulate further interest.

In 1982 the author wrote a paper under the title "The effect of increasing International Competition on Business and Marketing strategies of a British Based Company'. This paper was very critical of the efforts of British Marketing compared with other countries in Europe and ended with some words favouring the Japanese approach to marketing, and the main points are reproduced below. The key points in the Japanese approach may provide some food for thought by British business leaders and form the basis of a long term marketing strategy for UK firms and the UK as a whole.

- Japanese universities train 10 times as many engineers as Britain's
- Japanese industry spends as high a proportion of the country's GNP on Research and Development (R and D) as almost any western nation; and it employs more people in R and D than Britain, France and West Germany put together.
- It is hardly surprising that Japan registers more new patents in the US than Britain, France or West Germany (The extent to which they are all patents of substance may of course be questioned).
- Japan has learned that simply being an imitator of technology is a dangerous commercial strategy because competitors can easily play the same game. So the Japanese improve on the technology they borrow, keeping an ear cocked keenly for what the market is demanding.
- Japanese are thorough at market research but do not follow the results slavishly. The market is king in Japan and companies respond quickly to changing situations – and management structure has evidently the flexibility to do this.
- TOP managment in Japan tends to be more involved in spending time (on the golf course) smoothing relations with banks and bureaucrats. More decisions are made by middle management – ie by the people who have to carry the decisions through.
- One of the most important reasons for success in high technology areas relates to Quality Assurance. The vast range of consumer electronics produced by the Japanese depends on the micro chip, until recently America dominated this technology but Japan is closing fast. The Japanese having mastered the art of quality control can produce the microchip cheaper and since these tiny electronic devices are at the heart of advances in computers, communications, defence, factory automation and consumer products they will also become cheaper and their use extended.

Proper use of Quality Assurance methods such as Quality Circles and Total Quality Management by British firms making advanced equipment is of vital importance in reducing product costs and thus encouraging further investment in those products whose application in other areas will produce a chain reaction in cost reductions. The policy of 'get it right first time" is vital. According to Tom Peters "the price war has ended and the quality war has started" (21).

The lack of understanding and application of Quality Control and Quality Assurance by British manufacturers (eg of record players and the like) has resulted directly in the disappearance of many UK firms. If those firms still involved in manufacturing are to survive in world markets they will only do so if they are in a position to compete strongly in the quality war.

- In Japan, **the group is more valued than the individual,** the consensus more than the original idea, agreement more than the expression of difference.
- Recent Japanese successes in technology is not due to government aid as is sometimes alleged. The British and American Governments spend a lot on technology. Japan does not. **R and D is more likely to lead to commercial success if it is done and paid for by industry.** Projects backed by government tend to be big schemes with small commercial prospects; ones that industry should be sensible to stay clear of.
- The Japanese government is not immune from the bureaucratic tendency to get 'under the feet' of industry. As far as technology is concerned, the most helpful influence of the Japanese government to to encourage a financial and economic climate that favours investment. The Japanese economy manages to simultaineously achieve low interest rates, high savings rates, high debt/equity ratios and high investment rates, and the beneficial effect on Japanese technology is striking. The fact that the average machine tool is half the age of the average machine tool in America must do more for technology than the fact that the Tokyo government spends £10m a year on "post-robotics". It means that as soon as "post robotics" have been developed, factories will buy a lot of them and manufacturers will move rapidly down the learning curve.
- In Japan, links between production, marketing and R and D are close. New scientists and engineers are often sent to spend time selling before going to the laboratory.

As 1992 approaches it is appropriate to take an optimistic view. The UK has better natural resources than its competitors, is not lacking in creative ability, and much help is now forthcoming from Government and other agencies to help the marketing of British firms, in particular those determined to extend their activities by exporting to the SEM

LICENSING, JOINT VENTURES, FOREIGN DIRECT INVESTMENT

The topics of arranging a license agreement or forming a joint venture to acquire technology are the subject of several papers both by academics and members of marketing firms. A paper by Killing (2) advises that buying technology can be a viable corporate strategy. To use it effectively, a firm must have some minimal technical competence. The market is small and fragmented, and the deals which a technology seeking firm uncovers will be largely the result of its own hard work. Firms with technology to sell seldom advertise the fact. When deciding whether or not to enter a particular deal, a manager should have closely estimated the amount of help that will be needed in the new product area, and should also know the different degrees of access the company's employees will get to the supplier of personnel under various types of license agreements and joint ventures. To be successful a manager needs to know his firm's requirements and have the perseverance to locate a supplier who can meet them.

Many firms with technology will not enter joint ventures in which they own less than 50% of the equity. This means that technology buyers may be faced with situations in which their only options are either a closer relationship with the technology supplier than they would like or no deal at all. Firms that seriously wish to pursue a strategy of technology acquisition need also to develop the management skills necessary to handle 50-50 joint ventures.

The risks and rewards of entering into collaborative ventures is the subject of an article in the Financial Times in 1982 (2). Collaborative agreements take one or two forms – a joint venture or a joint activity. In a joint venture partners create a new company which is responsible for the project. With a joint activity there is no new company, at least in the first instance. Instead, parts of the existing companies work on the common project and co-ordinate their activities. The organisational structure remains flexible. In some cases joint "project teams" are formed, in others responsibilities are delegated as and when the need arises. Often when started as a joint activity the venture is transformed into a legal joint venture, just as couples who live together marry after a time.

The number of joint activities between companies is increasing at about twice the rate of joint ventures – and mergers and acquisitions – albeit from a smaller base. More companies will join the rush but they should consider how to avoid some of the pitfalls into which, however apparently obvious, some partners have fallen.

1. One of the most important requirements is for strategic complimentarity between the cooperating firms: they must have a strategic focus which is directly furthered by the cooperative agreement.

2. The degree to which the parcels of technology distributed among the partners are independent. With independence, a temporary setback in one of the partners need not slow down the others. However, if the parcels are interdependent, especially if the sites are geographically dispersed, delays cumulate; just as one company starts to regain momemtum after a set-back one of the others runs into difficulties and slows the project down. Thus 'creeping costs" sneak in and the project

can be uncompetitive when compared with a similar project from a single company. R and D cost may add a 30% penalty by collaboration.

3. The way decisions are made is relevant. Decisions taken by a joint committee convening regularly to monitor progress as in so many joint ventures, can make for slower progress than if the task were performed by one senior executive. Committee members also feel greater allegiance to their own company where their career is based rather to the joint team. This problem is eased when one of the partners takes the dominant role.

4. Management 'style' can also determine success or failure. One partner may be keen to carefully monitor budgets, controls and report performance measures and deadlines.The other partner may be more informal; styles where one partner is woolly and the other more aggressive and more oriented to the bottom line will have troubles – and there is much evidence of this sort of problem reported frequently in the press.

5. A final problem may relate to confidentiality. In the joint activity, personnel from each partner will visit the laboratories and offices of the other. Whilst collaborating on the one project the partners could be competitors in others. Thus there is the risk that commercially valuable information will be transferred.

Useful and practical cases dealing with the topics are refered to in the references given at the end of this chapter in particular refs 22 and 23 especially fall into the following categories.
- Marketers embrace licensing to move products off the shelves
- Licensing demanding all-or-nothing efforts to succeed.

DISTRIBUTION TO FOREIGN MARKETS

Important matters for consideration here will be:
- The size and distribution of each nations market for the firm's product.
- Supply situation in each market
- The degree of urbanisation
- The nation's topography
- Transportation methods
- Storage facilities offered

The country profile on offer from the DTI previously referred to will be relevant in helping to deal with these areas, as will the sections on marketing methods and transport.

CHANNEL OBJECTIVES

Basically, the objective is to achieve some target rate of return on investment. It is difficult for a channel to earn a return on £'s invested because this is more a measure of the firm's marketing effort.

Channel objectives must therefore be developed from corporate and marketing objectives.This then gives a more precise guide for channel operations. The method involves establishing market share goals in each of the firm's target market segments. Market share goals may be stated in terms of:

1. £ or units of sales
2. Profits that each target is expected to produce.

These might be stated thus

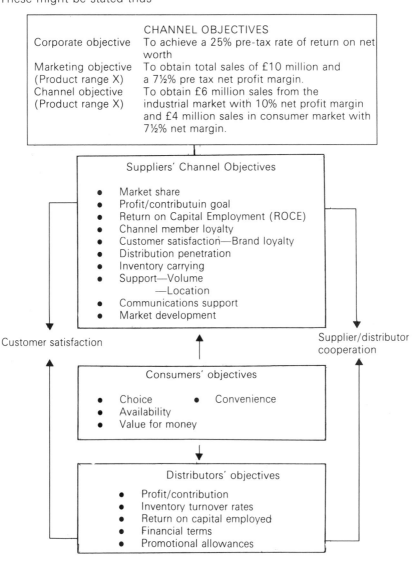

CHANNEL OBJECTIVES

Corporate objective To achieve a 25% pre-tax rate of return on net worth

Marketing objective To obtain total sales of £10 million and
(Product range X) a 7½% pre tax net profit margin.

Channel objective To obtain £6 million sales from the
(Product range X) industrial market with 10% net profit margin and £4 million sales in consumer market with 7½% net margin.

Suppliers' Channel Objectives

- Market share
- Profit/contributuin goal
- Return on Capital Employment (ROCE)
- Channel member loyalty
- Customer satisfaction—Brand loyalty
- Distribution penetration
- Inventory carrying
- Support—Volume
         —Location
- Communications support
- Market development

Customer satisfaction

Supplier/distributor cooperation

Consumers' objectives

- Choice   • Convenience
- Availability
- Value for money

Distributors' objectives

- Profit/contribution
- Inventory turnover rates
- Return on capital employed
- Financial terms
- Promotional allowances

When should channel selection decisions be made?

Questions that require a clear answer can be summerised below:
- Formation of new company or subsidiary following mergers or takeovers.
- New products introduced – channel compatibility with existing lines?
- Changes in marketing strategy, eg the need for greater promotional and service support at the dealer level could result in shift from intensive to selective distribution.
- A shift of market segment.
- Products in a new stage of the 'Product Life Cycle'.
- To meet competitive activities.
- When changes occur in existing channel structures.
- When multi-channels opportunities exist.
- When current channel opportunities are saturated.
- Emergence of cost problems, eg minimum drop size?
- Legal problems.
- Periodic review.

The selection of Channel objectives is not of course restricted to the international marketing aspects but can be considered part of the organisations overall marketing strategy and should be considered in that light.

REFERENCES, CHAPTER 12

1. Walsh LS, International Marketing, Macdonald and Evans, 1981
   2a Terpstra V, International Marketing 1987 4th Ed, Publisher Dryden Press.
   b. Terpstra V, The Cultural Environment of International Business, South Western Publishing Co, 1978.
   c. Barlets R, Are Domestic Markets and International Markets Dissimilar? Journ Marketing, July 1968.
3. Hakansson H, International Marketing and Purchasing of Industrial good: An Interaction Approach, John Wiley 1982.
4. Wind Y,Douglas S, International Market Segmentation, Eur. Journ. Marketing 1972 pp17-25.
5. Farley J, Hubbert J, Weinstein D, Price setting and volume planning by two European Industrial Companies, Jour. Marketing. Vol 44 no 1 Winter 1980 pp 46-54.
6. White J Niffeneffer P, Export pricing – an investigation into current practices of ten companies – in England. Quart. Rev of Marketing Vol 5 No 4 Summer 1980 pp 16-20.
7. Kaikati J G. The Reincarnation of Barter as a Marketing Tool, Journ. Marketing, Apr 1970 Vol 40 P19.

8. Paliwoda S J, East West countertrade arrangements: barter, compensation, buy back, counterpurchase. UMIST Discussion Paper 8105, Mar 1981.
9. Noonan C J, Practical Export Management, 1985. George Allen and Unwin.
10. Johanson J Weidersheim-Paul F, Internationalisation of the Firm, Journ. Management Studies, Oct 1975
11. Turnbull PW, Roles of personal contacts in Industrial Export Marketing, University of Manchester Institute of Science and Technology, Dept of Management Sciences.
12. Financial Times, Survey on International advertising, Dec 1981
13. Buddewyn J J, The Global Spread of advertising regulations MSV Business Topics, Spring 1981
14. Samiee S, Ryans Jr J K Advertising and Comsumerism in Europe, Jour. International Business Studies, spring/summer 1982 pp109-114.
15. Susuki N, changing patterns of Advertising by Japanese firms in the US. Journ. International Business Studies, Fall 1980 pp69-79.
16. Leff N H Farley JV, Advertising Expenditure in the developing world, Jour. International Business Studies, Fall 1981 pp69-79
17. Kirpalani V H, Mackintosh N B. International Marketing Effectiveness of Technology-Oriented Small Firms, Journ. Inter Business Studies 1980 Writer No 11pp 81-90
18. Bluell VP, How to study Foreign markets, Journ. Marketing, July 1968.
19. Journ. of Marketing Research Soc. Vol 24. No2 1982; a special issue on International Market research.
20. Wright R W, Columbian Journ. World Business, Spring 1979
21. Peters T. Managing in Chaos.
22. Killing P, Technology Acquisition: License Agreement or Joint Venture, World Business, Fall 1980, pp34-37.
23. Marketing News, American Marketing Association, 15 Oct 1982.

OTHER RECOMMENDED READINGS

1. Branch A E, Elements of Export Practice 2nd Ed 1985, Chapman and Hall.
2. Branch A E, Elements of Export Marketing and Management, 1983. Chapman and Hall.
3. West A, Marketing Overseas 1987, Pitman M and E Handbook.
4. Hillert E P, The Principles of Export Marketing 1985, Heinemann.
5. Paliwoda S J, International Marketing, 1988, Heinemann.
6. Mitchel P C N, Ingram T R, Export Strategy for the Small Firm, quart. Rev. Marketing, Writer 1978, pp17-26.
7. Buddewyn J J, The Global Spread of Advertising Regulations, M S V Business Topics, Spring 1981.

THE SINGLE EUROPEAN MARKET

The creation of a single market with Europe was inevitable with the formation of the European Community. By the end of 1992 the trade barriers which prevent Europe being a single market will have come down and many changes have already been agreed.

The changes happening could affect a business at any time so all firms need to prepare NOW to meet the challenge and seize the opportunities. During the next few years many businesses could double their present size – or halve it. A summary of the important stages is given below. An appendix to this chapter summerises the literature and help from the government and other agencies to help UK businesses to prepare for and venture into exporting their offerings to the Single European Market.

SINGLE EUROPEAN MARKET (SEM)

A major aim of the European community (EC) is the creation of the SEM by December 1992. This was originally stated as a prime objective of the Treaty of Rome, and was intended to create a single European trading block which would match the USA, USSR etc in terms of output, production and population. A first stage in the process was to be the removal of trade tariffs, here internal tariffs on industrial goods had been largely eliminated by 1977; but numerous obstacles to trade within the community still ramained. The objective of a SEM by 1992 proposed by Jacques Delors, President of the European Commission, were formalised in the Commission's White paper 'Completing the Internal Market' June 1985.

THE BARRIERS TO TRADE

The barriers to trade and benefits from liberalisation were identified by, and quantified by Paolo Cecchini in "The European Challenge 1992 – the benefits of a Single Market" which was published on behalf of the European Commission. The problem was that although internal tariffs had largely been eliminated by 1977 substantial trade obstacles were still in existence. The barriers to trade were identified as:
- Physical barriers – in particular frontier delays and administrative burdens imposed on goods in transit.
- Technical barriers – inter country differences in technical regulations, standards and differences in business law.
- Fixed barriers – in particular differing VAT and exise duties.

The 1985 White Paper also identified the following further barriers:
- Restriction on competition for public sector contracts – which in practice favoured domestic supplies.

● Special arrangements for specific industries, eg the Multifibre Arrangement, adopted by individual countries.

● The agricultural sector – as a consequence of the Common Agricultural Policy.

The White Paper's Liberalization Programme has three main components:

● The removal of physical barriers to the movement of goods and people.

● The removal of technical barriers covering quality, standards, public procurement and regulation.

● The removal of fiscal barriers, eg the harmonisation of VAT rates.

THE CECCHINI REPORT

This report by Paolo Cecchini mentioned earlier, estimated that the liberalization measures would result in economic gains to the SEM of the following order.

TABLE 1	
Static Welfare Gains	70bm-190bm ECU's (2½-6½% of the EC 1988 GDP)
Increased Growth Rate	1% pa
Increased Employment	2 million aditional jobs
Reduced consumer prices (% GDP)	6%
External balance	1%
Budgetary balance (% GDP)	1%

The SEM can therefore be seen to be a source of major benefit to governments, business and consumers.

The DTI has made available information packs to tell businesses what changes are taking place and check-lists that will help any business to prepare to take action now. (1)

There is an abundance of information and statistics available to guide all firms; as an appendix to this chapter many relevant papers and offers of help are listed. In terms of an important and useful set of statistics the Commission of European Communities published in March 1989, "A Community of Twelve: Key Figures" which give in pictorial form many statistics. Data on population, trade between member states, GDP, consumption, (as a % of total household consumption) are given later in this chapter.

BENEFITS OF THE SEM

There are many benefits which will be available to those businesses which are well prepared and in a position to take advantage of them. Some of the main advantage open to business are as follows:

- Dismantling all barriers will open up new opportunities for British business. With the accession of Spain and Portugal to the EC in 1986 there is a domestic market of 323 million people – nearly as many as the United States and Japan combined. Tables 1 and Fig 1 are relevant here.
- Completing a SEM will reduce business costs, stimulate increased efficiency and encourage the creation of wealth and jobs.
- The EC is the United Kingdom's largest export market and its importance is increasing.
- In 1972 the 11 other countries which are now SEM member states took 33% of UK exports; ten years later this figure was 44% and is now 50%. In all, UK exports of goods to the community totalled £41 billion in 1988.

Other member states now account for 52% of UK imports compared with 36% in 1972. However, there is still room for considerable growth in every EC market.

- The single European Act (SEA) commits the EC to the aim of progressivley establishing a single market over a period expiring on 31 December 1992. The single market is defined as "an area without internal frontiers in which the free movement of goods, persons, services and capital is insured in accordance with the provision of the Treaty".
- The SEA also incorporates a series of important Treaty reforms to speed up the decision-making by extending majority voting to virtually all the major areas of the Single Market Programme. In the past, progress was often held up in the unanimous voting requirements which applied before the SEA came into force.

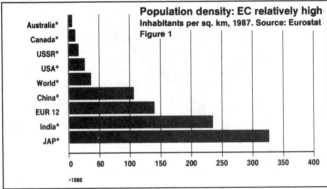

Fig 1 shows the relatively high population density of the SEM alongside that of other countries in the world.

Table 2 shows the populations of the countries in the SEM including the UK which illustrates the increased size of the new market.

Table 2 (source: Readers Digest Associations, Atlas of the World, 1987) Population of EC Countries	
Country:	Population (Millions) 1987
Denmark	9.8
W Germany	61.2
France	55.6
Greece	9.9
Eire (S Ireland)	3.5
Italy	57.3
Luxembourg	0.4
Netherlands	14.7
Portugal	10.3
Spain	38.8
UK	56.9
	318.4

Gross domestic product: a relatively rich Community . . .

GDP per head* (world = 100, 1986)

Figure 2. Source: Eurostat

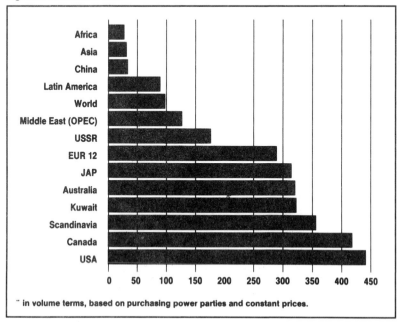

** in volume terms, based on purchasing power parties and constant prices.

Fig 2 compares Gross domestic products which show the the EC to be a relatively rich country.

Finally Figure 3 shows a comparison of distribution of expenditure as a % of total household consumption on accommodation, leisure/miscellaneous, food, transport and clothing items for 1986. It would appear that the Japanese are good eaters!

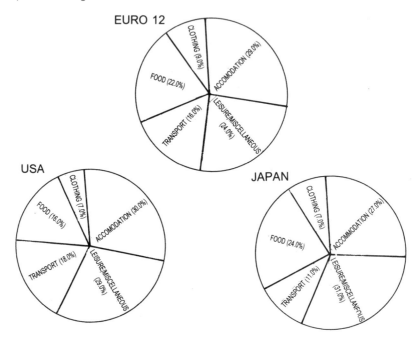

Any firm considering venturing into the SEM, or any other potential overseas market may find the following checklist helpful in formulating its marketing strategy in order to ensure that it maximises its potential for success. This checklist is not exhaustive and may need to be ammended to meet the needs of any particular organisation; it should however, provide a useful basis on which to proceed.

ACTION STRATEGY

Key questions would be:
- Has the market changed our offering(s)?
- Should the firm look upon the EC as its prime market rather than just the UK?
- How will the firm become vulnerable to more competition in present markets?
- Is the firm's management structure appropriate to exploit new opportunities or defend its position?
- Should the firm form links, merge or acquire a business to broaden its range of products to strengthen the enterprise? (further discussed later in the Chapter).

- What training in language skills are needed now to be ready for the Single Market?

In terms of marketing it becomes necessary to work at an appropriate checklist such as:

- Identify those countries the firm is not selling to, where sales are limited and why.
- Which markets become more accessible and when?
- What new customers can we reach? And how?
- Where are the firm's competitors and what is known about their marketing strengths, weaknesses, products and prices?
- How do competitors sell and what is the structure of distribution in the market? (refer back to the DTI "country profiles" for help in this area).
- Market information. Has the firm proper information and statistics? Where can the firm find this? Get it immediately (ref2 will help initially).
- Has the firm:
  - made or plan to make exploratory visits?
  - attended trade shows/exhibitions?
  - Has the business commissioned any market research or visited the statistics office? Has it got information on Government help to obtain low cost market research or contracted the European Chamber of Commerce on this topic?

How suitable are the firm's products/services?

- Obtain basic data by contacting the BSI to ask if there is an industrial standard for the firm's product, set by national authoritites or by a leading supplier.
- Check whether and how the offering would need adapting to the needs of industrial or commercial users.
- Does the quality of the offering match the needs of the market?
- Is product packaging suitable? Can the firm compete on product quality and price?
- Has the firm detail on new competition to its existing markets and has it:
- Identified potential competitors, assesed their competitive strengths in terms of price and quality.
- What are the firm's existing customers buying plans?

Is the business organised to learn about the wider market and carry out promotion effectively?

- Who will be responsible for marketing to the SEM?
- Who will collect and assess marketing information?
- Is the firm getting help and advice from the DTI's Marketing and Export Initiatives?

In the sales and distribution areas checklists would set down and answer the following questions:

How do you reach customers?
- Has the firm investigated the trade structure, such as wholesalers and retailers? Identified buying points?
- Examined different selling approaches, including brokers and agents?
- How do competitors use advertising, promotion and trade discounts?
- Has the firm considered regional test marketing? Established its sales targets? Decided on a sales and promotion budget?
- Decided on its selling organisation?
- What sales literature is needed? And has it considered the need for redesign for new customers and arranged translations where necessary.
- Has the marketing function decided how to advertise? And
- Assessed differences in national media available and cost? Decided on its budget?
- How will the firm provide an after-sales service?
- Considered relative merits and costs of direct provision or subcontracting (See chapter 11).

In preparing a distribution checklist a firm will note the importance of getting to the customer on time. More customers and destinations pose distribution challenges (once again the DTI country profiles will help here). New transport routes and new services will require study.
- What changes are needed in the firm's distribution needs?
- Has the firm identified new locations to be served and estimated the increased volume of products? And
- Found out about the structure of distribution in new markets, and considered speed of delivery and size of loads?
- What distribution arrangements will best achieve the customer service the firm is seeking? And
- Decided between direct delivery and the need for warehousing as well as
- Decided on warehouse locations, defined adequate stock levels and how to maintain them.

What organisation does the firm need to support its distribution?
- Has the firm decided on information handling requirements and how to control remote locations.

For enterprise supplies services it is necessary to decide
- How it will reach new customers
- How will you need to provide service direct from UK or need a presence in local markets?

● Has it considered the relative advantages and costs of:
  – establishing a subsidiary or branch?
  – linking with local firms?
  – using an agent or broker?

Checklists for the areas of production, finance, purchasing and product of development are suggested by the DTI in its Action Checklist for Business, published Sept 1988 by the DTI Central Offices of Information (I) Further practical help is available through the DTI's Enterprise Initiative previously discussed. Useful telephone numbers are given below: Statistics and Market Inteligence library and product Data Store (SMIL). This publicly accessible library of overseas market Intelligence can be contacted on 071 215 5444.

The Exports Europe branch covers all 12 communities and can be contacted by telephone on 071-215 5549 (Multi-country enquiries).

Export Intelligence service details can be obtained from the local DTI office.

Centres for European Business Information can be contacted in London, Dept of Employment, Small Firms Service, tel 071-730 8115 or Birmingham Chamber of Industry and Commerce, tel 021-454 6171 and also at Newcastle, Northern Development, tel 091-261 5131 and also at Glasgow, Strathclyde Euroinfocentre, tel 041-221 0999.

Contents of progress on EC legislation can be obtained on DTI's Hotline 081-200 1992.

THE EXPORTING COMPANY AND THE SEM

In his text 'Export for the Small Business' (3) Deschampsneufs in his Chapter 1 comments that "There probably never has been a better time to become involved with export, for two main reasons. First there is a noticable change taking place in international trade. For many years we have lived in a world of mass production . . . the aim of the producers has been to provide the greatest quantity of goods at the lowest possible price for the greatest number of consumers. Growth has been the aim of almost all companies, on the basis that the larger the company, the more efficient it becomes, and the greater its profits. As a result the consumer is offered increasingly standard products . . . yet today there are signs of revolt by consumers against standard products . . .

Secondly there is corresponding increase in the demand for a greater variety of life styles . . . we can see the growth of the 'Do it yourself market' for instance . . . people make their own wine, bake their own bread and service their own cars.

The significance of this development is that more and more specialised products are being demanded. This is where the small business has its

greater strength . . . it is they who are in the best position to supply specialised products and personalised services". The SEM to start in 1992 will present many opportunities for British companies since it will be dealing with a greater population with diverse patterns of behaviour.

In terms of the legislative impace of 1992 on small businesses, and the Small Business Research Trust 1992 Survey, the National Westminster Bank has published a Small Business Digest 1992 special edition available freely through any high street branch.

This very useful, easy to read, 20 page booklet deals with: The legislative impact of 1992 on small businesses.
1. The importance of small business on the European stage.
2. The institutions of the European Community.
3. Community legislation.
4. Treaty of Rome.

Protectionism and the free movement of goods and services.
1. Discriminatory Taxation.
2. Custom duties and equivalent charges.
3. Public procurement contracts.
4. Consumer protection.
5. Harmonisation of standards.
6. Financial services.
7. Indirect taxation – VAT and excise duties.
8. State aid

The legal implications of 1992 for small business
1. EC competition rules.

GET STARTED NOW

Before further discussing the smaller firm, a further guide offering help to smaller businesses in terms of government grants and final comments by Mrs. Thatcher and Mr. Major it is considered appropriate to quote some recent remarks by Lord Young.

In the DTI's Single Market Publication of October 1988 the main article, Now For Action, quotes Lord Young who makes relevant remarks to reinforce this chapter. In terms of awareness of the SEM there has been progess since the DTI formally launched the 'Open For Business Campaign'. However, at this time too few firms had begun to prepare seriously enough for action. Lord Young outlines how the DTI and associated agencies can help firms to prepare to get started NOW.

His final comments: "No one has any excuse for missing out. The SEM is your opportunity, go out and seize it."

The front page article *Now For Action* quotes Lord Young who makes the following points: "1992 is certainly on everyone's lips now; indeed you can hardly open a newspaper or switch on television without seeing something about the magic date. Many firms are featuring 1992 in their own advertising.

"Just 12 months ago very few people in business in this country – even senior people in large companies – knew much about the Single Market – Under one in six know of the 1992 target date for completing the Single Market – a staggering figure for a country which does half of all its trade with the European community.

"When we formally launched the Open For Business Campaign – I set a target of 90 per cent awareness of the Single Market by the end of this year.

"The battle for awareness has already been won but awareness is only the first step.

"– The all too easy '1992' label brings its own problems especially if it encourages firms to believe that they still have three of four years to prepare. 1992 is no magic date when everything will happen. 31 December 1992 is the date when a long and complex legislative process will be completed.

"The changes – for the Single Market are already happening. Decisions are being taken month by month.

"I want the British Business to be the best prepared in the Community. That means two big challenges.

- Awareness counts for little unless business really gets to grips with the implications of the fundamental changes taking place in the Community's trading rules. There is no substitute for doing your homework. The DTI has prepared the most comprehensive service anywhere in the Community. Use it.
- What matters at the end of the day, is not awareness or even understanding, but action by every firm in the country.

Our survey showed that fewer than one firm in three has begun to prepare seriously for action. That represents a substantial increase since I announced our campaign. But that is a long way short of being satisfactory. I want to see the figure grow rapidly during the next 12 months. Everyone will need to consider an action strategy and take decisions to respond to the Single Market Challenge.

DTI's Action Checklists outline the issues and gives sources of further information and advice.

DTI's Enterprise Initiative provides one of the key ways of preparing for the Single Market. Launched at the start of the year, it is already helping many businesses help themselves to achieve a more competitive edge. No one now has any excuse for missing out. The Single Market is our opportunity. Go out and seize it."

In the same publication appears a list of Single Market events, that is, details of conferences and seminars being organised in every part of the country by Chambers of Commerce, trade associations and other organisations. Further information can be obtained by telephoning 071-215 4770.

SMALLER FIRMS

Further, in the above publication is a useful article discussing small firms and the Single Market with sections covering the topics:

- Preparing now
- Opportunities
- Competition
- How to find out more

In the context of urging the smaller firm to join in the EEC by offering its service/product much has been written aimed at giving motivation and guidance; several references have already been given. The CBI has urged export aid (4) for the smaller businesses who could increase exports, and make a vital contribution to reducing Britain's trade deficit. It is suggested that more needs to be done to meet their requirement, particularly by the British Overseas Trade Board. This emerges from a CBI survey of nearly 200 smaller businesses. The need for action was underlined by the chairman of the CBI's smaller firms council when he announced the survey results. A particular problem area appeared to be in securing access to good market intelligence, and establishing sales and distribution returns, a special problem area reported for firms offering professional services was a lack of market information. This was a significant finding, the survey revealed, when plans to have mutual recognition of professional qualificiations in the single European Market are taken into consideration. The survey found there was 'much potential' for small firms to increase their European share. The most scope for increasing export activity lay with middle-sized businesses of from 21 to 50 employees.

The subject of government grants and other financial and trade industry has been covered in chapter 14, however a recent guide adds some further comments. The guide, *1992 Guide for the Smaller Businesses* from Price Waterhouse, the chartered accountants (5) reports that "The sad truth is that there are, indeed hundreds of millions of pounds' worth of grants, low-interest loans and other funds, but very little in the hands of business entrepreneurs and smaller firms. **Most of the money is with the Government's Enterprise Initiative Scheme, and a great deal of it is not being claimed."**

Price Waterhouse's independent services director comments that: "Business cannot afford to be complacent about the Single European Market. This is true not only for multi nationals, but also the smaller independent businesses and adds: **"Those who believe 1992 will have little or no impact on them are in for a rude awakening".**

Small businesses are advised to contact the trade department's hotline and the EC's British centres for more information. Most of the services are free.

The above guide also suggests that there is a direct link between export performance and someone in a company being able to speak in a customer's language. The skills are taught at Language-Export Centres. Further valuable help is available from the DTI's "1992 – for you". An action guide for the smaller business (6) which deals not only with markets, products/services, how the Single Market affects the smaller firm and finance but lists useful sources of further help for the smaller firm through local advice "clubs", trade associations, public sector contracts, finding business partners, documentation and payment as well as other booklets about 1992.

The Rt. Hon. Margaret Thatcher speaking in Madrid in September 1988, at a meeting organised by the Spanish prime minister, announced that Britain would be participating in Expo 92 in Seville with a stand of substantial size to show "Britain's resurgence and leadership in many areas of technology and services".

EXPORT BOOST ESSENTIAL

At the time of writing comes yet another appeal by John Major, the Chancellor, for British companies to export more and boost import substitution (7). Mr Major adds in his comments "Now is the time to go out and look for business elsewhere, to maintain profits, output and jobs. It is not the time for passive gloom. **It is the time for active marketing".**

British business leaders are being urged to start now since 1992 is not far off.

Voluminous information is now being offered by many agencies and Appendix 1 to this chapter gives a summary of help being offered by the:
    British Overseas Trade Board BOTB
    Department of Enterprise DTI
    Council of Chambers of Commerce in Central Europe CBCC
    The Confederastion of British Industry
    Major banks
    Accounting firms

The appendix will hopefully help business readers to pick our those areas which will be of maximum use to them and prevent their obtaining and reading through a vast amount of literature to locate a particular topic vital to their firm.

REFERENCES

1. An Action Checklist for Business, DTI and Central Office of Information, HMSO, Sept 1988.
2. A Community of Twelve: Key Figure. Commission of European Communities, March 1989, available from:
    8 Storeys Gate, London SW13 3AT. Tel 071-222 8122

4 Cathedral Row, Cardiff CF1 9SG. Tel Cardiff 371 631

7 Alva Street, Edinburgh EH2 4PH. Tel Edinburgh 225 2058

3. Deschampsneufs, H Export for the Small Business, 2nd Ed, Kogon Page
4. CBI, Centrepoint, 103 New Oxford Street, London WC1A 1DV
5. Price Waterhouse, 1992 Guide for Small Business, The Times, Nov 24, 1989. Further details Enterprise Agencies and European Information Centres (dial operator for Freefone Enterprise) BOTB 071 215 7577, DTI 1992 hotline 081 200 1992.
6. Sunday Times, 23 April, 1989, Gettin All the Facts for 1992.
7. The Times, 6 Dec, 1989, Export Boost Essential for Growth.

FURTHER SUGGESTED READINGS AND SOURCE OF INFORMATION

1. Fortune International, 28 Aug, 1989, Main J. How to go Global – and Why.
2. Fortune International, Special issue No 26, Autumn 1989.
    (a) The Challenge of Asia in the 1990s
    (b) Understanding how Japan Works
    (c) Doing Business in China Now
    (d) The Tiger Behind Korea's Prowess
    (e) Asia's Rising Export Powers
3. Fortune No 24 November 6 1989
    (a) America's Place in World Competition
    (b) Japan's Big Knack for Coming Back
    (c) Fortune Forecast on US Economy
4. Fortune Special Issue 29, Autumn 1989
    (a) The Smart Way to go Global
    (b) Promising Industries for 1990
5. Fortune No 20 Sept 25 1989
    (a) Where will Japan strike next?
    (b) How Harley beat back the Japanese. A successful turnaround for a firm where quality was awful, manufacturing a mess. The managers bought the company and pulled off a celebrated turnaround.
6. Fortune No 18, 28 Aug 1989
    (a) Dudley J. N., Strategies for the Single Market
    (b) Who runs Japan?
7. Fortune No 28, 18 Dec 1989, Kirkland Jn R1, Who gains for the New Europe? The author's answer to the question is "Almost everyone does _ and there's opportunity aplenty for deals. The combined GNP for East Germany, Hungary and Czechslovakia is bigger then China's"
8. 'Which' February 1990 _ The first of a new series on 1992, explaining to the general public and business what the SEM will mean to them.
9. In terms of the legislative impact etc, etc.

QUESTIONS

1. What are the problems that a small company may face in attempting to break into exporting? How may these be overcome?
2. Licensing is often described as a second best alternative. Why should this be? Outline its shortcomings and whether these may be minimised.
3. ". . . there are differences in the cultural environment between one country and another which are hard to identify and constantly in a state of change. Nevertheless the skilled international manager understands and respects them." Discuss.
4. "UK manufacturers will face difficulties in penetrating Western markets unless there are rapid improvements in their linguistic skills". Discuss this viewpoint.
5. There is no basic difference between international marketing and domestic marketing. Discuss this statement.
6. Secondary data in many overseas markets suffer from shortcomings. What are these shortcomings and what precautions need to be taken to make the data of maximum use?
7. How does a small company export without the need to go outside its own country? What are the advantages available for small firms?
8. Discuss the help currently available to British exporters who wish to minimise costs.

APPENDIX

INTRODUCTION

The purpose of this appendix is to identify the various sources of assistance available to exporters, and to summarise the contents of the literature available from a wide variety of sources. Hopefully this will save many hours of research by those wishing to devise a strategy which will enable their organisations to engage successfully in international trade either with the EC or the rest of the world.

1. **BOTB** "Help for Exporters _ Now's the time to Export" Sept 1987 gives a summary of all the services provided by the BOTB with appropriate addresses and telephone numbers. The booklet deals with:

The statistics and market intelligence library which provides access to a wide and thorough collection of foreign statistics, trade directories, development plans and other published information on overseas markets. The library is open to personal users Monday to Friday from 9.30 to 17.30. Further information and short enquiries by telephone can be dealt with at:

    The Statistics and Market Intelligence Library
    1 Victoria Street
    London SW1H 0ET
    Tel: 071-215 5444/5

The Product Data Store at the same address provides a central "bank" of product and industry based information about markets nationwide. A leaflet 'Product Data Store' is available on request.

Market Advice is available to firms/individuals who do not know enough hard facts about their overseas market. A scheme is available to provide accurate market facts before decisions can be taken about making a sales effort. **The Export Marketing Research scheme:**
- offers free professional advice on how to set about Market Research to the best advantage.
- having decided on a market research project a grant of up to 50% towards the cost – up to a maximum of £20,000 can be made.

The booklet "Help for Exporters"– Export Marketing Research Scheme is available to provide further details to keep up to date and the whole range of international opportunities through the BOTB monitoring service, the publication "Help for Exporters"– World Aid Section will be sent on request.

Getting into the market – information to aid potential exporters who need to find a representative abroad can be obtained from the booklet "Export Representative Service."

To explore working with a possible trading partner abroad, the booklet "Overseas Status Report Service" should be asked for.

Appointing an agent or distributor abroad can be successful and profitable as the literature indicates; it could also be perilous. This service can provide an impartial report on the agent or distributor's capability and commercial standing and venturing into the market can be further helped by asking for information given in the publication "Export Intelligence Service" which deals with:
- Type of Export Information Handled
- Speed of Service
- How items are categorised
- Matching your interests to our categories
- Different combinations for different needs

and
- Subscription rates

Outward Missions. Whilst many missions overseas are run by Chambers of Commerce or Trade Associations the BOTB can help to include a firm to join a mission and explore at first hand the prospects for its products. The new exporter will benefit from contact with more experienced members of the mission. Firms can learn about the practical advantages in joining a BOTB supported trade misssion by reading the leaflet available and titled "Outward Missions – help for Exporters" from the nearest BOTB regional office and gives details of new missions arranged. The leaflet covers:
- How missions are organised
- Countries included/excluded
- Rates of grant
- Conditions for participants

Those firms who may be put off by the complications and expense of exhibiting abroad can obtain help and advice from the BOTB whose leaflet "Trade Fairs Overseas" which details:
- How BOTB support works
- What is provided and the cost
- Travel grants
- British Pavillions
- All-British Exhibitions
- Conditions for participants

The BOTB also supports specialised seminars abroad and gives generous help with cost as explained in its leaflet "Overseas Seminars – Help for Exporters".

Further publications available for exporters include aid for getting into the market, are available in: "Store Promotions – help for exporters" and gives

advice on:
- Where to find out about promotions
- How to offer your products
- Timing and buying seasons
- Main locations
- The role of the BOTB

Participating in a well organised promotions event can often help the ambitious firm to enter a new market, or expand its business if it's there already.

Firms often wish to influence visitors (opinion leaders?) from abroad to show what they can supply. The BOTB can help bring the right people to Britain and put a firm on their itinerary. The leaflet "Inward Missions – help for Exporters" is available by contacting the regional BOTB office.

Specialist advice and help from the BOTB is available through specialist staff who handle them full time and can supply information on:

- Import duties
- Local taxes
- Import licensing regulations
- Import restrictions
- Temporary importation
- Foreign investment/ manufacturing under licence
- Agency legislation
- Custom procedures

- Documentation
- Samples
- Free zones
- Price Control
- Marketing/labelling of goods regulations
- Transport regulations
- Weights and measures
- Regulations covering dangerous goods
  - drugs/medicines
  - foodstuffs
  - livestock
  - spirits, wines, beers

The client firm should then contact the nearest BOTB Market Branch to handle its enquiry. If that branch cannot answer the query it will put the enquirer in touch with the specialist who can.

Under the heading 'Specialist Advice and held' other BOTB publications are suggested. They are:

"Technical Help for Exporters" which covers:
- Enquiry service
- Research and consultancy
- Up-dating services
- Technical translations
- Publications

and
- Fees

An important leaflet "SITPRO" Simplification of International Trade Procedures — help for Exporters lists:
- Service available
- Documentation systems
- Computers in international trade
- Savings on procedures
- Training materials
- Free management checklist and other publications

SITPRO helps to create an effective cost-effective international trading environment and was established in 1970 as an independent agency supported by the DTI. SITPRO, the Simple Trade Procedures Board, has a prime objective — to make Britih companies more competitive in world trade. It is achieved by attacking red tape, developing the skills of the people involved and encouraging the use of information technology in the trading, distribution and payment process.

This means
- seeking the abolition of bureaucratic procedures
- simplifying the processes and attendant paperwork
- developing Electronic Data Interchange (EDI) standards and the replacement of documents by EDI message sets
- raising awareness of how EDI can be of benefit to companies
- advising on training and providing guidance

The new address from 5.8.89 is:
SITPRO
Venture House
29 Glashouse Street
LONDON W1R 5RG
Tel: 071-287 3525
Fax: 071-289 5751

Further information on SITPRO's activities, products or services can be obtained by contacting this address.

The BOTB can assist in large scale operations through a special division that brings together all the various government support measures. These projects will normally offer a UK element in excess of £20m.

The Projects and Export Policy Division (PEP) of the BOTB provides a single focus for coordinating the full range of Government services available to support companies pursuing major international projects. PEP is divided into three branches all located at 1 Victoria Street, London SW1H 0ET (Tel: Ext 8811074) and telephone enquiries are as follows:

Branch 1
Airports and equipment, canals, bridges, tunnels, roads 071-215 4914
Railways, trucks, shipyards, ports, transport system 071-215 4863

Branch 2
Hydroelectric and renewable/alternative energy products, cement plant 071-215 4906
Chemical, petrochemical and other process plant 071-214 4904
Mining, all power products in India, defence 071-215 4910

Branch 3
Telecommunications, postal services, electronics, educational equipment projects 071-215 4855
Agricultural projects, fisheries, forestry, construction projects, water and sewerage 071-215 4848
Oil and gas (exploration, production, refining, distribution, pipelines) industrial projects not covered elsewhere 071-215 4843

Thermal generation and electrical distribution projects are the responsibility of the DTI's ship building and electrical engineering division: Tel: 071-215 4843

The British Overseas Trade Board was set up in January 1972 to help British exporters. Its members come mainly from industry and commerce and are experienced in exporting. Government department are also represented. The President is the Secretary of State for Trade and Industry. The Board's responsibilities are:
1. To advise the Government on strategy for overseas trade
2. To direct and develop the Government export promotion service on behalf of the Secretary of State for Trade and Industry
3. To encourage and support industry and commerce in overseas trade with the aid of the appropriate governmental and non-governmental organisations at home and overseas
4. To contribute to the exchange of views between Government and industry/commerce in the field of overseas trade and to search for solutions to problems.

The above background summary is taken from the leaflet "Help for Exporters – a summary of all services by the British Overseas Trade Board for UK Exporters." This leaflet and the BOTB annual report can be obtained by contacting the BOTB Regional Office or writing to:
>   BOTB Marketing and Briefing Unit
>   Room 228
>   1 Victoria Street
>   London SW1H 0ET
>   Tel: 071-215 5222

The BOTB offers further help on overseas publicity problems. A copy of its "Publicity for Exporters" can be obtained from a regional office or writing to:
>   BOTB Marketing and Briefing Unit
>   address as above

Some other publications available are listed in the above booklet as well as brief descriptions of other organisations complementary to those of the BOTB. The local BOTB office will advise which will best help particular problem areas. They include:

a) Export Credits Guarantee Department
b) The Defence Export Services Organisation
c) Chambers of Commerce. A firm may contact the Association of British Chambers of Commerce (ABCC) at Sovereign House, 212A Shaftesbury Avenue, London WC2H 8EW. Tel: 071-240 5831/6
d) The Banks
e) Trade Associations
f) Export Houses
g) The Export Buying Offices Association
h) Freight Forwarders
i) Air Couriers

j) **The International Chamber of Commerce** publishes a range of booklets on payments and documentation including Documentary Credits, Incomers, Commercial Agency Agreements, Exchange Rate Risks, Rules for Collections. This organisation can be contacted at

> ICC United Kingdom
> Centre Point
> 103 New Oxford Street
> London WC1A 1QB
> Tel: 071-240 5558

2. **DTI**

The voluminous literature published should be noted:
The Single Market – The Facts, 3rd Edition, an 87 page leaflet whose contents include:

- The Single Market Programme
- Freedom of establishment for the professions
- EC deregulation – avoiding red tape
- Influencing decisions
- Standards testing and certification
- Food law
- Pharmaceuticals
- Public Purchasing
- Information Technology
- Financial services
- Insurance/capital movements
- Company Law
- Competition Policy
- State subsidies
- EC/EFTA trade ralations
- Environment policy

- Collaborative R and D
- Selling in the single market
- Advice for small and medium sized businesses
- Transport

The Single Market – an action checklist for businesses, 3rd Edition is a 23 page brochure dealing with:
- Marketing
- Sales
- Distribution
- Production Development
- Finance
- Training, Languages and recruitment
- Information technology
- Where can you go for help?
- Purchasing.

Export marketing Research Scheme, guidline notes, comment on the export marketing research scheme (EMRS) which is administered by the Association of British Chambers of Commerce on behalf of the Department of Trade and Industry. The scheme is designed to help marketing research as an integral part of export strategy by facilitating the systematic collection, collating, evaluating and presentation of information on which marketing decisions can be based. Conditions of eligibility are given. The scheme can offer free professional advice on how to set about export marketing research and aspiring exporters can telephone market research advisers for help and explanation of what is on offer.

The scheme offers financial help for those who undertake a project in one of four forms.
a) Through a member of the firm who is qualified and experienced in research. The project is conducted 'in-house' when half of essential travel costs, interpreter's fee and a daily allowance towards hotel and meal costs for one researcher during overseas field work is available. This support does not extend to research relating to European countries.
b) Those commissioning professional consultants to undertake research overseas; half the cost will be paid.
c) Those purchasing published market research will have up to a third of the cost paid.
d) For trade associations commissioning research, or carry it out 'in-house' on behalf of members, up to three quarters if the cost will be paid.

Notes on the scheme together with application forms are provided. Export Briefing, BOTB, Help for Exporters, DIT - North West April 89.

This 31 page brochure deals with:
- Money for market research
- The DTI Service Card

- Export Representative Service
- Overseas status report service
- New products from British service
- Trade Fairs
- Seminars. Workshops – What's happening in the North West
- Outward Mission
- Country new/grants
- A list of 1992 single market events
- A list of contracts in the North West

The Export Initiative, a guide to exporting BOTB, January 1989 edition is a useful 30 page brochure in 5 sections titles:
1. Ready to Export?
2. Exporters' Checklist
3. Doing the Groundwork
4. Contacting the Market
5. Doing Business

Introducing the Enterprise Initiative, Revised Edition September 89. The 36 page brochure notes on:
The Enterprise Initiative
The Single European Market
Business and the Environment
The Consultancy Initiative
The Marketing Initiative
The Business Planning Information
The Financial Information Initiative
The Quality, Design and Manufacturing systems Initiatives
The Regional and Export Initiatives
The Research/Technology. Enterprise and Education Initiatives
Support Services
Other services for small firms and Regional Contracts

The useful information pack, Vital Statistics, can be obtained from the Business and Statistics Office in Newport, Gwent (1) and contains: Details of the location and services available from the Statistics and Market Intelligence library (SMIL). The DTI's headquarters in London is provided for public use. The library has collections of statistics – foreign and UK directories and development plans. Exporters can use the information for desk research on overseas markets. A visit here is recommended since it will save time and money on research abroad.

SMIL keeps a collection of published economic statistics from overseas countries on topics such as trade, production, price, employment and transport. Available also are trade figures – statistics of imports/exports from every country worldwide. Trade statistics are a vital step in market analysis – a comparison between a country's production and export figures against those for its imports gives an indication of the market.

SMIL holds those UK statistical publications relevant to exporters covering such areas as trade, industrial production statistics and general economic indicators. Market research is aided by the availability of commercially produced surveys to supplement official statistics. Published market research provides a valuable time-saving help. Readers should check the indexes to find out if the information available on their special service is listed.

Directories of many links are available with specialist directories covering particular sectors of industry. It is possible to obtain details of potential customers or competitors operating in a specific commodity area or country. UK trade directories are not available.

Development plans are published by many countries and provide an indication of the current state of an economy and future projections. Newly published plans are advertised through the DTI's Export Intelligence Service and also in the magazine 'British Business'. Most of the plans are available for loan to exporters.

The library subscribes to several indexing services which can be used to identify further sources of information. The library has a reading room and with plenty of literature available for individuals for use in pursuing their own 'desk' research. The library has booklets and has available the 'National Statistical Offices of the World'.

DTI offers a wide range of services to exporters from a network of Regional Offices. Exporters should visit the Product Data Store in 1-19 Victoria Street, London SW1H 0ET.

Enquiries on the Business Monitor Series and other UK statistics can be obtained by contacting the Business Statistics Office Library, Cardiff Road, Newport, Gwent NP9 1XG. Tel: 0633 222973. Telex 497122.

The useful DTI pack 'Vital Statistics' also includes booklets on:
- Business monitors, designed for businesses and providing statistics on manufacturing, energy, mining, service and distributive industries – compiled by the government's statistics office (BSO).
- Government Statistics – a brief guide is 'Sources of information 1988 Edition.'
- A business Monitor Form which when completed can be returned to the Business Statistics Office.

The very useful newspaper, Single Market, is published periodically eg Spring 1989, Summer 1989, Autumn 1989 and will be sent by the DTI if readers contact the Regional Office.

Further valuable information in the booklets 'Hints to Exporters' can be obtained by contacting the DTI Regional Office in the reader's area. Examples of these are:
Hints to Exporters. The Federal Republic of Germany and West Berlin.

DTI 1988/89.
Other booklets in the same series cover: France, Netherlands, Atilles and Aruba.

Other detailed and valuable publications/country profiles are avaialable from DTI/BOTB such as:
Country Profile – France (66 pages)
Market Consumer Goods – France (75 pages)

With such a volume of literature and help available, the exporter/importer in the UK is well placed to attack the single market.

Lastly, readers are advised to obtain from the DTI under its Enterprise Initiative Literature, details of the range of consultancy help available. The consultancy initiatives aim to increase a firm's competitiveness by helping through providing advice in certain key management functions. They help to prepare for the increased competition that will arise from the completion of the single European market by the end of 1992. The DTI booklet detailing these schemes is titled. Application and Guidance notes for consultancy, dealing with marketing, design, quality, manufacturing systems, business planning and financial information systems. The Regional DTI Office will supply or they can be telephoned at the DTI's Single Market Campaign on the 1992 hotline 081-200 1992

There is no shortage of up-to-date references and literature issuing at a great pace from the BOTB, DTI Banks and accounting firms. At the risk of giving the reader "indigestion", some very recent articles on the subject of Internationalisation or 'going global' would include some recent articles from Fortune magazine: each providing food for thought to those firms wishing to spread their wings abroad. Worth reading are:

How to go Global – and why. Fortune, 28 Aug 1989 (8)

This article attempts to answer the questions why and how to go Global. In summary; Why? To survive. How? by looking at the whole world as one market. The firm is advised to buy, borrow, hire and manufacture wherever they can do it best. And get local allies. This article further discusses a company without borders: ICI's major operations which readers would find educational.

A very recent publication will be of particular interest to all companies ambitions to market their services in the single market. The book 1992 – strategies for the Single Market by James W Dudley (11) deals with:
- Strategic management for the Single Market
- Inward opportunities and collaborative arrangement
- Market research
- Product and pricing strategies
- New product development strategies
- International advertising and media policies

- Physical distribution and customer service
- Threats and opportunities for domestic firms
- Competition from Japan, America, the Pacific Basin, Europe
- Threat of parallel trade
- Foreign exchange
- Plans, timetables and budgets

MAJOR BANKS

Useful and informative information for individuals and firms wishing to export is available from major banks. Examples of brochures/leaflets available from National Westminster, Midland, Trustees and Barclays banks, for example is noted below.

The National Westminster pamphlet (1) introduces its services for the exporter and importer by advising . . . "International trade today is taking place in an increasingly competitive and complex environment. If you are to achieve success in your international trade activities you will want the best advice available." Their brochure lists selected publications and provides a list of publications available which can be obtained by completing a form indicating the brochures required; these are:

Guide for exporting and importing
International movement of money
Documentary credits
Foreign Bonds and Guarantees
Export Insurance and Finance
International Trade Bulletins (published monthly)
Foreign exchange for importer and exporters.
Foreign currency accounts explained

The following information and services are offered:

Economic Reports
International Trade Bulletins
Economic and Financial outlook
Overseas visits
Trade Opportunities
together with several other publications

Services include:

- Documentary credits
- Advance payment/open account
- Bills for collection
- Cargo Insurance
- International Bonding

National Westminster advises that it is a leader in the London Foreign Exchange and Money markets. This bank has many specialist managers who can advise on and deliver currency and interest rate management services which cover topics from Spot Foreign Exchange to Currency Options and Financial Futures.

The brochure includes the names/addresses/telephone numbers of some 20 banks.

Midland Bank provides help and information to importers and exporters

(2) Their brochure lists services on offer such as;
- Documentary credits
- Bills of exchange
- Foreign currancy accounts
- Multi currency cheque accounts

Again the brochure 'Midland Services for Importers and Exporters' (2) is available at High Street branches and includes an enquiry form which can be used to order publications.

Services for Importers
Services for Exporters

Brochures from the TSB (3) and Barclays Banks list services offered and include:

Documentary credits
Bills for collection
Export Finance Scheme and ECGD facilities
Foreign Exchange Services
Foreign currency accounts
Simple fund transfer
Bonds, Guarantees and Indemnities

The TSB brochure concludes with a useful glossary of terms.

Two booklets of interest to importer and exporters are available from Barclays High Street banks. They are 'Import/Export Funding' and 'Merchanting' (4) and 'Barclays Tradeline and Trade Flow – short term export finance (5) published under 'International Trade services':

Brochure (4) lists the addresses and telephone numbers of 7 commercial services offices. Further details of all services offered are available from:

Barclays Commercial Services Ltd
Arbuttnot House
Breeds Place
Hastings
East Sussex
TN34 3DG
Tel: 0424 430824 Fax: 0424 721361

Brochures on the following topics are available from the above address:
Domestic and International Factoring
Invoices Discounting (confidential and disclosed)

BANK REFERENCES

1. International trade, National Westminster Bank PLC, International Banking Division, National Westminster Tower, 25, Old Broad Street,

London EC2N 1HQ. High Street branches will provide
2. Midland services of Importers and Exporters, most high street branches.
3. TSB Bank, International Services, through the local branch.
4. Barclays Bank, High Street branches
5. Barclays International Trade Services, Tradeline and Tradeflow, Short Term Export finance. Most high street branches.

 **SOURCES OF INFORMATION AND HELP**

This final chapter summarises help currently available to firms wishing to improve their marketing effectiveness and related subjects. A list of definitions or notes on marketing terms is given together with a further reading list of marketing texts and articles under appropriate headings.

Support for Marketing (SFM) is a DTI scheme aimed at helping small/medium firms to get expert advice on how they can raise their marketing effectiveness and performance to the level achieved by the most successful UK and international businesses.

This important initiative by the Department of Trade and Industry's Business and Technical Advisory Services is managed by The Chartered Institute of Marketing on behalf of The DTI.

Support offered Firms can obtain up to 15 days of marketing assistance from a specialist marketing consultant. There is no charge for the first two days during which time a survey is carried out and details of the proposed assignment prepared. For the remainder the firm is charged at ONE THIRD OF THE COST, the balance being met by the DTI. The minimum time for a project is 8 days of assistance. The service is confidential and no work is disclosed without the firm's approval.

Support is available to independent firms or groups anywhere in Great Britain with 1–500 employees. Each firm is entitled to one assisted project only.

Qualifying Criteria. To qualify for assistance the firm needs to demonstrate that any project forms part of a sound business plan and the benefits will lead to an increase in international competitiveness in a reasonable time scale.

The SFM initiative itself is aimed at companies which require assistance in developing their marketing strategies and overall marketing plan, as opposed to one of the elements of marketing.

There are no application forms and requests for further information can be made either to the Institute of Marketing or one of the four other contact points listed below:

HEAD OFFICE   The Chartered Institute of Marketing,
Moor Hall,
Cookham,
Maidenhead,
Berks. SL6 9QH
Tel: (062 85) 24922
Telex 849462   Fax (062 85) 31382

SCOTLAND

University of Strathclyde
Stenhouse Building,
173 Cathedral Street,
Glasgow G4 0RG
Tel: 041 552 4400

THE NORTH

Salford University Business Expansion
  Services Ltd.
Salbee House, Salford M6 6GS
Tel: 061 736 2843

MIDLAND & SOUTH WEST

University of Warwick
School of Industrial and Business Studies
Coventry CV4 7AL
Tel: 0203 523523

SOUTH AND SOUTH EAST

Marketing and Logistics Group
Cranfield School of Management,
Cranfield,
Bedford MK43 0AL
Tel: 0234 751122

Information and advice on other government assistance schemes can be obtained from the DTI's regional offices.

Grants from Europe for Small Firms. Other grants and help are available through the European Regional Development Fund and the Department of Trade and Industry. They are available to:

- people setting up in business
- independent small firms employing up to 200 people, or part of a group employing that number.
- consultants, or any kind of organisation, providing a service to small firms.

Grants include:-

- 55% grants towards the cost of a BUSINESS CHECK UP to establish key areas for improvement and possibly identify the need for specific follow-up consultancy work.
- 70% grants towards the cost of reviewing a firm's marketing activities and drawing up of a MARKETING STRATEGY for the future.
- 55% grants towards the cost of:
  a) TRANSLATIONS of marketing information and sales literature from or into foreign languages.
  b) Advice on improving existing BUDGET AND CONTROL SYSTEMS.
  c) LICENSING-IN A NEW PRODUCT.
  d) Investigating the merits of acquiring a MICRO-COMPUTER.

- 70% grant towards the cost of FEASIBILITY PROJECTS leading to the development of new products and processes.

Details about these grants and the financial limits imposed can be obtained by contacting the Regional Office of the Department of Trade and Industry nearest the firm.

REGIONAL DEVELOPMENT GRANTS

The extent of assistance now varies according to the designation of the geographical area. Prior to November 1984 the three categories of Development Area were:

- Special Development Areas (S.D.A.'s)
- Development Areas (D.A.'s)
- Intermediate Areas (I.A.'s)

S.D.A.'s were the areas with the most serious problems of structural decline such as Merseyside, Clydeside and Newcastle, and they received the greatest assistance. The scale of assistance was less in the D.A.'s and I.A.'s. Northern Ireland was categorised as a S.D.A., receiving additional assistance because of unique problems in that region. In November 1984 the category of SPECIAL DEVELOPMENT AREA was dispensed with leaving only

- Development Areas
- Intermediate Areas

Map 1 below shows the distribution of the development areas.

Prior to March 1988 the main instrument of Regional Policy was the Regional Development Grant (R.D.G.). The R.D.G. was a capital grant of 15% payable to firms in the Development Areas on investment in plant, buildings and machinery. The grants were subject to a cost per job limit of £10,000. Alternatively a job grant was made available of £3,000 for each new job created in labour intensive projects.

Capital grants were subject to the criticism that they encouraged capital intensive production when the underlying purpose was the creation of jobs. Also the grants failed to discriminate between good and bad investment and also that the grant would be paid to firms who would have made the investment even if the grant did not exist.

To overcome some of these criticisms the government introduced in March 1988 **The Regional Initiative** with a new system of **Regional Enterprise Grants.** The new system of grants are given at the discretion of the Department of Trade and Industry (DTI) upon the presentation of a **BUSINESS PLAN** by the applicant and are no longer automatically available. The grants will be provided only if the business plan meets the criteria of the D.T.I. and the project is taking place in a Development Area or South Yorkshire.

MAP 1

The criteria applied include: market opportunities for the business over the next 2–3 years, the effect of the project on sales, profits and employment levels, and how the project and the business will be financed.

The new grants are of two types:

(a) – grants for **investment** projects in most manufacturing and some service sectors. The D.T.I. will pay 15% of expenditure on fixed assets in the project, up to a maximum grant of £15,000. Eligible costs include plant and machinery (new or second-hand), buildings, purchase of land and site preparation, and vehicles used solely on site.

(b) – grants for **innovation** projects which lead to the development and introduction of new or improved products and processes. The D.T.I. will pay 50% of eligible costs, up to a maximum grant of £25,000. Work can range from feasibility studies, through the development of technical specifications, to the design and manufacture of prototypes. There is no limit on the size of projects which can be considered.

The measures introduced in March 1988 represent a significant movement towards a more market orientated approach to regional policy.

TAX ALLOWANCES

Tax allowances for capital expenditure in building, plant and machinery are available and details of current rates of first year and initial allowances will be given by the local Inspector of Taxes.

Small firms having difficulty in obtaining finance for starting up or expanding due to insufficient security can be helped by the LOAN GUARANTEE SCHEME from the government. Details can be obtained by contacting any High Street bank or Industrial and Commercial Finance Corporation Ltd. (ICFC).

For firms located in a rural area or country town where the population is under 10,000 aid can be received through The Council for Small Industries in Rural Areas (COSIRA) towards loans for building, equipment, raw materials and working capital. Firms should contact their nearest COSIRA office.

Assistance for R and D in New Technology and support for innovation is available in many areas. Again, contact with the DTI Regional Office will establish what aid is available in the area of operation of the firm or research organisation. The applying company must be viable and have the technical and financial capability to carry the development through. The project must be innovative, stand a good chance of success and improve the company's performance. No assistance is given if the project is able to proceed without Government support.

Schemes for consultancy help and towards feasibility studies are available in many areas and the DTI Regional Office will supply details.

Help for Adult Training, Tourism Projects and assistance towards the cost of employing a specialist consultant to carry out a survey aimed at Energy Conservation is available in many areas. Details are available from the DTI or County Central Offices.

A Guide to Local Authority Assistance is published by The National Westminster Bank PLC. Six directories for 1986 are available at £2 each or £10 for the whole set and obtainable from:

> National Westminster Bank PLC
> Commercial Information Section,
> 6th Floor,
> National House,
> 14 Moorgate,
> London EC2R 6BS.

Under various acts Local Authorities have certain general powers by which they are able to provide assistance to industry where this lies in the interest of their own locality. These include help with mortgage loans for the acquisition of, or the carrying out of works on land and, with the consent of the Secretary of State, the disposal of land below market value. Other assistance may include improvement grants, industrial site preparation, provision of advance factories etc.

The ways in which Local Authorities operate vary widely. Each council determines the kind of assistance it will offer and the amount it will allocate for such measures, according to the needs of its own area. The National Westminster Bank publications provide a very useful guide to businesses in all areas who should keep in close touch with their local authority for up-to-date information and changes that may affect them.

The areas covered by the above publications are:

	Standard Regions	**Counties**
Volume 1	North, North West, Yorks and Humberside	Cheshire, Cleveland, Cumbria, Durham, Humberside, Lancashire, North Yorkshire, Northumberland.
Volume 2	East Midlands, West Midlands, East Anglia	Cambridgeshire, Derbyshire, Hereford and Worcester, Leicestershire, Lincolnshire, Norfolk, Northamptonshire, Nottinghamshire, Shropshire, Staffordshire, Suffolk, Warwickshire.
Volume 3	South East	Bedfordshire, Berkshire, Buckinghamshire, East Sussex, Essex, Hampshire, Hertfordshire, Isle of Wight, Kent, Oxfordshire, Surrey, West Sussex.
Volume 4	South West, Wales	Avon, Clwyd, Cornwall, Devon, Dorset, Dyfed, Gloucestershire, Gwent, Gwynned, Mid Glamorgan, Powys, Somerset, South Glamorgan, West Glamorgan, Wiltshire.
Volume 5	Metropolitan Councils	Greater Manchester, Merseyside, South Yorkshire, Tyne & Wear, West Midlands, West Yorkshire.
Volume 6	Greater London	

Volume 1, for example, lists:

- Assistance available from Cheshire County Council with addresses of council offices and enterprise agencies.
- Assistance from City/District/Borough Councils with addresses of council offices and a brief note on help available.
- Notes and relevant addresses under the other counties listed above.

Many publications from local authorities, The DTI and other government agencies dealing with financial and other assistance are available and the amount of information is enormous. Many large accountancy firms as well as High Street banks can provide summaries of information available. Some specialist firms however can not only provide this information and advise client companies accordingly but are willing and able, for a fee, to make the detailed application on behalf of client companies and because of their daily contact with government and local authority officials deal with the considerable detail and information required on the way to securing the appropriate grant(s). A relatively new organisation, The Grant Exchange Ltd., based in Chester, offers such a specialist service. Individuals or firms seeking detailed help in this area and who lack the time or experience to deal with the complexities of deciding what help is available to them and cope with the detailed application requirements, should 'shop around' for organisations who have in-depth experience in this area.

At the time of writing, changes in the rules applying to financial aid are changing and some grants will not be available after 31 March 1988. The Department of Trade and Industry should be consulted on the proposed changes and others envisaged.

Publications referring to financial aid to industry and commerce from County Councils, Banks, Accounting Firms and the STI changed in 1988 and the reader should take account of this when seeking help. The currently available literature on aid is voluminous and changing. For example, in February 1988 a publication by Cheshire County Council gave details of financial aid to commerce and industry in Cheshire (1) under the headings:

AID FOR NEW OR EXPANDING FIRMS
1.1   Regional Development Grant
1.2   Regional Selective Assistance
1.3   National Selective Assistance
1.4   European Investment Bank Loans
1.5   Small Firms Investment Grant
1.6   Loan Guarantee Scheme
1.7   British Coal Enterprise
1.8   Venture Capital
1.9   Enterprise Counselling
1.10   Marketing Initiative
1.11   Design Initiative
1.12   Quality Initiative
1.13   Manufacturing Initiative
1.14   Business Planning
1.15   Financial and Information Systems

AID FOR SELF-EMPLOYMENT
2.1   Enterprise Allowance Scheme
2.2   North Cheshire Cooperative Development Fund

RURAL AID
3.1   Council for Small Industries in Rural Areas (COSIRA)
3.2   South Cheshire Rural Development Area

This publication advises that whilst every effort was made to ensure that details provided were accurate at the date of publication, the various forms of assistance listed may be subject to later amendments. Readers were advised to confirm details provided with the agency concerned. These remarks will apply to publications issued by other County Authorities.

A recent publication, New Sources of Grants and Aid for Business in the U.K. is available in A5 loose leaf format and updated every three months with new grants and important changes to existing schemes (2). This source covers:

- Employment
- Marketing
- Research and Innovation
- Capital Investment
- Energy Saving
- Exporting

and - Local Schemes

In terms of marketing, the latest detail concerning:

- Support for Marketing
- Joint Marketing Scheme
- Support for design
- Marketing Development Grants
- and Better Business Services

is given and the entry form for each scheme contains:

- At-a-glance summary
- Structure of the Scheme
- Who qualifies
- Form of aid available
- Contact addresses
- How to apply – official procedure and practical tips
- Application form and case study where applicable

Further information in the form of publications and seminars are regularly appearing on the subject of cash aids as several organisations offer practical advice on obtaining public finance. The following articles are examples:

Finance T, "How to get that extra cash aid", Deloitte Haskins and Sells (3).

Help to locate those elusive grants (4) is a useful article by North West Business Development Services of Horwich, near Bolton.

A one day seminar "EEC and UK Grants and Loans, a strategic appraisal" is discussed in the publication from CIMA in their conference programme, September–December 1987(5).

Finally, a Directory of Grant Making Trusts (6) provides an alphabetical list of many grant-making charitable trusts, lists organisations by type and resources and advises how to approach them.

REFERENCES

1. Financial Aid to Commerce and Industry, Employment Promotion Group, Cheshire County Council, Commerce House, Hunter Street, Chester CH1 1SN (Feb. 1988).
2. New Sources of Grants, WEKA Publishing Ltd., The Forum, 74-80 Camden Street, London NW1 0EG.
3. Finance T, NW Business Monthly. September 1986.
4. Industry North West, March 1989.
5. The Chartered Institute of Management Accountants, September–December 1987.
6. A Directory of Grant Making Trusts. Published by charities & Foundations, 48 Penbury Road, Tonbridge, Kent TN9 2JD.

APPENDIX I
FURTHER REFERENCE LITERATURE

GENERAL

1. The Guardian Guide to Running a Small Business. Kogan Page Ltd. First published 1980.
2. Working for Yourself, 6th Edition. The Daily Telegraph Guide to Self-Employment, G. Golzen, 1983, Kogan Page.
3. How to Buy a Business, The Daily Telegraph Guide, P. Farell, 1983, Kogan Page.
4. Directory of Grant Making Trusts, 1987, published by Charities and Foundations, 48 Penbury Road, Tonbridge, Kent TN9 2JD – gives an alphabetical list of grant-making Charitable Trusts and details organisations by type and resources, advises on how to approach trusts.
5. Expansion Kit for Business, financial management for the growing business, Touche Ross & Co., London 1983.
6. Many publications directed at helping business start-ups, small/medium business are available from many banks, e.g. Barclays Bank (Business Advisory Service), Cooperative Bank, Lloyds Bank, Midland Bank, National Westminster, Royal Bank of Scotland, T.S.B., The Yorkshire Bank and others have literature, often freely available at local branches or obtainable by contacting the local branch.
7. High on Tech, Low on Cash, provides a guide to raising finance in the U.K., published by Touche Ross International, 1986.
8. Patents, a source of technical information, Patent Office, Dept. of Trade, printed for Her Majesty's Stationery Office, 1983.
9. Useful publications available from Wyvern Business Library, Ely, Cambs. CB7 4BR.
    - e.g.   1. Do your own Market Research, Hague P.N., and Jackson P.J.
      How to go about performing professional market research for yourself.
    - e.g.   2. Offensive Marketing 2nd Edition, Davidson J.H.
      Contains more than 120 examples of companies from J. Sainsbury to Jaguar who have used offensive marketing as well as checklists for you to rate the marketing effectiveness of your company.
    -        3. Making Major Sales, Rackham N.
      A set of simple and practical techniques (the SPIN method) which have been tried in many leading companies with dramatic improvements in sales performance.

4. Selling by Telephone, Rogers L.
   A whole universe of techniques, styles and rules which can increase your success rate from the average 2% to a splendid 5%.
5. How to Sell a Service, McDonald M.
   Covers the whole sales process from a service-seller's point of view.
6. How to Win More Business by Phone, Telex and Fax, Katz B.
   How to generate business without leaving your desk.
7. Be Your Own PR Man, Bland M.
   How to generate free advertising.
8. Practical Sponsorship, Turner S.
   How to get more from a small business promotion budget.
9. The Secrets of Successful Sales Management, Adams T.
   Practical, how-to-do-it advice.
10. Do your own Advertising, Crompton A.
    How the smaller businessman can produce advertising that really works.
11. Running Your Own Mail Order Business, Breckman M.
    Mail Order is big business . . . with room for small businesses.
12. Product Liability, Nelson-Jones R., and Stewart P.
    A new law under the Consumer Protection Act 1987. Anybody who produces something for sale, who imports it or who distributes it is vulnerable to this wide ranging new law.
13. Managing Export Marketing, Katz B.
    Selling abroad doesn't have to be difficult.
14. Successful Business Strategy, Hardy L.
    How to win customers by supreme marketing.
15. Pricing for Results, Winkler J., published on behalf of the Institute of Marketing.
16. The Generation of Ideas for New Products, Sowrey T.
    Over 60 tried and tested techniques for finding new ideas.
17. Be Your Own Company Secretary, Scrine A.J.
    published in association with The Institute of Chartered Accountants of England and Wales. By law most companies need one director and one company secretary.
18. Finance for the Perplexed Executive, Proctor R.
    How to understand and use major financial ideas.

TEXTS

10. Kotler P. Marketing Management Analysis, Planning and Control, 2nd Edition, Prentice/Hall International Editions, 1972.
11. Webster & Wind. Organisational Buying Behaviour, Prentice Hall, 1972.
12. Corey B.R. Industrial Marketing Cases and Concepts, Prentice Hall, 1972.
13. Brand G.T., The Industrial Buying Decision, Cassell, Ass. Bus. Programme 1972.
14. Hill R.W., Hilliar T.J., Organisational Buying Behaviour, MacMillan 1977.

MARKETING COMMUNICATION

15. Lavidge R.J.,Steiner G.A., A Model for Predictive Measurement of Advertising Effectiveness, Journal of Marketing, Oct 1961.
16. Turnbull P.W., The Allocation of Resources to Marketing Communications in Industrial Markets, I.M.M. No.3, 1974.
17. Webster F., Communication Theory/Industrial Markets, Journ. Mark. Research, Nov 1968.
18. Cunningham M., White J., The Role of Exhibitions in Industrial Marketing, I.M.M., Summer 1974.
19. Kinnard R.W., Survey of Industrial Advertising Media, Brit. Journ. Marketing, Summer 1969.
20. Schiffman L.G., Gaccions V., Opinion Leaders in Institutional Markets, Journ. Mark., April 1974.
21. Webster F., Informal Communication in Industrial Markets, Journ. Mark. Res., May 1970.
22. Parrish T., How Much to Spend for Advertising, Journ. Ad. Res. April 1971.
23. McDonald C.M., Measuring Advertising Response, ADMAP, March 1980.
24. Schwartz D., Measuring the Effectiveness of Your Company's Advertising, Journ. Mark., April 1969.

PRICING

25. Rickwood C.P., Piper A.G., Marginal Costing, CIMA, Portland Place, London.
26. Winkler J., Pricing for Results, published on behalf of Inst. of Marketing, Heinemann, London 1983, Reprinted 1985.
27. Nimmer D., Does Your Pricing Pay? Marketing, April 1970.
28. How British Industry Prices, Ind. Mkt. Res. 1975.
29. Blattberg, Eppen, Leiberman, Price Deals for Non-Durables, AMA Journ of Mark., Winter 1981.
30. Borona T., Johnson W., The Social Psychology of Industrial Buying/Selling, Int. Mktg., Vol. 7 No. 4, August 1978.

PURCHASING

31. Wind, Green, Robinson, The Determinants of Vendor Selection, Journ of Purchasing, August 1968.
32. Hakeson, Johnson, Wootz, Influence Tactics in Buyer-Seller Processes, Inst Mark Mgt., Vol.5 No.6., December 1976.
33. Hass R.W., Wotruba T.R., Industrial Marketing; An Organisation Problem, Inst. Mark. Mgt. No.4, 1975.
34. Farmer D., Developing Purchasing Strategies, Journal of Purchasing and Mkt. Mgt., Vol. 14, No. 3, Fall 1978.
35. Rink D., The Product Life Cycle in Formulating Purchasing Strategy, Inst. Mkt. Mgt., Vol. ? No. 3, August 1976.
36. Luffman G., The Processing of Information by Industrial Buyers, Inst. Mark. Vol. 3, 1974.

MARKETING STRATEGY/PLANNING

37. Cunningham M.T., Product Planning, The Essence of Corporate Strategy, Journal of Business Policy, Vol.2 No.4, 1972.
38. Kotler P., Growth and Competitive Strategy, Ref. 10 above.
39. Levitt T., Planning and Preparation for Change, Innovation in Marketing, McGraw Hill, Ch. 7, 1972.
40. Risk Management, Jardine Glanvill (UK) Ltd., Publications Manager, CIMA, 63 Portland Place, London.
41. Quershi M.A., Analysing Business Strategy, obtainable from CIMA above.
42. Humphreys R.G., Analysing Uncertainty, obtainable from CIMA above.
43. Porter, M., Competitive Strategy, Free Press 1980.
44. Porter, M., Competitive Advantage, Free Press 1985.
45. Ansoff, H.I., Strategic Management, MacMillan 1972.
46. Argenti, J., Practical Corporate Planning, Allen and Unwin 1980.
47. Argenti J., Predicting Corporate Failure, Ind. Instit. of Chartered Accountants, 1983.

BUYING BEHAVIOUR

48. Webster & Wind, A General Model for Understanding Organisation Buyer Behaviour. Journ Mark, Vol. 34, April 1972.
49. Brand G., Key Members of the D.M.V. The Industrial Buying Decision, Ch. 6 (see section on TEXTS).
50. Sheth J., A Model of Industrial Buying Behaviour, Journ. of Mark., 37 No. 4., 1973.
51. Wind Y., Webster F., On the Study of Industrial Buying Behaviour; Current Practices for Future Trends, Inst. Mark., July 1972.

PRODUCT LIFE CYCLES

52. Levitt T., Exploit the Product Life Cycle, Harvard Business Review, Nov./Dec. 1965.
53. Doyle P., The Realities of the PLC, Quart.Rev. Marketing, Summer 1976.
54. Dhalla N.K., Yuseth S., Forget the PLC, Harv.Bus.Rev., Jan/Feb 1976.
55. Polli R., Cook W., Validity of the PLC, Journ of Business, Oct 1969.

SEARCH FOR NEW PRODUCTS

56. Nelson R.R., The Rate of Direction of Inventive Activity: Economic and Social Factors, Princeton University Press, 1962.
57. Schmookler J., Invention and Economic Growth, Harvard University Press, 1966.
    a) Booz, Allen and Hamilton, 'A Programme of Product Evolution.'
    b) Steel, 'Finding out what the customer will buy.'
    c) Wehrly, 'Analysing Competitive Factors in New Product Development.'
    d) In Product Strategy and Management, Berg and Shukmann.
58. Launching New Products, British Institute of Management Checklists 29 and 30 with associated reference literature, 1973.

**APPENDIX II
DEFINITIONS AND A GLOSSARY
OF MARKETING TERMS**

MARKETING: Several definitions are available and two are offered.
Marketing is a management process responsible for anticipating and satisfying client/customer needs – at a profit.
Marketing is a total business philosophy aimed at improving profit performance, through identifying customer needs, designing the best service/product to satisfy these needs, delivering the offering on time and providing a sound after-sales service.

MARKET RESEARCH: The process of systematic investigation into markets to:

                  a) establish present and potential demand for consumer and industrial products.

and   b) provide a basis for management decisions.

MARKET SEGMENTATION: is concerned with distinguishing relevant customer groups and their needs and interests and NOT concerned with distinguishing product/service possibilities.

THE MARKETING MIX refers to the main variables available to the firm to be set in order to match the benefits sought by buyers with those offered by the seller. The firm's marketing mix (the "4 P's") is represented by PRODUCT, PRICE, PROMOTION and PLACE (distribution service).

A MARKETING AUDIT is a systematic, critical and objective analysis of a firm's marketing capability and the environment in which it operates. The main job of the audit is to examine internal strengths and weakness and analyse the external situation.

MARKET SHARE: The percentage of the market represented by a firm's sales in relation to total sales. For detailed discussion and definitions of Market Demand, Market Forecast, Market Potential, Company Demand and related concepts see Kotler (ref 10) above.

A MARKETING PLAN for any company relates solely to that company and sets down:

              ● Where the firm is now
              ● Where the firm wishes to go
and   ● How it should organise its resources to do it.

The elements of the plan are a marketing audit/SWOT analysis, a statement of some key assumptions, marketing objectives, strategies and programmes for each level of the business.

MARKETING OBJECTIVES are statements of targets to be pursued and achieved during the period covered by the marketing plan. Objectives relating to profit, market share, market development and penetration are primary objectives, more commonly called strategic or business objectives since they relate to the objectives of the firm as a whole. Objectives set for specific marketing activities can be described as programme objectives.

POLICIES are summary statements of objectives and strategies.

PRODUCT/SERVICE POSITIONING: Good marketing requires the selling company to give its product(s) a real or psychological difference from that of competing products since buyers make their choice from a competitive field. A differentiated product is one that is seen by buyers as particularly suited to their needs compared with competing products. The selling company needs to:

- show that its product satisfies the needs of buyers in particular segments

and
- find the best position in the 'product space' with respect to competitors to induce buyers to believe that the product most accurately meets his needs.

A PRODUCT LIFE CYCLE describes the birth, growth, maturity and decline of a product over time. During the life of a product, sales income increases and then declines; profitability will depend on the marketer's approach in manipulating the market mix during its life. Total life expectancy of products varies enormously and efforts during launch and thereafter to extend the life cycle and profitability require considerable creativity on the part of the producer.

PROGRAMMES detail the final steps in marketing planning, listing the tasks to be undertaken by all participating departments in line with the strategies and objectives previously set down. Programmes define the individuals/ departments responsible for achieving objectives listed in a given time period.

TARGETS are objectives set for an individual or group, e.g. the group's target is to increase sales by x% to hardware retailers.

COST-RELATED PRICING systems are used by firms to set prices mainly on the basis of cost. All costs are included together with an allocation of overheads based on expected production levels.

COST-PLUS PRICING is used to price products/jobs that are non-routine and difficult to "cost" in advance, e.g. construction and development work.

PENETRATION PRICING is aimed at stimulating market growth to capture a larger share of the market and likely to be used if the market is highly price sensitive.

MARKET SKIMMING PRICING takes advantage of the fact that some buyers are ready to pay a higher price than others since the product/service has a high present value to them. This situation can be advantageous if there are enough buyers whose demand is relatively inelastic, smaller volume production is not expensive and there is little danger of entry by rival firms.

PSYCHOLOGICAL PRICING When the seller (e.g. retailer) reduces the price down to a level just below a supposed 'barrier' price, e.g. £9.95 is possibly more attractive than £10.

TARGET PRICING is a cost-orientated approach where the producer decides the price that will give a rate of return on total costs at budgeted level in line with the financial objectives set by the company's board.

COMPETITION-ORIENTATED PRICING is used by firms who set prices on the basis of what their competitors are charging.

MARGINAL COST PRICING. Manufacturing costs may be divided into fixed and variable, the latter vary according to output and the former remain unchanged regardless of the level of activity. When output produces sufficient revenue to cover fixed and variable costs it has reached 'break-even' point. When a firm can find a customer/isolated market/segment without jeapordising price levels in existing markets it can quote prices based on marginal cost. Additional sales increase total profit although percentage profit per unit will be lower. Marginal pricing provides a reason for accepting the lowest possible price but is a dangerous practice when uncontrolled.

STANDARD COSTING is the ascertainment and use of standard costs (predetermined costs) and the measurement and analysis of variances (variance analysis is the resolution into component parts, and the explanation of variances).

SATISFICING occurs when a company is satisfied with a price because it is considered conventional for a given level of risk despite the possibility of an increased return.

Index